MODERN
AMERICAN
HISTORY ★ A
Garland
Series

Edited by
FRANK FREIDEL
Harvard University

THE DEPRESSION IN TEXAS ★ The Hoover Years

Donald W. Whisenhunt

 Garland Publishing, Inc.
New York & London ★ 1983

Library of Congress Cataloging in Publication Data

Whisenhunt, Donald W.
  The Depression in Texas.

  (Modern American history)
  Bibliography: p.
  Includes index.
  1. Texas—Economic conditions.   2. Depressions—
1929—United States.   I. Title.   II. Series.
HC107.T4W5   1983   338.5'42   82-49080
ISBN 0-8240-5663-9

All volumes in this series are printed on acid-free,
250-year-life paper.
Printed in the United States of America

THE DEPRESSION IN TEXAS:

THE HOOVER YEARS

by

Donald W. Whisenhunt

This book is dedicated with love
to Mr. & Mrs. L. J. King, my mother
and stepfather--*Mom and L.J.*--whose
faith in me and silent support have
never wavered.

TABLE OF CONTENTS

The story of Texas during the Great Depression is a most interesting one. It was one of the most traumatic periods in American history. People who lived through it remember it in many different ways. Some recall the thirties as a time of relative calm and little discomfort; others remember it as a time of unrelieved suffering. Studies of Texas during this period are limited and narrow in scope. Now that we are some fifty years removed from the period, it seems appropriate to try to place it in a proper historical context.

For almost twenty years I have been interested professionally in this decade of American history. Because of my personal interest stemming from my family background, my major professor in graduate school, Timothy P. Donovan, suggested that I study how people of Texas reacted to the depression. Since a doctoral dissertation had already been done on Texas and the New Deal by Lionel V. Patenaude, I decided to focus on Texas during the Hoover period. This seemed to be a reasonable time period since Texas had broken with its long Democratic tradition in 1928 to support the Republican Herbert Hoover for the presidency. When hard times came within the first year of Hoover's administration, most Texans were anxious to return the Democratic fold in 1932, especially since there was a chance that a Texan, John Nance Garner, might have a chance to be the next president. For many, however, there was more hope and excitement in the potential, and later actual, candidacy of the New York patrician, Franklin D. Roosevelt.

I entered this study with some hesitation. Studying public opinion or reaction was considered somewhat risky for a graduate student since opinion is not a very precise activity, even today when scientific polling is much more advanced. Certainly, the problem of assessing public opinion in the

thirties was difficult to handle. I will be forever grateful
to Professor Donovan for giving me the idea and for providing
encouragement at every step of the project. His faith in my
ability to complete the project was unswerving; he was more
confident, at times, than I ever was that I could complete
the study.

I was thankful for his support at the time because I was
able to complete the dissertation in record time and was award-
ed the Ph.D. at Texas Technological College (now Texas Tech
University) as planned. I have been even more grateful in the
seventeen years since the study was completed for the professional gratification it gave me. I have been able to use what
I learned in numerous other related projects.

In the years since 1966 I have continued to research and
publish on various aspects of the depression in Texas and in
other localities. I have also studied limited depression top-
ics with national implications. While engaged in my research,
I discovered that Professor Robert Cotner at The University of
Texas at Austin had begun to direct a series of master of arts
theses on various Texas cities during the depression. At the
time I did my work, only one had been completed. In succeeding
years, I was very interested to see each thesis as it was completed. I wanted to know, for example, if any of these students
found any evidence in a local area that contradicted my conclusions and if they discovered examples of public opinion that
I had missed. Eventually a dozen or more of these theses were
completed before Professor Cotner's retirement. I was grati-
fied to know that most of them supported my conclusions. Eventually, abridged versions of a number of these theses were
published in a book edited by Professor Cotner entitled *Texas
Cities in the Great Depression* (see the bibliography for cita-
tions for this book and the various theses I used).

Except for the work directed by Cotner, little other research has been done on the Hoover period in Texas since my
work was completed. Several scholars, including Professors
Patenaude and Kenneth E. Hendrickson, Jr., of Midwestern State

University, have produced significant work on Texas in the thirties, but they have concentrated primarily on Texas during the New Deal period.

In the years since I completed my original study, I have done additional research on various parts of the dissertation. I have been able to use materials that were not available, for one reason or another, at the time I did my original research. Based upon this new research and more careful analysis of my original work, I expanded some portions of the original dissertation. I have been fortunate to publish several articles in scholarly journals based on the dissertation. In this revised version of the original study I have incorporated the work I have done since 1966. I am very grateful to the various publications for permission to use these articles in this published version of the dissertation even though they may not be immediately recognizable in this revision. I would like to take this opportunity to acknowledge and thank the various journals. The articles and journals are listed below.

"The Bard in the Depression: Texas Style," *Journal of Popu-Culture*, II (Winter, 1969).

"The Texas Attitude Toward Relief, 1929-1933," *Panhandle-Plains Historical Review*, LXVI (1973).

"The Texan as a Radical, 1929-1933," *Social Science Journal*, XIV (October, 1977).

"East Texas and the Stock Market Crash," *East Texas Historical Journal*, XIX (January, 1981).

"West Texas and the Stock Market Crash of 1929," West Texas Historical Association *Yearbook*, LV (1979).

"The Transient in the Depression," *Red River Valley Historical Review*, I (Spring, 1974).

"There is No Depression," *Red River Valley Historical Review*, V (Fall, 1980).

"Huey Long and the Texas Cotton Acreage Control Law of 1931," *Louisiana Studies* (presently *Southern Studies*), XIII (1974).

"The Search for A Villain," chapter in *The Depression in the Southwest*, edited by Donald W. Whisenhunt, Kennikat Press, 1980.

I would also like to take this opportunity to acknowledge assistance received from other sources over the years.

In addition to Professor Donovan already mentioned, I would like to acknowledge the support and encouragement I received from other members of my doctoral dissertation committee: Professors Lawrence L. Graves, Ernest Wallace, Lowell L. Blaisdell, J. William Davis, and the late David M. Vigness.

Space does not permit me to thank individually all the kind and gracious people in various libraries and archival collections scattered across the country whose courtesies were extended to me without question and with much graciousness. I would like to thank especially those newspaper editors throughout Texas who opened their files for me to use. Above all, I would like to thank Frank R. Simpson, a graduate school colleague of mine at the time and now a resident of San Angelo, Texas, for the many conversations, discussions, and arguments we had about Texas during the depression. It was his interest, as much as any one factor, that helped me to organize my thought and material so that some order was created out of the mountains of documents from which this work originated.

My wife, Betsy, also deserves special mention. She supported me in many ways during graduate school and even assisted me in what seemed at the time the never-ending process of reading newspaper files. In the years since, she continued to be a major psychological support for my professional predilection with the Great Depression. My mother and stepfather, Mr. and Mrs. L. J. King, to whom I have dedicated this published version, have always supported me in my professional endeavors even though they were not always sure what it meant. They certainly understood this dissertation, however, since they have very vivid memories of the events described here.

Many people, as noted, assisted me in this study. I would hasten to add, however, that their assistance was primarily to make material available to me. The narrative and conclusions in this study are mine, and any errors of fact or interpretation are my responsibility.

Tyler, Texas   Donald W. Whisenhunt
March 1983

CHAPTER I

INTRODUCTION

Second only to the Civil War, the Great Depression of the 1930s was probably the most traumatic experience in the history of the United States. Depressions had been common in American history, but for the people of the thirties this one seemed to be different somehow. Old values were threatened by forces far beyond the control of the average citizen--and of the government, for that matter. Americans could not understand what went wrong. They could not understand why nothing could be done to correct the problems.

The attitude of the people--public opinion--is hard to gauge. Public opinion is always elusive even in a time when polls seem to guide all politicians. In the age before scientific polling, it is even more difficult to determine what people thought about specific events. One of the best ways to evaluate opinion is to study reaction. How people reacted to certain things gives a hint or a clue to what they thought.

A great deal of mythology and misinformation have developed about the Great Depression. For example, the belief that many people committed suicide following the stock market crash of 1929 persists. The responsibility of Hoover and the Republican Party for causing the depression lives on. The extent of unemployment, hunger, and homelessness is debated by groups whose opinions are formed more on the basis of their current views than on historical facts.

For these reasons, as well as many others, what the people of the thirties actually thought and how they reacted to the events around them need to be known. Because the depression was so long and America is so large, a de-

tailed study would be most difficult. The best effort,
therefore, would seem to be to focus on one state in a
limited time period. For that reason, this study attempts
to assess the public reaction in Texas during the period
of the Hoover presidency, 1929-1933.

American thought has been shaped and conditioned by
many forces and experiences. Four of these--the frontier
experience, the agrarian myth, the conspiracy theory of
history, and the fundamentalist mind--played a significant
role in shaping the thought of the average Texan in the
1930s.

The frontier experience, always a vital force in American history, is directly responsible for a portion of the
way in which the American views the world. Professor Frederick Jackson Turner explained that many traits of the American character were derived from the frontier. Many of the
customs, traditions, and institutions that characterized
the American of the twentieth century were remnants of
older European experiences or entirely new ones forced upon him by the American frontier environment.[1] As the frontier moved from one section to another, it left behind it
enduring ideals that had a lasting impact upon the thinking
and actions of the whole country.[2] "Buoyant self-confidence
and self-assertion were distinguishing traits" of the western character,[3] but they were not the only legacies of the
frontier. These characteristics and others, including self-
reliance and a distrust of governmental authority, were
among the most apparent in the Texas of the thirties.

The second force upon American thought has been the
"agrarian myth" as defined by Professor Richard Hofstadter.

[1] Frederick Jackson Turner, *The Frontier in American History* (New
York: Holt, Rinehart, and Winston, 1920), 1-38.

[2] *Ibid.*, 264.

[3] *Ibid.*, 210.

This was the idea that rural life was the best possible existence; the evils existing within it were the fault of outsiders, not the farmers themselves. As farming became more commercialized and the nation more urban in the late nineteenth century, the country as a whole became more sentimental and nostalgic about its rural past. In popular imagination the agrarian life was virtually perfect; most people simply refused to remember the harshness of that life.[4]

Thirdly, the conspiracy theory of history has been vital in American development. The idea that a great sinister force is in operation to destroy all that is good in American life is by no means new.

> In the history of the United States one finds it, for example, in the anti-Masonic movement, the nativist and anti-Catholic movement, in certain spokesmen for abolitionism who regarded the United States as being in the grip of a slaveholders' conspiracy, in many writers alarmed by Mormonism, in some Greenback and Populist writers who constructed a great conspiracy of international bankers, in the exposure of a munitions makers' conspiracy of the First World War, in the popular left-wing press, in the contemporary American right-wing, and on both sides of the race controversy today, among White Citizens Councils and Black Muslims.[5]

The fear of a conspiratorial threat is not limited to any one section or one group of American people; most of them have, at various times, considered themselves confronted by a sinister organized force.

The fourth influence is the fundamentalist mind. Partly a result of the other forces, it tends to view the world in very simple terms. Because of his struggle with hostile forces on the frontier--nature, Indians, geography--the world became, in many respects, a struggle for the American between good and evil. Religion, always important in Amer-

---

[4] Richard Hofstadter, *The Age of Reform* (New York: Random House Vintage Books, 1955), 24, 62.

[5] Richard Hofstadter, *The Paranoid Style in American Politics and Other Essays* (New York: Alfred A. Knopf, 1965), 9. Hereafter cited as Hofstadter, *Paranoid Style*.

ican life, became more fundamental and more emotional on the frontier, and in the nation as a whole, after the Great Awakening. Hofstadter explains the fundamentalist mind as one that "looks upon the world as an arena for conflict between absolute good and absolute evil, and accordingly . . . scorns compromises." In fact, "the issues of the actual world are hence transformed into a spiritual Armageddon. . . ."[6]

These four facets of American thought were held by many diverse groups of Americans prior to the Civil War. As the economic base of the nation changed with the development of industry in the late nineteenth century, agrarian society felt itself threatened by new forces that it could not understand. Thus, the agrarian protest beginning in the 1860s and 1870s and culminating in the formation of the People's Party in the 1890s was the first time in American history that the four forces combined to create a response to a specific challenge. The Populist movement used, probably without knowing it, these four conditioning influences to develop a philosophy designed to protect the rural way of life. Significantly, the Populist rhetoric built on this foundation was formulated only in the face of a serious economic upheaval--this way of thinking which might be called a "crisis mentality" is a small part of the broader concept that Hofstadter calls the "paranoid style."[7]

> But the fact that movements employing the paranoid style are not constant but come in successive episodic waves suggests that the paranoid disposition is mobilized into action chiefly by social conflicts. . . . Catastrophe or the fear of catastrophe is the most likely to elicit the syndrome of paranoid rhetoric.[8]

The Great Depression of the 1930s, the greatest economic crisis of the twentieth century, brought forth much the

---

[6] Richard Hofstadter, *Anti-intellectualism in American Life* (New York: Alfred A. Knopf, 1963), 135.

[7] For a discussion of the paranoid style, see: Hofstadter, *Paranoid Style*, 3-40.

[8] *Ibid.*, 39.

same reaction from Americans as did industrialization in the nineteenth century. Research shows that Texans, especially infused with the legacy of the four dominant themes in American thought, employed the same dialogue and exhibited the same mentality that was dominant throughout American history and was crystalized into a cohesive reaction syndrome by the Populists. Texans were not unique in their reaction to the depression; they serve, in reality, as an example of American thinking in the twentieth century. The conceptions of and responses to the depression were probably similar in both rural and urban America; however, the "crisis mentality" is more easily observed and understood in rural society, of which Texas is only one example.[9]

The reaction of Texans to the depression is in keeping with their agrarian heritage. As children of the frontier, most of them were steeped in the agrarian myth, raised on fundamental religious beliefs, and tended to believe in the conspiracy theory in times of stress.[10] At first they tried

[9] In the discussion of the reaction I will use a number of terms to describe the mentality of Texans. When the terms "populism," "agrarian thought," "neo-populism," or others of this nature are used, they are intended merely to express or denote a way of thinking, a rhetoric, a syndrome, a way of life. There is no deliberate attempt to draw an analogy between the political movement of the People's Party of the 1890s and the actions of Texans in the 1930s.

[10] For a discussion of the importance of agriculture to Texas life and history see the following: Billy M. Jones, *The Search for Maturity*, Vol. V of *The Saga of Texas*, ed. Seymour V. Connor (6 vols.; Austin: Steck-Vaughn Company, 1965), 108-133; Roy Sylvan Dunn, "Agriculture Builds a City," *A History of Lubbock*, ed. Lawrence L. Graves (Lubbock: West Texas Museum Association, 1962), 239-292. For the importance of religion in earlier Texas history see Rupert N. Richardson, *Texas the Lone Star State* (2d ed. rev.; Englewood Cliffs, New Jersey: Prentice-Hall, Inc., 1958), 64-65, 175-178. For an example of more recent importance of religion in the state see Merton L. Dillon, "Religion in Lubbock," *A History of Lubbock*, 449-509. Texans, since the colonial period, often exhibited feelings that they were being persecuted by an outside force (or conspiracy). For examples of this see the Texas Declaration of Independence in Ernest Wallace and David M. Vigness (eds.), *Documents of Texas History* (Austin: The Steck Company, 1963), 98-99; Jones, *The Search for Maturity*, 148-149, 166-167; Hofstadter, *Paranoid Style*, 8-9.

to ignore the existence of the depression by preaching unrealistic optimism; when its presence could no longer be
denied, the search for a conspirator began, and the old
values about relief and the role of the government in society had to be reevaluated.

Although there are differences, to be sure, dictated
by time, place, and circumstances, a striking resemblance
between nineteenth-century agrarianism and the Texan in the
thirties is quickly apparent. One obvious parallel is the
desire of both groups to return to the halcyon days of pre-
industrial America.[11] They were as unrealistic as were the
European leaders who met at the Congress of Vienna in 1814
to try to recreate the Europe of the *ancien regime*. Just
as the Europeans were unable to ignore the reorganization
of society brought about by the French Revolution and Napo-
leon, the Texan, and America as a whole, was unable to ignore industrialization and return to the "good old days"
of the agrarian myth. Despite the overtones of radicalism
in both periods, each can be seen as really a conservative,
or perhaps reactionary, movement to retain the good things
in American society--the agrarian way of life. Despite the
more sophisticated reaction of the 1930s, due probably to
the decreasing naivete of the country as a whole, both periods were characterized by a simple-minded approach--a desire for simple answers--to a complex problem.

The purpose of this study is to point out the similari-
ties and, where they exist, the differences between the
agrarian mentality of the nineteenth century and the depression mentality of the 1930s.

[11] Professor Norman Pollack may be correct in his assertion that the
agrarian response to industrialism was not an attempt to return to pre-
industrial America, but instead tried to cope with the new world.
Wherever the truth lies, the farmers of the nineteenth century and of
the 1930s were both trying to protect a way of life they thought best
and that was threatened by rapid changes. See Norman Pollack, *The
Populist Response to Industrial America* (New York: W. W. Norton &
Company, Inc., paperback edition, 1966), 2-8.

In Texas in the thirties the agrarian mentality can be observed at work on every hand, even among urban dwellers. The dominant themes of agrarianism as expounded by the Populists are "the idea of a golden age; the concept of natural harmonies; the dualistic version of social struggles; the conspiracy theory of history; and the doctrine of the primacy of money."[12] Although this is a description of nineteenth century agrarianism, the themes appear in the thinking of many Texans, and Americans everywhere, in the 1930s. Included among its other characteristics are a high degree of provincialism, an intense dislike of the city, a belief in the duty of the federal government to intervene in the economic affairs of the country, and a critical viewpoint toward the economic system with the goal of correcting it.[13] At this point two major paradoxes appear, perhaps a result of conflicts in the forces that shaped American thought. Despite the optimism and confidence often attributed to the American as a result of the frontier experience, a deep-seated anxiety or even pessimism appears in nineteenth-century agrarian thought. This was due partly to the fear that the country had been taken over by a conspiracy of industrial and financial capitalists who dominated the farmer and made agrarian life even more difficult.[14] Such a contradiction is certainly present, in varying degrees, in Texas during the depression.

The other paradox involved the idea of small government and states rights, probably a result of the frontier, in opposition to the Populist concept of government action to correct economic evils. In Texas, as in much of the nation, the Jeffersonian concept of small government was widespread. Because the first thirty years of the twenti-

[12] Hofstadter, *The Age of Reform*, 62.

[13] *Ibid.*, 17, 34, 61, 82.

[14] *Ibid.*, 66, 71, 93.

eth century were, generally speaking, years of progress and prosperity, most of those who advocated a larger role for government--local, state, or national--were hardly noticed or given a hearing in the 1920s. This attitude did undergo a change in the thirties, however. What appears on the surface to be a paradox in both American and Texan thinking is, in reality, merely a matter of definition. What was usually meant by "small government" or "laissez faire" was an attitude opposed to government control or regulation but one very receptive to its aid in economic development.

The Texan's concept of small government was made clear in his outlook toward public welfare and relief. To the Texan, born of the frontier experience, welfare and relief were the concern of the indigent's friends, neighbors, and relatives, but certainly not that of the government. In extreme cases, the poor might rely upon the localities or the state, but never upon the federal government. This was the theoretical approach, but in practice the Texan was often at the head of the line for federal handouts. At the height of the depression the New York *Times* reported that relief work in Texas was so poorly managed that the "twin problems of unemployment and relief are the despair of enlightened and intelligent social workers. . . ."[15] Never before had the problem been so acute; friends and neighbors were no longer capable of taking care of the less fortunate. In the same article a statement that the "Texas agencies have more Western breeziness than Southern hospitality"[16] in their attitude toward transients in the state would also apply, to a lesser degree, to Texas citizens in need of relief. Part of this was due to the absence of a tradition of organized public welfare, but the refusal to face the truth of the economic situation "instead of wallowing, according

[15] New York *Times*, December 25, 1932, IV, 5.

[16] *Ibid.*

to frontier habit, in mere emotional optimism and hope,"[17] was responsible for much of the delay in organizing to meet the demands of the depression.

Texas pride also had something to do with the attitude toward federal aid in the early stages of the depression. The Dallas *Morning News*, the leading daily newspaper in the state, opposed asking for federal aid for drought relief because Texas could take care of its own through private agencies such as the Red Cross. "The News has steadfastly set its face against tin-cup-and-blue-goggles trips to Washington for 'relief' for Texans. . . . Are we going to let our own flesh and blood beg on the steps of the National Capitol?"[18] A local Texan said that direct federal aid would make life "a sort of barnacle existence with a people stuck to the Federal Treasury and eating the heart out of Government."[19] He admitted that Texas faced a grave situation but he appealed to the natural hardiness of the people and to their patriotism. "Remember the struggle of the Pilgrims; remember the struggle of the early Texans who fought poverty and Mexican tyranny to raise our immortal flag. Keep the ship out of the dark fog of paternalism, where it might go upon the rocks and might be destroyed."[20] Another leading daily advocated private relief,[21] emphasized that Texas greatness had been achieved by self-reliance, and insisted that too much dependence upon Washington, "encourages paternalism and vitiates state morale."[22] These few examples suffice to show the pervasiveness of the frontier influence

[17] James Truslow Adams, *The Tempo of Modern Life* (New York: Albert & Charles Boni, Inc., 1931), 268.

[18] Dallas *Morning News*, January 15, 1931.

[19] "Letters From Readers," *ibid.*, January 13, 1931.

[20] *Ibid.*

[21] Galveston *Daily News*, September 5, 1930.

[22] *Ibid.*, August 29, 1930.

of self-reliance and "rugged individualism" on Texas thinking even in a time of stress, but the agrarian position on
the role of the government would assert itself as the depression deepened.

The rural suspicion of cities, long a trait of the American character, was still evident in Texas in the thirties.
Although Texas had a rural majority in population,[23] the urban centers had grown in total numbers approximately nine
percent from 1920 to 1930.[24] Turner hinted at the urban-
rural conflict;[25] in the Texas of the thirties it can be seen
clearly. The census of 1930 indicated growing urbanization
at the expense of the rural and small town element. The
Austin *Statesman*, noting the change, was unhappy about it.
The editor seemed to long nostalgically for the old days
when he reported the indisputable facts that the census provided.

> Gone is the old grist mill and the saw mill. Gone
> is the village doctor. Gone is the village inn. Gone
> is the village smithy. Going is the village store in
> connection with the village post office. Gone are the
> calicos and other articles of bygone days.[26]

He did, however, have a word of encouragement for the farmer because "farm houses are fitted WITH MODERN CONVENIENCES,
MAKING THEM MORE ATTRACTIVE THAN RAMSHACKLE HOUSES IN THE
NEARBY HAMLET."[27] The rural element, ever intent on holding
its political power despite its declining population, took
steps to keep the cities under-represented in the state
legislature by approving a constitutional amendment in 1936

---

[23] David L. Cohn, *The Life and Times of King Cotton* (New York: Oxford University Press, 1956), 241. Hereafter cited as Cohn, *King Cotton.*

[24] U.S. Bureau of the Census, *Fifteenth Census of the United States:
1930. Population,* I, 15.

[25] Turner, *The Frontier in American History,* 316-317.

[26] Austin *Statesman,* April 20, 1930.

[27] *Ibid.*

that limited the number of representatives allowed to each urban area.[28]

Ideology certainly influenced Texas reaction to the depression, but the population and institutions of the state are also important in the shaping of public opinion as can be seen by a brief demographic survey of the state. The total population of Texas in 1930 was 5,824,715. Compared with the 4,666,228 persons in Texas in 1920 the number in 1930 represented an increase of well over one million or 24.9 percent. This was the best ten year growth period in total numbers in the state's history; the decade, 1900-1910, was second best with an increase of almost 850,000 or 27.8 percent. In terms of percentage increase, the 1920-1930 record was the second lowest with a percentage of 19.7. In 1930 the density of population was 22.2 per square mile, the highest of any period in the state's history.[29]

The number of urban dwellers had also increased significantly by 1930. In many respects, especially in Texas, the Bureau of the Census classification of urban areas[30] does not give a true picture of prevailing conditions. Cities ranging from 2,500 to as high as 10,000 or 20,000 remain, in many respects, rural communities because they are often (more often than not) located in the center of an agricultural area and, with the absence of an industrial capacity, remain, despite their size, dependent upon the agricultural community for existence. This fact must be remembered when discussing the urban composition of Texas. The urban residents in 1930 (2,389,348) constituted 41 percent

[28]Roscoe C. Martin, *Urban Local Government in Texas* (Austin: University of Texas Bulletin No. 3637, 1936), 338.

[29]*The Texas Almanac and State Industrial Guide--1931* (Dallas: A.H. Belo Corporation, 1931), 134. Hereafter cited as *Texas Almanac*.

[30]In discussing urban population it should be noted that the Bureau of Census uses a total of 2,500 or more residents to indicate an urban community. *Ibid.*

of the total population; this is a significant increase when compared to the 1920 figure of one and one-half million urban dwellers who composed 32.4 percent of the total population.[31] It should be noted, however, that there were only thirty-five cities whose population totaled 10,000 or more; they had a total of 1,799,442 or approximately 30 percent of the entire population. Moreover, the fifteen cities that had a total population of more than 25,000 totaled 1,490,266 or approximately 25 percent of the state. Of this number only five cities--Dallas, El Paso, Fort Worth, Houston, and San Antonio--had more than 100,000 residents.[32] Thus, it is readily apparent that Texas was only approaching the status of a truly urban state; many of the cities over 10,000, to say nothing of those from 2,500 to 10,000, were either partially or wholly dependent on agriculture for their livelihood. Because of this dependence and a close affinity for the rural values and rural way of life, most of the cities of Texas reflected the thinking of rural America. Although it is difficult to determine the exact number, many of the city dwellers undoubtedly had been only recently farmers or rural citizens themselves. This should partly explain the reluctance of Texans to adapt themselves to the new insititutuions, such as public welfare, that are required in an urban society. It may also account for the reluctance of urban residents to challenge the countryside for political control of the state. Perhaps, it would be more accurate to say that the approximately one million people, or 18 percent of the state who lived in cities over 100,000 were the truly urban residents since they were forced by circumstances to face the problems that are usually associated with city life in the twentieth century.

The composition of the population of Texas also helps

---

[31]*Fifteenth Census of the United States: 1930. Population*, III, 941.

[32]*Ibid.*, 941, 1015; *Texas Almanac--1931*, 151-152.

to explain why it reacted in certain ways to specific events
during the Great Depression. Of the nearly six million
people in the state 73.5 percent or four and one-fourth
million were classified as "white," 14.7 percent were Negro,
and 11.7 percent were Mexican. Of those classified as white
over four million were born in the United States while only
slightly less than 100,000 were foreign-born. Of the foreign-born element about 70 percent were naturalized citizens.[33]

Of the native white population only one-fourth was born
outside of Texas. As was true in frontier days the largest
number of native whites in the state had originally come from
the cotton producing states of the Old South. With the passage of years, however, a larger number and percentage of
residents listed their place of origin as one of the northern states. This changing trend in migration was expected
to continue as the century progressed.[34] It can easily be
seen that many of the ideas and values of the Texan were
shaped and influenced by the agrarian orientation of both
the Old South and the Midwest.

The foreign element in Texas was slight if only the
foreign-born citizens were considered, but there was also a
substantial number of native whites of foreign or mixed
parentage. Of the 426,000 citizens of foreign white stock,
327,000 native whites had one or more parents of foreign
birth. Germany was the nation most heavily represented in
the foreign stock with more than 150,000 people, constitut-
ing 36 percent of the total. The other nations with large
representations in Texas were Czechoslovakia (11.5%), England (6.9%), Italy (5.1%), Mexico (4.6%),[35] and Irish Free

[33]*Fifteenth Census of the United States: 1930. Population*, III, 941.

[34]*Texas Almanac--1929*, 43.

[35]The native population of Mexican extraction was listed in the
1930 census as "Other Races." In 1920 they had been listed with the
whites; thus comparison of figures for 1920 and 1930 will not be cor-

13

State (4.4%). The remaining foreign stock originated throughout the world, but most of this number was, by far, from Northern and Western Europe.[36] The German, Danish, Scandinavian, Austrian, and Czechoslovakian population had always been mainly rural while most of the others lived in cities.[37] The English, Irish, and Italians particularly were urban dwellers.[38]

As already indicated the two major non-white groups in Texas were Mexicans and Negroes. The estimated number of Mexicans in 1920 was 388,675; of these, 145,940 were native born and 242,735 were born in Mexico.[39] By 1930 the Mexicans had increased to 683,681 or 11.7 percent of the total population. The census figures do not indicate the number of Mexicans who were foreign born at this time.[40] The Mexicans, in 1933, were concentrated mainly along the Rio Grande River extending inside Texas for an average of two hundred miles. The larger cities, particularly San Antonio and El Paso, had a heavy concentration of Mexicans. The large increase in the Hispanic population from 1920 to 1930 was due mainly to the economic opportunities in Texas combined with the unsettled political and economic situation in Mexico. From 1930 to 1933 depressed economic conditions in Texas and stricter United States immigration laws resulted in a decrease in Mexican immigration. This serious depression caused an estimate to be made that approximately 100,000 had returned to Mexico between 1930 and 1933.[41] Slightly less

rect unless this change in method is understood. *Fifteenth Census of the United States: 1930. Population*, III, 2-3.

[36] *Ibid.*, 948.

[37] *Texas Almanac--1933*, 48.

[38] *Fifteenth Census of the United States: 1930. Population*, III, 948.

[39] *Ibid.*, 2-3.

[40] *Ibid.*, 941.

[41] *Texas Almanac--1933*, 48.

14

than one-half of the Mexicans were urban dwellers in 1930, composing 13.4 percent of the total population; slightly more than one-half composed 10.7 percent of the rural inhabitants. It should be noted, however, that about one-third of the rural Mexican population neither lived on farms nor were engaged directly in agricultural pursuits.[42]

The other major non-white element in Texas, the blacks, constituted 14.7 percent of the total population in 1930, a decline in percentage from 1920 (15.9%) and 1910 (17.7%) despite an increase in absolute numbers of over 100,000 from 1920 to 1930. Of the 854,964 blacks in the state slightly more than one-third made up 13.8 percent of the rural population; approximately four-fifths lived in non-farm rural areas.[43] In 1933 black citizens were concentrated mainly in the eastern and southeastern one-third of the state. The heaviest density was in a belt extending about 150 miles westward from the Louisiana boundary.[44] As already noted, the black population was growing in total numbers, but not as rapidly as the white element. This was due to the small migration of blacks from Texas into the northern states although this was not as large in Texas as in the southern states east of the Mississippi River.[45]

Since the non-white groups constituted over one-fourth of the total residents of the state, some knowledge of the economic and social status of these people would be helpful in understanding the state as a whole. The way in which minority groups reacted to the depression, where it can be ascertained, will be of significance. Since minority groups only rarely spoke out and since few of them held political office, it is easy to conclude that they agreed with the

[42]*Fifteenth Census of the United States: 1930. Population*, III, 941.

[43]*Ibid.*

[44]*Texas Almanac--1933*, 48.

[45]*Ibid.*, *1929*, 44.

opinion of the state as a whole or that they were too inarticulate, or perhaps too afraid, to speak. As will be
shown, these groups did on occasion disagree with the majority and, in rare instances, took the lead in forming public
opinion.[46]

Figures and information on the Mexicans are difficult
to obtain, but it is reasonable to assume that the Mexican-
Americans of Texas suffered much social, economic, and political discrimination, particularly in the areas of heaviest
concentration. This is due both to historical causes dating
from the colonial period and to the natural inclination to
dislike and distrust those who are different from the majority in custom, religion, or language. Mexican influence in
political affairs was probably small also. Although the
census statement on illiteracy does not give figures for
Mexicans, their position can be deduced from the other figures given. Of a total of over 300,000 illiterates in Texas
over ten years of age, Mexicans constitutioned more than one-
half of that total with more than 160,000; this is approximately 34 percent of the total Mexican population compared
to the state total of 6.8 percent.[47] Such a degree of illiteracy indicates that it would be difficult for Mexicans to
exert much political influence. When they did, it was usually only in the cities or other areas where they were heavily concentrated. It was here that a Latin leader could
exert an influence similar to that of the city bosses over
the immigrants in northern cities.

[46]See for example the advanced thinking of the League of United
Latin Americans when it advocated federal ownership of banks in 1932,
some time before much of the state agreed. J.T. Canales, "Usury," *Lulac
News,* I (July, 1932), 5.

[47]*Fifteenth Census of the United States: 1930. Population,* III, 946.
The Census Bureau classes a person as literate if he is able to read and
write; ability to write his name is not considered literacy. Since no
specific test was given during the enumeration of the census, the figures are based on the responses of the citizen. *Ibid.,* 3.

The condition of blacks in Texas is easier to ascertain since statistics are more readily available. Discrimination against blacks is well-known throughout the South; it is reasonable to assume that it was more or less the same in Texas with the highest degree being in the south and southeastern parts of the state where the black population was largest. The number of blacks lynched in the United States is usually a fair indication of their position. The latter years of the thirties witnessed a decline in this activity throughout the nation, but during the first few years the numbers were erratic.

> In 1930 a total of twenty Negroes was lynched, as against seven in 1929. The next year the figure was twelve. In 1932 it dipped abruptly to six, soared to twenty-four in 1933, declined to only fifteen in 1934, mounted again to eighteen in 1935.[48]

No figures are available for Texas, but it is true that blacks were disliked and subject to mistreatment. On one occasion, for example, a mob in Sherman, unable to remove a black prisoner from the county jail for lynching, satisfied itself by setting fire to the court house, thus destroying both the prisoner and the county building.[49] At least one newspaper in Texas was concerned about the national rate of lynchings and was happy with the decline in 1931. "This is good news, especially when it is remembered that a bad depression year usually intensifies class and racial antagonism and makes lynchings more likely rather than less."[50]

Blacks also suffered from economic and social problems as much, or more so, than did white citizens. In 1930 blacks in Texas were losing jobs and farms; attendance in public schools was on the decline; discrimination was common; very few were skilled enough to hold jobs in many plants and

[48] W.J. Cash, *The Mind of the South* (New York: Random House Vintage Books, 1941), 379.

[49] New York *Times*, May 10, 1930, p. 1.

[50] Austin *Statesman*, June 14, 1932.

factories that were coming to Texas.[51] In the same year many
blacks, probably a majority, were living in very poor conditions in the various alleys of Galveston.[52] An example of
the relative economic position of Texas blacks is indicated
by the unemployment figures from the census of 1930. In
this early stage of the depression 4.8 percent of black
workers were unemployed as compared to 4.3 percent for the
total population and 4.2 percent of white workers.[53] This
was bad enough, but as conditions got worse for the state as
a whole, they became proportionately worse for the black
citizen. In October 1933 an unemployment relief census,
taken by the Federal Emergency Relief Administration, showed 7.1 percent of all Texans on relief; blacks were in a
worse condition. They had 8.8 percent on relief while whites
had 5.4 percent.[54] It is not wise to compare the two sur-
veys too closely because they do not report exactly the same
conditions and different methods were used to compute the
totals. They do serve, however, to indicate the low economic
position of blacks in Texas in relation to whites; they also
show that the position of blacks declined proportionately to
that of the white citizen. The literacy rate among blacks
also indicates their relative position in Texas. Illiteracy was 13.4 percent among blacks, but in the state as a
whole the rate was only 6.8 percent; among native whites it
was less than two percent.[55]

The fear and suspicion of blacks in Texas was shown in

[51] "Pens of the People," Galveston *Daily News*, April 7, 1930.

[52] *Ibid.*, January 24, 1930.

[53] *Fifteenth Census of the United States: 1930. Unemployment--United States Summary*, 18.

[54] U.S. Federal Emergency Relief Administration, *Unemployment Relief Census October 1933*, (1933), 13-14.

[55] *Fifteenth Census of the United States: 1930. Population*, III, 946.

the action taken against a group of avowed Communists who were arrested for agitation among the unemployed of Dallas in 1931. Although there were a number of charges that could have been brought against the men, one of them was convicted for advocating Negro equality. [56]

The foregoing illustrations should indicate the feeling in Texas for minority groups and their relative positions in 1930. It is clear that if this degree of tension and inequality existed in 1930, at the beginning of the depression, conditions would become much worse as the crisis deepened.

Religious affiliation in Texas generally followed the trend in most southern states. In Texas in 1930 there were sixty-three different religious groups reported with 15,062 churches; total membership was 2,280,366. Following the national pattern, Texas was predominantly a Protestant area. Protestant denominations reporting more than 10,000 members each included eight different churches although several were divided into a number of smaller divisions. The largest group was the combined Baptist churches with a total of 5,949 churches and a membership of 760,192. This included the Southern Baptist Convention, the largest single Protestant body in Texas, with a membership of over 465,000. All black Baptists in Texas totaled 234,000. The remaining were scattered among four other smaller groups. Next in size was the combined total of all Methodist groups. The 4,230 congregations and 508,544 members included a number of divisions including two branches for blacks totaling over 56,000. The other six major Protestant denominations totaling slightly over 400,000 included the various Lutheran bodies (99,-737), the Churches of Christ (98,909), the Presbyterian groups (85,514), the Disciples of Christ (77,150), the Protestant Episcopal Church (32,700), and the Evangelical Synod of North America (11,137). The remaining Protestant churches were small in membership and of little significance

[56]"The Dallas Mob," *The Common Herd*, XVI (June, 1931), 3.

on a state-wide scale. The Jewish faith was represented by forty-nine congregations and 39,237 members.

By far the largest single religious body was the Roman Catholic Church with 742 churches and 555,899 members.[57] The Catholic Church was only about one-fifth the size of the combined Protestant denominations, but since it was under one organization and one leadership, its influence was undoubtedly proportionately greater among its own members than that of the Protestants who had a tendency for factional dispute and lack of centralized leadership.

Throughout the South the educational systems lagged far behind the national average. Strides were made in the 1920s, however, to bring standards up to the national level. Despite the poor level of achievement in southern schools, "the costs relative to total wealth were highest for any section, for the good reason that the region, with its high birthrate, had a relatively greater number of young people of school age."[58] Comparative figures show that the "expenditures per white school child ranged from a high of $47.64 in Texas to a low of $20.83 in Arkansas. Elsewhere expenditures per school child ranges from $125.43 in California to $64.65 in New Hampshire."[59] Despite this poor record, Texans defended their schools by explaining that Texas was a new state with a population density one-half that of the nation; to develop a good educational system took time; and the best schools were usually found in areas of heaviest concentration of population. These defenders were also fond of pointing out that Texas ranked first in total expendi-

---

[57] *Texas Almanac--1931*, 290-293. It should be noted that the religious census is only taken every ten years; the one nearest 1930 was in 1926. Therefore, the figures given here, although relatively accurate, will not be exactly correct for 1930. *Ibid.*, 290.

[58] Cash, *The Mind of the South*, 423-424.

[59] Cohn, *King Cotton*, 244.

tures supplied by the state for public schools, second in percentage of public funds spent for education compared to total cost of government, and third in percentage of state and local debt incurred for education.[60] Despite lagging behind the nation for many years, Texas was one southern state that had made much progress by the time the depression arrived.

Texas in 1930 was a rural state with a growing urban element, with at least one-fourth of its population of nonwhite groups, with a poor but improving educational system, with a strong agrarian influence, and with no tradition and small understanding of public welfare and relief. Any area of this type would be hard-pressed in a serious financial crisis. That crisis came with the crash of the stock market in 1929.

---

[60] *Texas Almanac--1929*, 225.

CHAPTER II

THE STOCK MARKET CRASH

The Great Depression, in retrospect a watershed of American history, became apparent to almost everyone within a few weeks or months after the collapse of the stock market in October 1929. The depression did not begin with the decline in stock values because some facets of the American economy, notably agriculture, had been depressed for some time. However, the shaky financial and banking structure, major weaknesses in the economy, did not become noticeable to the general public until the stock market crisis placed new and stronger demands upon it.

Generally, the eight years just preceding the Wall Street debacle were ones of great prosperity for the United States. The increasing prosperity was basically sound until about 1927 when the stock market assumed a more important role in the nation's economy and culminated by mid-1929 with inflated prices completely beyond reason.

The United States was controlled politically during this decade by the Republican Party. No shrinking violet, it readily took credit for the unparalleled prosperity of the nation. Herbert Hoover, in the campaign of 1928, did not heistate to remind the American people

> that the policies of the Republican Party have played a large part in . . . the building of the magnificent progress which shows upon every hand today. I say with emphasis that without the wise policies which the Republican Party has brought into action during this period, no such progress would have been possible.[1]

With the accession of Warren G. Harding to the presidency in 1921, business, especially big business, assumed a much larger voice in the nation's governmental affairs.

---

[1] Ray Lyman Wilbur (ed.), *The New Day: Campaign Speeches of Herbert Hoover, 1928* (Stanford, California: Stanford University Press, 1928), 150. Hereafter cited as Wilbur, *The New Day*.

Business did not demand a great number of services from the government, but it was very insistent upon those that it did want. Efficiency and economy that would bring lower taxes was the most important; business still insisted, though less vehemently, on a protective tariff. Its demand for a return to free enterprise meant, in essence, the withdrawal of government from business of any sort and the greatest possible elimination of governmental restrictions. This did not mean that the administration was to stop aiding business whenever and wherever it could.[2] The Republican administration of Harding followed the policy, "as nearly as a leaderless administration could be said to have had a policy," of doing "with alacrity whatever business wanted to have done."[3] This favored position for business was maintained in subsequent administrations. President Coolidge, even more business oriented than Harding, best expressed himself in one of his most often quoted statements. "The business of the United States is business." At another time he also said, "The man who builds a factory builds a temple. . . . The man who works there worships there."[4]

Herbert Hoover, elected to the presidency in 1928, had been in both the Harding and Coolidge administrations as Secretary of Commerce and was in full accord with this business philosophy. In the election year of 1928, Hoover was aided by the apparently increasing level of prosperity although a number of other factors played a part in his election. The Dow-Jones stock averages, long considered a reliable barometer of business conditions, gained almost one hundred points, reaching a level of 300 by the beginning of

[2] John D. Hicks, *Republican Ascendancy 1921-1933* (New York: Harper & Row Torchbooks, 1963), 50.

[3] *Ibid.*

[4] As quoted in John M. Blum *et al.*, *The National Experience* (Harcourt, Brace & World, Inc., 1963), 605-606.

1929.[5] During the campaign, Hoover continually emphasized
the economic record of the previous eight years under Republican Presidents; he spoke often about freedom from poverty and fear.[6] To him, this degree of well-being had not
been made possible by governmental interference in business
or daily life, but instead, "by adherence to the principles
of decentralized self-government, ordered liberty, equal
opportunity, and freedom to the individual. . . ."[7] Although Hoover did not say much about the weaknesses in the
economy, his opponent, Alfred Smith, could do little to remind the people that in 1927 669 banks had closed, four million workers had been unemployed, and farm distress was severe. "A majority of the voters probably believed that the
country was prosperous, and no one could persuade them that
it was not."[8]

Hoover stated during the campaign that his concept of
America included a prosperous nation where the wealth was
widely distributed among the people, not concentrated in
the hands of a few.[9] He and other Republican leaders seemed
not to notice, however, that in the boom year of 1929 approximately 18,000,000 families, or half the total population,
received less than $1,500 per year income. After the stock
market crash it decreased to approximately one-half that
figure.[10]

[5]James Joseph Hannah, "Urban Reaction to the Great Depression in
the United States, 1929-1933" (Ph.D. dissertation, University of California, Berkeley, 1956), 5. Hereafter cited as Hannah, "Urban Reaction."

[6]Wilbur, *The New Day*, 150, 168, 176.

[7]*Ibid.*, 168.

[8]Harris Gaylord Warren, *Herbert Hoover and the Great Depression*
(New York: Oxford University Press, 1959), 45. Hereafter cited as Warren, *Hoover and the Depression*.

[9]Wilbur, *The New Day*, 176.

[10]William A. Lydgate, *What Our People Think* (New York: Thomas Y.
Crowell Company, 1944), 103.

Despite this and other ominous warning signs the Hoover administration began in March 1929 with great promise. Foreign problems, a legacy of the world war, had been eased somewhat with the Kellogg-Briand Peace Pact and the arrangements on war debts made by the Young Commission. Industry was booming, labor peace was widespread, and stock prices were rising; the future seemed secure.[11]

Conditions in Texas in 1929 were comparable to the national ones. Prior to the crash, business remained very good, especially in insurance and pharmaceuticals. In the rural communities on the South Plains business continued to be encouraging in the summer; even after the crash, prospects in all lines of business seemed good.[12] Year-end statements by various chambers of commerce also reflected the prosperous times. Lubbock reported gains in bank deposits of 38 percent in one year's time[13] while Dallas indicated that 1929 was very good for banking and construction.[14] The state teachers' periodical reprinted an article from *Nation's Business* that painted national prosperity in the most glowing terms, both for the present and the future.[15] This is somewhat significant since public school teachers were usually among the last to share in national prosperity; it may have possibly been a word of encouragement to them rather than an accurate statement of their condition. Although some of these glowing reports may have been exaggerated to impress or encourage

[11] Dwight Lowell Dumond, *America in Our Time* (New York: Henry Holt and Company, 1937), 433.

[12] "Business is Good," *Southern Pharmaceutical Journal*, XXII (October, 1929), 79; "Editorial," *Southwestern Life News*, XXIII (March, 1929), 1; *Terry County Herald* (Brownfield), July 26, 1929, December 6, 1929.

[13] "Bank Deposits Gain 28 Per cent in Year," *The Hub*, III (November, 1929), 8.

[14] "1929--A Year of Accomplishment," *Dallas*, VIII (December, 1929), 7.

[15] John Hays Hammond, "A Look Back and Ahead," *The Texas Outlook*, XIII (October, 1929), 18-20.

readers, economic conditions in Texas did remain generally favorable for most of 1929.

Pride in past accomplishment and optimism for continued prosperity in 1929 and subsequent years was general through-out the country. Despite the faint signs of economic weak-ness the average citizen was content with the *status quo* as long as nothing happened to challenge prosperity.[16] When Herbert Hoover became President, he could see nothing in the future except a continuation of the good times; he constant-ly issued optimistic statements calculated to further in-crease confidence. His statements would later cause him much criticism and embarrassment, but one of his defenders maintained that the President should not be blamed for his typical American optimism. To expect a politician to fore-see the economic future was foolish when most of the profes-sional economists themselves did not see any end to the boom days.[17] In fact, they continued in mid-1929 to assure the nation that it had reached "a permanently high plateau" of prosperity.[18]

The attitude of Texans toward the future was comparable to the national one, except for the occasional prophet of doom who was quickly silenced or ignored. The weekly news-papers, spokesmen for the business interests they represen-ted, were confident about the future. One South Texas news-paper reported that since postal receipts were a true baro-meter of economic conditions, the prospects for 1930 were good because postal receipts for 1929 were well above the previous year.[19] During the early months of 1929 another

[16] Dixon Wecter, *The Age of the Great Depression, 1929-1941* (New York: The Macmillan Company, 1948), 8. Hereafter cited as Wecter, *The Great Depression*.

[17] Eugene Lyons, *Our Unknown Ex-President* (Garden City, New York: Doubleday & Company, Inc., 1948), 237.

[18] Wecter, *The Great Depression*, 1.

[19] Clipping from Huntsville *Item*, July 9, 1930, Clay Stone Briggs Papers, University of Texas Archives, Austin, Texas, folder no. 43.

paper ran a statement on its masthead declaring, "The year 1929 promises to be a banner year in building and development progress."[20] Whether these statements reflected the true sentiments of the people is not easy to acertain, for they may have been merely examples of the "booster" spirit so common in the twenties.

Despite the almost unanimous confidence, there were occasional notes of pessimism in Texas opinion. One man, soon after the election of 1928, was concerned that Hoover would not only continue Coolidge's business policy but that he would be "aggressively expansive in favor of the predatory classes and those seeking special governmental privileges."[21] High cattle prices in the spring of 1929 were not encouraging to the ranching interests because they were convinced that history would soon repeat itself with a drop in prices, depressing the agricultural community even more.[22] Therefore, prospects for the future were not bright for all Texans.

The stock market crash did not begin the depression because signs of weakness in the economy had been noted earlier in the year. The early stages of a depression could be seen by June when industrial and factory production indexes reached a peak and turned downward. Steel production, freight-car loadings, home-building, and automobile production were on the decline; agriculture had not recovered since the end of the first world war; employment was difficult to obtain and to retain because of the decline in many of the major industries.[23]

[20] *Texas Spur* (Spur), February 15, 1929.

[21] Democratic National Committee Correspondence, 1928-1933, Franklin D. Roosevelt Library, Hyde Park, New York, December 11, 1928, Box 718. Hereafter cited as FDRL.

[22] *Texas Spur*, April 19, 1929.

[23] John Kenneth Galbraith, *The Great Crash, 1929* (New York: Time Incorporated edition, 1962), 9; Irving Fisher, *The Stock Market Crash-- And After* (New York: The Macmillan Company, 1930), 57; Harry L. Hopkins,

Conditions in 1929, both economic and psychological, were of a nature to create a severe panic if anything abnormal (if the twenties can be considered normal) were to occur. This challenge to the prevailing philosophy and mores came in the panic of October when the stock market tumbled like a house of cards. The complacency and sanguine acceptance of prosperity of Texans was so commonplace that the crash and ensuing depression challenged the basic values of the people.

The theory that the crash confronted a completely unsuspecting people is incorrect. A number of prominent individuals, expressing fear of the inflated market, tried to warn the people of the dangers of speculation. Men like Paul Warburg, a Federal Reserve expert, and Francis H. Sisson, vice president of the Guaranty Trust Company of New York, urged responsibility and sanity in stock purchases and begged the people to use more caution.[24] Despite these and other warnings people throughout the nation continued to "play the market" in the hope of quick wealth. The warnings were not completely unheeded because a number of people saved themselves from the impending disaster by liquidating their holdings earlier. A pessimistic banker, Peter J. Brady, after predicting a crash early in the year, declared, "I know nobody will believe me, but it will come."[25] And come it did! It came with greater fury and with greater losses than any stock market panic in history.

Though the people did not realize it, the great bull market came to an end on the first trading day in September when industrials closed at 381 1/4, the highest level of the twenties. After that, despite occasional upsurges, the mar-

Spending to Save (New York: W. W. Norton & Company, Inc., 1936), 13; G. D. H. Cole, *A Guide Through World Chaos* (New York: Alfred A. Knopf, 1934), 6.

[24]Hannah, "Urban Reaction," 9.

[25]*Weekly Dispatch* (San Antonio), November 9, 1929.

ket steadily declined throughout September and October. The first real panic began on October 24 when almost thirteen million shares were sold. Most people who purchased stock on this and subsequent days hoped this would be the low point of the decline; thus, after buying at low prices they would profit when the market recovered. The most disastrous day in the history of the New York Stock Exchange to that date, and probably of any exchange in the world came on October 29 when almost sixteen and one-half million shares were traded.[26] Industrials dropped thirty points to an average of 230--a decline of more than 150 points in two months.

Even before the extent of the crisis was known, the search for a villain started. Roger Babson and others who had forecast a crash were severely criticized and blamed for the break since their predictions undermined the confidence of the financial world. Babson was considered so responsible for this temporary setback that the slump is often referred to as "The Babson Break."[27] This was the beginning of the witch hunt to find a culprit.

Quickly, to bolster the sagging confidence of the rank-and-file investor and speculator, a number of prominent bankers and other financial leaders began to buy stocks, with great attendant publicity. Despite the temporary help this provided, buyer confidence could not be maintained.[28] Attempts to shore up confidence were also mainfest by the deliberately optimistic statements issued by many of the nation's leading financial authorities. Men like Irving Fisher, stock market expert, Secretary of Commerce R. P. Lamont, and Secretary of the Treasury Andrew Mellon all tried to reassure the public that the crash was nothing to

[26]Galbraith, *The Great Crash*, 101-116.

[27]Hannah, "Urban Reaction," 7-13; Galbraith, *The Great Crash*, 86-89.

[28]Hannah, "Urban Reaction," 19-23; George Soule, *Prosperity Decade* (New York: Rinehart & Company, Inc., 1947), 308.

worry about. In a complete reversal of previous contentions, they tried to convince the public that the Stock Exchange had no direct bearing on the financial stability of the country or on the actual production of goods and services. Statements of this nature had a hollow ring, however, when compared to the recent attitude that the market was a true barometer of economic conditions and the soundness of business. Professor Fisher's statement that the crash represented only a "shaking out of the lunatic fringe" in the market received wide support from other financial experts.[29] The hope that the market would soon reach bottom and begin to rise again was a lost one; the decline which began in September 1929 did not end until June 1932. Stock prices, of even the most stable companies, reached unbelievable lows by June 1932. United States Steel, for example, was listed on September 3, 1929, at 262 but by July 8, 1932, it was quoted at 22; this was common among most stocks listed on the New York Exchange.[30]

Once the extent of the crash became apparent, people reacted to it in different ways across the nation. Hoover, long the champion of unfettered free enterprise, was later critical of businessmen for not recognizing in the aftermath of the debacle that it was nothing more than a normal, cyclical slump that occurred at three to seven year intervals.[31] His criticism is surprising in view of his position in 1928 that United States prosperity was due to Republican policies that favored business interests.[32] It is

[29] Henry Morton Robinson, *Fantastic Interim* (New York: Harcourt, Brace & World, 1943), 182; Galbraith, *The Great Crash*, 100; Russel B. Nye, *Midwestern Progressive Politics* (East Lansing: Michigan State University Press, 1959), 322.

[30] Galbraith, *The Great Crash*, 144.

[31] Herbert Hoover, *The Great Depression, 1929-1941*, Vol. III: *The Memoirs of Herbert Hoover* (New York: The Macmillan Company, 1952), 30.

[32] Wilbur, *The New Day*, 150, 168.

also surprising that he would, twenty years after the crash, still maintain that it was not abnormal.

Hoover and the financial leaders feared more than anything else a financial crisis caused mostly by fear and loss of confidence in the wake of the crash. The series of optimistic statements they issued in the first weeks after the disaster [33] are partially explained by this fear. Hoover believed that the fundamental question was whether the federal government should step in to relieve the crisis and stabilize business. To him it was unthinkable. Since it had never been done before, to do so now would weaken confidence rather than strengthen it. He believed that the major responsibility was to help maintain confidence.[34] In his first annual message to Congress in December, he tried to minimize the effects of the crash when he said:

> The capital which has hitherto been absorbed in stock-market loans for speculative purposes is now returning to the normal channels of business. There has been no inflation in the price of commodities; there has been no undue accumulation of goods, and foreign trade has expanded to a magnitude which exerts a steadying influence upon activity in industry and employment.[35]

Statements, both official and non-official, from men of prominence reflected the President's attitude. Most believed the only thing required was to avert the development of deep pessimism because when, in due time, the market had corrected itself there would be no serious long-range repercussions.[36] The concern for confidence-building was re-

[33] Daniel R. Fusfeld, *The Economic Thought of Franklin D. Roosevelt and the Origins of the New Deal* (New York: Columbia University Press, 1956), 172; hereafter cited as Fusfeld, *The Economic Thought of FDR*; Fisher, *The Stock Market Crash--And After*, 63; Stuart Chase, *Prosperity Fact or Myth* (New York: Charles Boni Paper Books, 1929), 180.

[34] Hoover, *The Great Depression*, 29, 32.

[35] William Star Myers (ed.), *The State Papers and Other Public Writings of Herbert Hoover* (2 vols.; Garden City, New York: Doubleday, Doran & Company, Inc., 1934), I, 145. Hereafter cited as Myers, *State Papers of Herbert Hoover*.

[36] *Ibid.*, 575; Fisher, *The Stock Market Crash--And After*, 63; Chase,

flected by the *Saturday Evening Post* when it stated, "Wall Street may sell stocks, but Main Street is buying goods."[37] This served the dual purpose of maintaining confidence and of helping to remove from the minds of the people the belief that the stock market indicated true business conditions. On the whole, according to one authority, the people making these statements were not held responsible for them. Hoover was the one exception. His personal prestige suffered because his oft-repeated statements of confidence and optimism proved untrue, and because his attitude of reassurance became a major instrument of government policy.[38]

The search for a villain (or conspirator) upon which to place the blame began soon after the crash. Some people, following Hoover's lead, believed that since nothing was basically wrong with the market, the trouble was caused chiefly by mob psychology brought on by the excesses of the evil and unscrupulous professional speculator.[39] Probably the most realistic statement was made by *Variety*, the newspaper of show business, when it reported, "WALL STREET LAYS AN EGG!"[40] It would be some time before a large segment of the business community, and the public at large, would be this honest.

Reaction in Texas to the stock market crash took many forms. By and large, public opinion was expressed in the daily and weekly press, the official publications of various business enterprises, and those publications devoted to the

Prosperity Fact or Myth, 180; Soule, *Prosperity Decade,* 313.

[37] As quoted in Eric F. Goldman, *Rendezvous with Destiny* (New York: Random House Vintage Books, 1956), 248.

[38] Galbraith, *The Great Crash,* 147.

[39] Fisher, *The Stock Market Crash--And After,* 63; Chase, *Prosperity Fact or Myth,* 15; Soule, *Prosperity Decade,* 311.

[40] As quoted in Gilbert Seldes, *The Years of the Locust* (Boston: Little, Brown, and Company, 1933), 11.

interests of a particular social, intellectual, or economic group. The response passed through three different phases. The immediate reaction during October, November, and December of 1929 was much the same throughout the state; during 1930 Texans made a more penetrating analysis of the market; from the beginning of 1931 until the inauguration of President Franklin D. Roosevelt in March 1933, there was continuing discussion of the stock market and its relationship to the severe depression that paralyzed the nation.

The immediate reaction in 1929 was similar to that of Hoover and the prominent financial leaders. A number of the small town weekly newspapers used "canned" editorials to preach optimism. A number of them, using the same story, expressed the opinion that the crash represented nothing more than the destruction of luxury businesses that really had no place in American society anyway. This editorial was particularly happy to see the discomfiture of the rich. Beauty parlors with a minimum charge of $25 per treatment, "exclusive jewelry stores where no customer was really welcome unless he had a hundred thousand dollars to spend" were really the only businesses to suffer from the turbulence on Wall Street. Thus, Texas and American business really had nothing to worry about; they probably would benefit with the speculators and gamblers out of the market.[41] Other canned editorials assured Texans that "while stocks 'faw down and go boom' and a multitude of speculators find themselves the victims, our national prosperity continues on an even keel." The average American was not about to succumb to widespread pessimism about the possibility of depression to the degree that he would lower his standards of living and allow these predictions to come true.[42]

[41]*Hansford County News* (Gruver), November 15, 1929; *Texas Spur*, November 15, 1929; Beeville *Bee-Picayune*, November 28, 1929.

[42]*Devil's River News* (Sonora), November 8, 1929; Beeville *Bee-Picayune*, December 5, 1929; *Texas Spur*, December 6, 1929, December 27, 1929; Sterling City *News-Record*, December 13, 1929.

The confidence in the soundness of American business was reflected throughout the press of the state. Most papers emphasized that since the market had no relation to the real business conditions of the nation, anyone who predicted serious trouble was only a prophet of doom and should be ignored. Nothing of substance had been lost because the deflation in the market was only in paper values, not in real wealth.[43] This attitude was best expressed by a farm publication when it said:

> But the country is safe. Its resources have not been lessened by a single ton of ore or coal, or by a single bushel of grain, or a bale of cotton, or by a single industrial building. These things are all here, and the country will go forward on a sounder, saner and safer basis than since the wild gambling boom started a few years ago.[44]

Even organized labor, undoubtedly influenced by the business conference called by Hoover to prevent a depression, expressed optimism. Labor gave much credit to its own participation in the meeting for stopping what could have been a disaster.[45]

The El Paso *Times* was concerned about the crash and the effect it might have on public confidence. In a series of editorials from October 31 to December 11, it emphasized that in the chaotic conditions on Wall Street only one brokerage firm, which was not on the exchange itself, had gone bankrupt; New York, not Texas, was the principal sufferer;

---

[43] Greenville *Banner* as quoted in Dallas *Morning News*, November 28, 1929; Dorothy Dell DeMoss, "Dallas, Texas, during the Early Depression: The Hoover Years, 1929-1933" (M.A. thesis, The University of Texas at Austin, 1966), 12; hereafter cited as DeMoss, "Dallas during Depression"; Marion Martin Nordeman, "Midland, Texas, during the Depression, 1929-1933" (M.A. thesis, The University of Texas at Austin, 1967), 15-17; hereafter cited as Nordeman, "Midland during Depression"; Robert Allan Ozment, "Temple, Texas, and the Great Depression, 1929-1933" (M.A. thesis, The University of Texas at Austin, 1966), 7-8; hereafter cited as Ozment, "Temple and Depression."

[44] "The Sun Still Shines," *Cotton and Cotton Oil News*, XXX (November 18, 1929), 1.

[45] Dallas *Craftsman*, December 6, 1929.

because bankers were conservative, statements by them that the crash was not of great importance should be believed; and Secretary of the Treasury Mellon's announcement of a planned tax cut was an example of government optimism and confidence.[46] The number and intensity of confidence-building editorials makes it apparent that at least some of the citizens of El Paso were concerned about the crash, possibly to the extent of forecasting depression.

The insistence of the press that business was sound was echoed throughout the state. The papers continually insisted, by using statements of public officials, business leaders, and anyone else who might influence the public, that only the gamblers were hurt, not the basic structure of business.[47] Perhaps this sentiment was best expressed by a country editor when he wrote:

> No children, Santa Claus is not dead. He was not killed in the big crash on Wall Street, as at first reported. He may not come to see those "Bad Manses" who were operating on "margin" up there, but, never fear, he will be back to see all the little boys and girls in Terry County, who have been good.[48]

Even agriculture, long in a state of depression, shared this optimism. One journal reported that the market would not affect the cotton market, but when this proved untrue, it emphasized that in the long run world demand would mean more to the cotton farmer than any events on the New York Stock Exchange.[49]

[46] El Paso *Times*, October 31, 1929, November 15, 1929, November 19, 1929, December 11, 1929.

[47] Austin *Statesman*, November 10, 1929; *Devil's River News*, December 6, 1929; Galveston *Daily News*, October 31, 1929; Ernest Elmo Calkins, "Lessons of the Stock Market Crash," *Southern Florist and Nurseryman*, XXVIII (December 20, 1929), 8.

[48] *Terry County Herald*, November 15, 1929.

[49] Jack Blackwell, "The Situation in the Kingdom of Cotton," *Cotton and Cotton Oil News*, XXX (October 30, 1929), 2; *ibid.*, November 4, 1929, 2; *ibid.*, December 23, 1929.

The great concern for the stock market crash and its impact certainly indicated that many Texans were discussing the event and that the press was highly concerned about it. A deeper pessimism existed than most of these journals were willing to admit. Certainly one of the goals of the business organs, and much of the daily and weekly press, was to maintain a high level of business activity. Thus, the continual Pollyanna attitude was dishonest in some ways because it was an attempt to convince readers that people in other areas of the state and nation were not concerned about the events in New York. This was not true. This is merely one example of the paradox in American thinking. On the surface the press maintained a calm and happy appearance while underneath this facade, a deep-seated anxiety, which is difficult to prove, seems to be present.

In the desire to maintain confidence much of the state press tried to find a silver lining in the cloud of the Wall Street fiasco. Some of the newspapers explained that the crash was good because it proved the stability of American business; actual earning capacity of giant corporations had not declined, but had probably increased. Stability was indicated in that, unlike previous panics, the great brokerage and banking houses had not failed.[50] Others said that the good effect was that it drove the small amateur investors out of the market. A concern for the "Lambs" who had been shorn unmercifully was not of great importance. That the amateurs were forced from speculation back to work where they should have been all along, leaving the stock market to the men with the knowledge and the wealth to operate it, was a major advantage. Some of the papers thought that what had happened was good enough for the people who had no place in the market; the country folks should stay out of the lion's den of the city-slickers. In addition to the beneficial

[50] El Paso *Times*, October 29, 1929; Dallas *Morning News*, November 13, 1929.

removal of the non-professionals, bad stocks had been driven out of the market making the good ones even better risks.[51] The greatest number believed that the most beneficial result was that the deflation of the market now made it possible for more money to circulate throughout the country. They were pleased that local bankers who had been sending their money to New York because of high interest rates would now use it for local loans that would benefit Texas. Business would now improve.[52]

There were many Texans, of course, who took no notice the stock market and were even unaware of the crash. A recent study of East Texans revealed that many of them heard something about a "crash" in New York, but they really did not know what it meant. Life for them went on afterward just as it did before.[53]

Quickly after the crash, Texans began to look for a cause of the debacle. In the aftermath of the crash most observers believed it was caused by speculation, but this reaction took different forms. One small town paper said the cause was a state of mind in New York that began to panic and spread to the rest of the country.[54] Inherent in this statement is the concept that the state of mind was induced by the manipulators in New York.

Many of the newspapers and other commentators openly

---

[51] Amarillo *Daily News*, December 10, 1929; Austin *Statesman*, December 10, 1929, November 7, 1929; Port Isabel *Pilot*, November 13, 1929; George West *Enterprise*, December 6, 1929; Weatherford *Democrat*, November 1, 1929.

[52] Galveston *Daily News*, November 23, 1929; "The Parade is Over," *Hardware and Implement Journal*, XXXIV (December, 1929), 56; *The Valley Farmer and South Texas Grower*, November 5, 1929, p. 16; hereafter cited as *The Valley Farmer*.

[53] Oral history interviews by students at Panola College under the supervision of Professor Bill O'Neal, 1978-1981, originals in Whisenhunt files.

[54] Pampa *News* as quoted in Dallas *Morning News*, December 12, 1929.

hinted that the cause was a conspiracy of big business, particularly of large speculators. One paper openly declared that there may have been a political motive involved that caused "Wall Street" deliberately to bring on the crash. Probably it was merely a device to frighten Congress into passing tariff increases demanded by the Eastern manufacturing interests. This paper was convinced of the conspiracy because "in the absence of concrete explantory [sic] conditions, the debacle had the suddenness of premeditation.[55]

Although others did not express their beliefs in these exact words or with such conviction, the same idea of a financial conspiracy can be seen throughout the state. Many believed that the "big eastern money barons" had caused the bull market boom for the express goal of enticing unsuspecting small, inexperienced speculators into the market. Then the "lambs" were bankrupted by a deliberate deflation of the market that left it and the wealth of the country in the hands of Wall Street. Some of the papers took an "I-told-you-so" attitude and were now relieved that the small investors had learned a leason that would force them to use their money for investment at home. This is not to say that they were totally unfeeling for those who lost their money, but the press usually implied that those who play with fire get burned.[56]

Not all the observers advanced the conspiracy theory, but among most of them there was a decided anti-Wall Street sentiment. One San Antonio resident reflected the ideas of many in a letter to Senator Tom Connally when he said:

> Now that a soviet of business and industry has been
> established under Commissar Julius [Klein, Assistant
> Secretary of Commerce] I suppose the Sons of the Wild

[55] Galveston *Daily News*, October 26, 1929.

[56] Sterling City *News-Record*, December 13, 1929; Dallas *Morning News*, November 20, 1929; El Paso *Times*, October 25, 1929, October 26, 1929, November 6, 1929.

Jackass will be able to find out how to vote without consulting the gentleman from Pennsylvania. Isn't that nice?

I hope the Congress will not destroy the market for stocks and bonds but sympathize with Sen Glass [*sic*] effort to restrict manipulation. A panic was the inevitable result of what had gone before.[57]

A similar attitude was expressed by E. G. Senter, gubernatorial candidate in 1930, who was very unhappy about Governor Dan Moody's promise to Hoover for an increase in state public works construction in order "to rehabilitate Wall Street." He contended that only the gamblers had been hurt in the crash; what they really wanted was for "the rest of the country to come build them up again so that they may try and have a more of a general panic on the next collapse."[58] Senter also thought that the public only got what it deserved because "the truth is the stock gamblers have absorbed all things to themselves so long that the public had grown insensible [*sic*] to the economic crime which they represent."[59]

Anti-Wall Street sentiment was expressed by many in attempts to discover the cause and in devising ways to keep it from happening again. Contrary to the optimism expressed by the press, many Texans, particularly Austinites, were concerned about the possibility of a depression. Many of those discussing causes did not always wave the flag of optimism and prosperity.[60]

[57] Tom Connally Papers, Library of Congress, Manuscript Division, Washington, D.C., General Correspondence, 1929, December 25, 1929, Box 10. Hereafter cited as Connally Papers.

[58] *Terry County Herald*, December 6, 1929.

[59] Connally Papers, n.d., Box 10.

[60] "The Economic Trend," *Editorials of the Month for Texas*, I (October, 1930), 487; Judith Geraldine Jenkins, "Austin, Texas, During the Great Depression, 1929-1936" (M.A. thesis, The University of Texas at Austin, 1965), 14; hereafter cited as Jenkins, "Austin during Depression"; "Fooling the Farmers," *The Common Herd*, XV (March, 1930), 12; *Weekly Dispatch*, December 21, 1929.

Gambling came in for its share of the blame. In the typical attitude of rural Protestant America, many believed this crisis was merely punishment for past sins. Senator Connally, in a letter to a constituent, explained that the stock market operations as dictated by big business were a near neighbor to gambling.[61] Concurrent with the charges against legalized gambling was the fear of immorality. *The Baptist Standard,* official publication of the Southern Baptist Convention, exposed a segment of Texas opinion with its concern for morality in New York. It also expressed widespread feeling that the market should be closed when it declared:

> Any business which causes "the community's mental health and vision" to need restoring is wrong. It ought to be opposed and smashed by the moral forces of the country. The whole parasitic gang of speculation bandits that fasten themselves upon the body of legitimate business and industry ought to be pruned off and there should be no possibility of their return.[62]

Senator Connally implied that the real cause of the trouble was the Republican Party because:

> The fawning sycophants who love to lick the feet of power, have been shouting every [*sic*] since last November that the increasing values on the stock market evidenced a "Hoover market." They were willing to claim the credit for this artificial and imaginative prosperity, but when the crash came, it was somebody else's market.[63]

Prior to 1930 proposed remedies for the evil were either to control the stock exchange through government regulation or close it altogether. Congressman O. H. Cross, who introduced a bill to make margin buying illegal, received much support. Thus, the concept of government regulation of such an immoral institution certainly had supporters [64] al-

---

[61] Connally Papers, November 30, 1929, Box 7.

[62] "Speculation and Other Gambling," *The Baptist Standard,* XLI (November 7, 1929), 4.

[63] Connally Papers, November 30, 1929, Box 7.

[64] *Ibid.,* November 22, 1929, Box 5, December 9, 1929, Box 7, November 11, 1929, Box 11.

though the idea was in contradiction to the business philosophy of the twenties. Among those who wanted the Stock
Exchange closed[65] was a man from Waxahachie who became quite
excited.

> The Stock Exchange and Commodity Exchanges as
> operated today, are non-essential to conducting our
> commercialism, they are merely and truly "LEACHES"
> on a great common-wealth and should be EXTERMINATED.
> Sentiment, generally, at present favors the
> EXTERMINATION of the damnable "Leaches."[66]

The above indicates that early reaction to the crash
took the extremes--optimism or dejection. By far the optimists were more numerous, but there did exist a disconcerting number who did not agree with the prophesies of un-
limted prosperity for the future. On the South Plains an
elderly country doctor who contributed to his county newspaper under the pen-name of Aesculapias was quite an astute
observer of society. Using sarcasm, he tried to prepare
Texans in his part of the state for the bad times to come.
After painting a rather dismal picture, he freely gave some
advice to his fellow citizens.

> However, be optimistic, go to bed and dream of
> oodles of money to pay for the car you bought and the
> gas for it this coming season. Tell your creditors
> that the President and others in authority have pro-
> claimed Prosperity and urge all others to build air
> castles and indulge in hallucinations about the things
> you haven't and never will have. This will do for
> the present.[67]

Aesculapias was more correct than even he probably believed;
in 1930 and subsequent years conditions became much worse.

During 1930 the stock market continued to decline despite the earlier optimism that it would recover and probably go higher than in the boom year of 1929. Even with the
continuing decline, Texas still looked for the silver lin-

---

[65]*Terry County Herald,* December 20, 1929.

[66]Connally Papers, November 26, 1929, Box 9.

[67]*Terry County Herald,* December 20, 1929.

ing. Some of the periodical literature, and the public as well, waited until the new year before commenting on the crash.

Among the business spokesmen optimism continued high early in the year, although an occasional feeling of pessimism can be noted. In their New Year's greetings a number of business publications announced that 1929 had been a good year and, despite the trouble in New York, Texas was sound. They indicated that now was the time to stop the widespread rumors of depression, to sell more life insurance, to improve the depressed floral business, and to make 1930 a banner year.[68] As the year progressed businessmen advocated investment in "safe" savings and loan associations, encouraged employee stock ownership, and ridiculed the talk of hard times that could induce a state of pessimism in 120 million people just because of the speculation of "a handful of fools in Wall Street."[69]

During 1930 the commercial press continued to be the most optimistic segment of Texas society, at least in print. In retrospect much of this optimism is rather unconvincing; perhaps the papers themselves were only "whistling in the dark" to keep up their own confidence. Some exhibited shock that Americans could be scared by what had happened in New York, while others continued to play variations on the old theme that business was sound, that there was nothing to worry about. They emphasized that the market was only an incorrect barometer of actual conditions and that Texans should not be distressed if a few parasitic speculators got what was coming to them.[70] One paper tried to show that

[68]"Whispers," *Hardware and Implement Journal*, XXXV (January, 1930), 9; "President Vardell's Address to the 1929 Club," *Southwestern Life News*, XXIV (January, 1930), 8; "Greetings and Best Wishes," *Southern Florist and Nurseryman*, XXVIII (January 3, 1930), 14.

[69]Brady *Standard*, February 4, 1930; El Paso *Times*, August 20, 1930; Austin *Statesman*, November 7, 1930.

[70]Galveston *Daily News*, January 1, 1930, February 12, 1930; Has-

confidence in good securities had not faltered because the
stock of the West Texas Utilities Company continued to sell
during and after the crash at no decrease in price until
the company sold more shares than it had originally planned.[71] In the search for a culprit, the conspiracy of the
stock manipulators continued to get most of the blame.
Others included the Federal Reserve System and the Republican Party. Some newspapers were afraid that the crash would
bring forth radical legislation that would do more harm than
good.[72]

Why the newspapers remained so unrealistic in the face
of worsening conditions is difficult to explain. Perhaps
one Austin citizen was correct when he said that the papers
did not run scare headlines because the people were already
shaken enough and any pessimism of the newspaper would intensify that of the townspeople.[73] One of the most realistic statements made in 1930, although the typical confidence-building technique is apparent, was uttered by a
South Plains editor. After saying that Hoover was correct
in his statement that America was fundamentally sound, he
went on to challenge the Pollyanna attitude of many and to
discredit the idea that only a few New Yorkers had been
hurt in the crash.

> . . . *it is . . . senseless to say that the country
> did not suffer from the recent high financial crisis.*
> When it is remembered that thousands of small merchants,
> tens of thousands of clerks and perhaps millions of
> other middle class workers all over the country lost
> from a few dollars to thousands to go to the big New
> York manipulator, is there any wonder that it took all

kell *Free Press*, January 2, 1930; Beeville *Bee-Picayune*, April 3, 1930;
Devil's River News, January 3, 1930; George West *Enterprise*, February 7,
1930; "The Street Called Wall," *Holland's*, February, 1930, p. 4.

[71]*Texas Spur*, January 3, 1930.

[72]Galveston *Daily News*, October 16, 1930, August 10, 1930; Uvalde
Leader-News, April 4, 1930; Amarillo *Daily News*, October 20, 1930.

[73]Jenkins, "Austin during Depression," 15.

hands at Washington and the several capitols of states
busy for several weeks to keep the ship on an even keel.[74]

Other groups, reflecting popular anxiety, were not so
optimistic during 1930. Organized labor, although weak in
Texas, quickly recovered from its confidence binge of 1929
and began to criticize industry for its short-sightedness
that led to the crash. The accusation is clear that if industry had relied upon labor's sound advice this sort of
thing could never have happened.[75] The Southern Methodist
General Conference, representing Texas and other southern
states, joined the *Baptist Standard* in denouncing the immorality involved in market speculation and margin buying.[76]
Anti-Wall Street and anti-Hoover sentiment was decidedly
present among the few individuals who commented on the situation.[77] This sentiment grew significantly as the depression deepened.

From the beginning of 1931 until the inauguration of
President Roosevelt in March 1933 public reaction took a
decided turn. Very seldom did the press, or individuals
for that matter, speak in defense of the stock market. This
is not to say that they ceased trying to build confidence;[78]
however, defense of the stock market was very feeble. Statements about the temporary rise in stock prices or the need
for more confidence in the financial system appeared from
time to time,[79] but they were not very well-received. In-

[74] *Terry County Herald*, January 17, 1930. Emphasis added.

[75] Dallas *Craftsman*, March 28, 1930; *Weekly Dispatch*, November 8, 1930.

[76] Beeville *Bee-Picayune*, June 3, 1930.

[77] "Public Opinion," Amarillo *Daily News*, January 20, 1931; "Letters From Readers," Dallas *Morning News*, February 5, 1931.

[78] This is discussed fully in Chapter III.

[79] See for example: Amarillo *Daily News*, January 21, 1931; Galveston *Daily News*, October 22, 1931; "Two Speakers Give Dallas Some Advice," *Dallas*, X (February, 1931), 6-7.

stead of the incessant harping about how good the stock market was or how much was learned from the crash, Texans began to probe deeper to find the causes and the solution to
this ever-recurring problem. This probing and more serious
consideration of the situation led to some rather vehement
attacks on the stock market as an American financial institution.

Those Texans discussing the cause of the crash either
believed they knew the cause or they were seriously trying
to find it. In this analysis the Texan exhibited those
characteristics so prominent in the agrarian mentality--the
attempt to find a conspiracy at work, the goodness of rural
life, an inconsistency in ideas, and the intense dislike for
the East.

Some of the observers viewed the financial crisis from
a rather shallow viewpoint. One man believed that the crash
was caused by conservatives. Without elaborating on this
statement he implied that he meant the conservatism of the
bankers and stock brokers because "if conservatism that is
wanted is . . . the kind that causes millions of the savings
of the people to be lost thru [sic] closing of banks and the
sale of inflated bonds and stocks, then I rather be [sic] on
the liberal side or be charged with being liberal."[80] Another tried to rationalize the crisis as being caused by
selfishness, and one man believed it was an international
conspiracy of Jewish bankers led by the Rothschilds.[81] These
are, however, rather weak charges with little to substantiate
them.

The more serious observers believed, by and large, that
overspeculation had caused the crash. To some, that was the
only cause--people trying to get rich merely over-extended
their resources despite the warnings of experts. Once the

[80]FDRL, July 5, 1932, Box 723.

[81]Austin *Statesman*, June 3, 1932; Galveston *Daily News*, December
6, 1931.

boom started, it was difficult to halt inflation of stock values; thus a crash became virtually inevitable.[82]

Still others thought the cause was the control of money by New York bankers and the Federal Reserve System. Because bankers in other parts of the nation were controlled by Federal Reserve banks, they had no choice but to do as they were told. Martin Dies, Texas Congressman later to become famous for his House Committee on Un-American Activities, stated on the floor of the House of Representatives that the restriction of competition and the Federal Reserve control of credit had been largely responsible for the crash. If monetary policy were a cause, then the Republican Party, in power since 1921, was partly or wholly responsible for the crisis. Congressman Dies and others were thus convinced that the Republican Party was responsible for the inflation of stock prices and the bull market.[83] J. H. "Cyclone" Davis, a perennial Texas politician and an old Populist, probably best summed up much of the sentiment in Texas although most people would not, or could not, use his colorful language.

> The maladministration and failure of the Republican Party after ten years of unrestrained rule has resulted in the most widespread panic-pandemonium of debt, distress and desolation among the masses and the most ravenous rapacity of the privileged classes. This ten years, odorous in public scandal, festered with malignant malfeasance, bribery and corruption in official life, gave the Democratic party a glorious opportunity.[84]

Sentiment about whether the speculation and market distress caused the depression was about equally divided. To

[82]Bonham *Daily Favorite*, August 22, 1931; Austin *Statesman*, November 20, 1930; *The Valley Farmer*, June 5, 1931, p. 8.

[83]U.S., *Congressional Record*, 72d Cong., 1st Sess., 1931, LXXV, Part 1, 735, Part 4, 3997; "Public Opinion," Amarillo *Daily News*, January 20, 1931; "Letters From Readers," Dallas *Morning News*, February 5, 1931.

[84]Cyclone Davis, *Memoir* (Sherman, Texas: The Courier Press, 1935), 79.

many newspapers, there was no question about it; they often began articles and editorials about the "business depression which had its beginning in last fall's stock market panic."[85] Others believed the panic in Wall Street which forced industrial concerns to cut back on expansion helped cause the depression.[86] There were those, however, who believed that stock market manipulation had nothing at all to do with the depression.[87]

At the national level many were antagnostic to Wall Street for various reasons. Some who considered it to be bad by nature thought it should be abolished while many believed it to be merely an evil thing that could not be corrected.[88] Texans, by and large, followed the national pattern from 1931 to 1933. During this period when the market continued to decline even lower than after the first crashes, Texans became more violent in their attacks on it.

Only a few of the newspapers maintained respect for the market, and they were not often very enthusiastic about it. They continued to use the confidence-building approach, but by the winter of 1932-1933 it was growing a bit hackneyed.[89] One paper, at least, grew more concerned by the passage of time. The Uvalde *Leader-News* in Feburary 1931 was optimistic about the upsurge in stock prices,[90] but about a year later the same paper said, "Much comment is around over the activities of a few reds. What about those anarchists who have

[85]"Business," *Editorials of the Month for Texas*, I (March, 1930), 112.

[86]"Capital," *Lone Star Constructor*, VIII (August, 1931), 5.

[87]FDRL, May 12, 1932, Box 721; W. L. Clayton, "The World's Economic Tangle," *Acco Press*, IX (April, 1931), 19.

[88]Galbraith, *The Great Crash*, 157.

[89]El Paso *Times*, November 12, 1932, January 1, 1933; Brady *Standard*, April 3, 1931; Cameron *Enterprise*, August 18, 1932.

[90]Uvalde *Leader-News*, February 13, 1931.

helped to ruin millions of American citizens by their under-
cover methods of operation on the stock market."[91] Some of
the commercial press used virulent invectives because they
believed the manipulators who still controlled the market
were not allowing it to rise, and others believed that the
crash of 1929 was the cause of the depression.[92]

One of the most violent attacks on stock exchanges came
from the ranks of organized labor. Voicing what was obviously a national campaign, two labor papers advocated closing
of the New York Stock Exchange for thirty days to prove to
the nation that it was not necessary for regular business
enterprise. This would restore lost confidence and courage
to the average citizen and would make business more stable.[93]
The worst attack on the stock market appeared in the Dallas
Craftsman.

> What a fine lot of patriots the Wall Street gents
> have turned out to be.
> They have profiteered in peace as they did in war,
> in hard times as they did in good times.
> What the rabble rousers have now to talk about!
> And why not give 'em hell?
> If any gang in America has a panning coming its
> [*sic*] Wall Street gents who have goughed, rigged and
> juggled to their own tremendous advantage, while mil-
> lions have been in want.
> What a spectacle! And they still have the nerve
> to hold up their heads and think they are great men.
> The difference between Al Capone and the Wall
> Street racketeers is one of geography and field of
> operation. Moral difference? Just where?[94]

Agricultural people in Texas were about as unhappy as
organized labor. Sheep and goat raisers, among others, believed that Wall Street was responsible for poor conditions

---

[91]*Ibid.*, March 11, 1932.

[92]Austin *Statesman*, June 24, 1932, July 11, 1932; Beeville *Bee-Picayune*, March 3, 1932; Ozment, "Temple and Depression," 10.

[93]Dallas *Craftsman*, January 1, 1932; *Weekly Dispatch*, January 9, 1932, January 16, 1932.

[94]Dallas *Craftsman*, May 20, 1932.

on farms and ranches; the depression was prolonged by stock manipulators. Some even went so far as to rewrite the Lord's Prayer to show that Wall Street and Big Business were the real gods that ruled America.[95]

Among the religious leaders who spoke out on economic issues, the most prominent was J. Frank Norris, pastor of the very large First Baptist Church in Fort Worth.[96] His statements probably reflected his congregation's attitude to some extent and partly his own which undoubtedly influenced his followers. Norris believed that the United States was under the dictatorship of Wall Street composed of nothing but a bunch of thieves. He said he had more respect for bandits who stole money in the open at the risk of their own freedom and lives than for the men like Samuel Insull who stole from the public under the cloak of legality.[97]

Despite the dislike for the stock exchange, few except organized labor were willing to advocate that it be closed. Others wanted close regulation that would prevent such a disastrous decline in the future. Congressman Dies believed only the regulation of the stock exchange and the banking system could take the control of the nation's finances out of the hands of a few corporation executives and put it back into the hands of the people where it belonged.[98]

Texas reaction to the depression can be seen to have taken three different stages. In the first, from the crash in October until the beginning of 1930, almost all groups

[95] "Resume of the Del Rio Convention," *Sheep and Goat Raisers Magazine*, XIII (January, 1933), 66; *Ferguson Forum* (Austin), March 26, 1931; FDRL, October 10, 1932, Box 724; "Letters to the Times," El Paso *Times*, October 4, 1931; *Texas Spur*, February 27, 1931.

[96] Ralph Lord Roy, *Apostles of Discord* (Boston: The Beacon Press, 1953), 352.

[97] Sermon, "The Revolution in America--Are We Passing Under Dictatorship?" newspaper clipping in Norris Scrapbook, Norris Papers in the possession of Rev. E. Ray Tatum, University Baptist Church, Lubbock, Texas. Hereafter cited as Norris Papers.

[98] FDRL, October 10, 1932, Box 724.

believed there was nothing to worry about. Most thought the catastrophe was only the periodic leveling that took place to rid the market of the amateurs, the weak, and the poor; that nothing was basically wrong with business; that maintenance of confidence in the financial structure of the nation was all that was needed. In 1930 most people were still optimistic although they were growing a bit more cautious as more dissenters made their voices heard. It was during this period that the search for a scapegoat began. From the beginning of 1931 to March 1933, as a result of more careful analysis, more criticism was leveled at Wall Street for causing the troubles from which the nation suffered. Surprisingly, in light of widespread radicalism (to be discussed later), the stock market escaped much of this type of criticism. Perhaps the answer lies in the fact that by 1931 or 1932 the actions of the stock market ceased to be of major importance to most Texans because very few of them were involved any longer and because they were more concerned with their own welfare.

Texas opinion during this period certainly reflects the influence of agrarian thinking in Texas. Old populist ideas were still present and more would be revived later. Opinion also reflects the frontier influence in Texas. The populist and frontier mentality is shown by the extreme optimism, the search for a scapegoat (or conspirator) on which to blame the trouble, and the intense dislike for anything that was Eastern, especially after "the East" became the scapegoat.

Unparalleled optimism was the greatest difficulty Texans had to overcome during this period. The refusal to accept the consequences of the market crash was also characteristic of the state in facing the depression as a major disruption of the social, political, and economic life of the nation and of the state.

CHAPTER III

"WASN'T THE DEPRESSION AWFUL?"

Human nature being what it is, most people are reluctant to acknowledge the existence of unpleasant conditions. Most people are willing, even anxious, to look for the silver lining in any cloud of adversity. Rather than concentrate on the unpleasant, they usually prefer to be optimistic about the future. Such an attitude was quite evident in the early stages of the Great Depression, both on the national level and in Texas.

Texans reacted to the depression in a fairly definite pattern. In keeping with the American characteristics of optimism and self-reliance, Texans, at first, refused to admit that a depression existed. As conditions worsened, however, more of them examined the crisis in all its aspects. After the state as a whole was forced to admit that a depression really did exist, Texans began to predict the imminent return of prosperity, to search for the beneficial effects of the crisis, and to plan ways of ending it.

At the national level some time passed before the reality of the depression was admitted. Perhaps, as some claimed, the knowledge of the true situation was kept from the American people by those in power;[1] more likely, however, the national propensity for optimism did not allow Americans to admit the true situation.[2] The United States, totally unprepared for such a challenge, took from one to four years to admit the existence of an economic depression and to survey realistically its extent. Much of the responsibility for refusing to face reality must rest with the nation's leaders.[3]

[1] Seldes, *The Years of the Locust*, 11.

[2] The Brookings Institution, *The Recovery Problem in the United States* (Washington: The Brookings Institution, 1936), 35.

[3] Hannah, "Urban Reaction," 43, 56.

The year 1930 was the first crucial period. Signs of severe unemployment and depression were already present, particularly in the cities, during the first months of the year. Bread lines, transiency, demonstrations, and human misery became more common.[4] Despite such clear signs of trouble, Americans, in early 1930, still responded with billboards and newspaper advertisments asking, "Wasn't the Depression Terrible?"[5]

Ironically, the old words, panic and crisis, were too trauma-laden; the new word "depression" was more widely used and acceptable. In characteristic American fashion, the word depression also became unacceptable in later years and was replaced by such words as "recession."[6]

As will be seen, Texans followed the national leadership. For months and even years most of the mass media refused to acknowledge the existence of a depression since there had been no sudden decline in prosperity. Since Texas was not industrialized, problems of unemployment did not appear for some time. In fact, the depression descended so gradually that most Texans did not realize its existence until it was already serious.[7] By 1931, however, only the most blind optimists were unable or unwilling to accept reality.

A fear that the stock market crash and its aftermath would destroy business confidence stimulated a national campaign to maintain and restore faith in the soundness of business, the capitalistic system, and the future. Hoover, believing the only real danger to the nation was the loss of

[4]*Ibid.*, 78-79; Seldes, *The Years of the Locust*, 50.

[5]Goldman, *Rendezvous with Destiny*, 248.

[6]Robert S. and Helen Merrell Lynd, *Middletown in Transition* (New York: Harcourt, Brace and Company, 1937), 7; Wecter, *The Great Depression*, 16-17; John Kenneth Galbraith, *The Affluent Society* (New York: The New American Library, 1958), 44-45.

[7]Jenkins, "Austin during Depression," 56.

hope and confidence, did all he could to convince the nation of its great future. His public statements are, in
retrospect, somewhat naive and unreal, but they were certainly in keeping with his philosophy and with the attitudes of
the twenties. The President did not believe that a depression could be averted by public statements nor did he believe that occasional slumps could be avoided. He did believe, however, that there was no reason for depression at
this time since the high level of prosperity could be maintained if only the public did not lose heart. So convinced,
he made a special trip to Philadelphia in the fall of 1931
to attend a World Series baseball game to demonstrate to
the public his own confidence and faith in the future.[8]

Hoover's policy was reflected throughout his administration although many did not share his slight caution.
Secretary of the Interior Ray Wilbur, even in later years,
refused to recognize the severity of the depression. He
recalled that certainly the depression was serious and many
people suffered from it, "but the fact remains that the
gloom dispensers and those 'playing politics at the expense
of human misery' (as Mr. Hoover described them) pictured it
as much worse than it was."[9] The Commerce Department was,
likewise, certain of the soundness of the economy,[10] but
when challenged by a Texan for hurting business with optimistic statements, Secretary Lamont replied that his De-

[8]Hannah, "Urban Reaction," 258; Warren, *Hoover and the Depression*,
114; Theodore G. Joslin, *Hoover Off the Record* (Garden City, New York:
Doubleday, Doran & Company, Inc., 1934), 18, 33, 230; Richard Hofstadter,
The American Political Tradition and the Men Who Made It (New York: Random House Vintage Books, 1948), 300; hereafter cited as Hofstadter, *American Political Tradition*.

[9]Edgar Eugene Robinson and Paul Carroll Edwards (eds.), *The Memoirs
of Ray Lyman Wilbur* (Stanford, California: Stanford University Press,
1960), 560.

[10]Letter, May 8, 1930, Secretary's Correspondence, Department of
Commerce Papers, Record Group 40, National Archives, Washington, D. C.
Hereafter cited as Secretary's Corres., Commerce Dept.

partment's only goal was "to present an unbiased and honest appraisal of the existing facts, without attempting to over-emphasize either the favorable or unfavorable factors of the situation.[11]

A feature of the national confidence campaign was its reverence for times past. The tone of the President's actions and those of the nation as a whole was to *re*store prosperity. People wanted to *re*turn to the their jobs, to *go back* to normal conditions, to *re*cover from the market crash, and to *re*capture the calm feeling of the past.[12] Rather than looking to the future and the challenges brought by an economic crisis, the confidence campaign reflects a facet of human nature--the reverence for the "good old days." The nation eventually faced with the reality of the depression was forced to come to grips with the true situation.

Despite the national confidence crusade, not all financial and political leaders agreed with it. The encouragement expressed was not representative because most of those who disagreed with the President did not speak out in the early stages of the depression.[13] Senator Tom Connally, for example, who later said that he was concerned from the time of the crash that a depression was possible, criticized the Hoover administration for its lack of a policy with which to meet it.[14]

Of the few in the nation who were willing to speak out in 1930, most believed that the administration was correct in its assessment of the future. During the first few months of the year, they believed that a depression had been

[11]R. P. Lamont to R. E. Thomason, March 28, 1932, *ibid*.

[12]Seldes, *The Years of the Locust*, 60.

[13]Broadus Mitchell, *Depression Decade* (New York: Holt, Rinehart and Winston, 1947), 31.

[14]Senator Tom Connally as told to Alfred Steinberg, *My Name is Tom Connally* (New York: Thomas Y. Crowell Company, 1954), 134-135. Hereafter cited as Connally, *My Name is Tom Connally*.

averted.[15]

Hoover had great confidence in national conferences he called of various business, labor, agricultural, and political leaders. Promises of these conferences to continue the nation's economic life by maintaining production and employment at prevailing wages reassured many people. Governors of forty-two states, including Dan Moody of Texas, promised expanded public works programs to alleviate temporary unemployment in their states. Support of government action to this small degree was a significant deviation from Hoover's philosophy and became a precedent for future governmental involvement in the nation's economic life.[16] The psychological impact of these conferences, coming as they did in the wake of the crash, probably had the effect of reassuring the nation temporarily. The long range benefit, however, is more doubtful.[17]

Texans were generally impressed with the conferences. The state press, pleased with Moody's quick response proudly emphasized that Texas pledged more in public works spending than ten other states combined. The Dallas *Morning News* believed that Governor Moody should follow Hoover's example by calling state conferences to improve what it believed to be an already high level of prosperity.[18] Other editors agreed that business conferences were just what Texas needed. So anxious to believe that no depression existed, some editors even attributed good Christmas retail sales to the conferences; almost any sign of prosperity

[15] Lynd, *Middletown in Transition*, 15.

[16] Hoover, *The Great Depression*, 42; Hannah, "Urban Reaction," 40; Lloyd M. Graves, *The Great Depression and Beyond* (New York: The Brookmore Economic Service, Inc., 1932), 86; Robinson and Edwards, *The Memoirs of Ray Lyman Wilbur*, 551.

[17] Adams, *The Tempo of Modern Life*, 289.

[18] Galveston *Daily News*, November 27, 1929, December 1, 1929, Austin *Statesman*, November 30, 1929; "Prosperity Outlook for 1930," *Editorials of the Month for Texas*, I (January, 1930), 7-8.

might be credited to Hoover's confidence campaign.[19] Even organized labor, among the first to be hurt in a depression, was confident that Hoover had prevented hard times. The labor press emphasized the participation of its own leaders in the conferences as instrumental in averting depression.[20]

Despite general support for the conferences, not all Texans were convinced of their value. One South Texas newspaper, after praising Hoover's goals, concluded that only certain groups had been aided. The farmer, the editor believed, did not share in "Republican prosperity" as did special interest groups who were always favored by the Republican Party.[21] A man from Galveston thought Hoover's goal was to shift blame for the trouble from the Republican Party to the people as a whole.[22]

The Texas press, both commercial and special interest, was happy to join in the national confidence crusade. During the first year almost all the press denied the existence of a depression. It is easy to conclude from the large volume of editorial comment that a severe depression was in progress although the newspapers simply refused to admit it. Another proof of the existence of depression, despite the denials, was their lack of originality. The editors, hard-pressed to find something to praise, could only repeat the platitudes issued by the business world; they became rather hackneyed by 1932 and 1933. Chambers of Commerce sent confidence teams into rural areas to keep up the courage of the country folks, but as conditions worsened they were of little

[19] *Texas Spur*, December 20, 1929, January 24, 1930; Galveston *Daily News*, November 18, 1929; Greenville *Banner* as quoted in Dallas *Morning News*, November 28, 1929; Beeville *Bee-Picayune*, December 19, 1931; Uvalde *Leader-News*, February 5, 1932.

[20] Dallas *Craftsman*, December 6, 1929; *Weekly Dispatch*, December 14, 1929.

[21] Hebbronville *News*, November 27, 1929.

[22] FDRL, November 27, 1929, Box 718.

value. Some people tried to maintain a front of calmness by continuing to live as in the past even though only the very rich could afford to do so.[23]

Newspapers in all sections of the state--from Canadian in the Panhandle to McAllen and Port Isabel in South Texas, and from El Paso in the west to Dallas in the east--participated in the delusion of self-praise. Such things as statements from businessmen, reports of small employment, large diamond sales, and optimistic chamber of commerce statements were seized upon as harbingers of prosperity.[24]

Special interest publications for most of 1930 followed the lead of newspapers. If they are to be believed, the insurance and floral businesses were good; Houston had no depression; the labor market was stable; and the lower Rio Grande Valley suffered no ill effects.[25] Governor Moody was even persuaded to write an article for a chamber of commerce magazine expressing the same attitude.[26]

---

[23] Austin *Statesman*, February 13, 1930; Richardson, *Texas the Lone Star State*, 322-323; Nordeman, "Midland during Depression," 17-18. For an example of how one rancher maintained his extravagant living standard although he probably could not afford it, see: Wilhelmina Beane, *Texas Thirties* (San Antonio: The Naylor Company, 1963), 27.

[24] This type of sentiment is available throughout the state. For good examples see the following: Amarillo *Daily News*, April 2, 1930; Canadian *Record*, December 26, 1929; October 30, 1930; Dallas *Morning News*, February 3, 1930; El Paso *Times*, February 8, 1930; Galveston *Daily News*, January 23, 1930; George West *Enterprise*, January 3, 1930; Haskell *Free Press*, January 23, 1930; Huntsville *Item*, June 19, 1930; McAllen *Monitor*, February 21, 1930; Pecos *Enterprise and Gusher*, March 7, 1930; Port Isabel *Pilot*, January 1, 1930; Seguin *Enterprise*, February 21, 1930; *Texas Spur*, August 29, 1930; "Business," *Editorials of the Month for Texas*, I (April, 1930), 164; see also Mary Maverick McMillan, "San Antonio during the Depression, 1929-1933" (M.A. thesis, The University of Texas at Austin, 1966), 4-31; hereafter cited as McMillan, "San Antonio during Depression."

[25] "Editorial," *Southwestern Life News*, XXIV (February, 1930), 1; "On the Upward Swing," *Southern Florist and Nurseryman*, XXIX (September 19, 1930), 14; "Depression . . . Gets Cold Shoulder in Houston," *Houston*, I (August, 1930), 5; Dallas *Craftsman*, December 6, 1929; "Musings of Monty," *Monty's Monthly News of the Lower Rio Grande Valley of Texas*, XII (December, 1930), 32; hereafter cited as *Monty's Monthly*.

[26] Dan Moody, "Year of Prosperity Assured for Texas," *Houston*, I

Private citizens, to a lesser degree, also refused to acknowledge the depression. Some believed the nation had talked itself into hard times and the only solution was to talk itself out. These optimistic statements, if they are read closely, show a feeling of anxiety--an indication that they did not really believe their own homilies.[27]

Despite the refusal to recognize a depression in the early stages, a number of newspapers[28] and chamber of commerce journals[29] who were forced to make a few concessions about national business stagnation were still unwilling to admit that Texas had a depression. They were quick to emphasize, in fact, that Texas or their own particular locality was not beset with such difficulties. However, "behind the facade of hope and optimism there remained the haunting fear of poverty, inequality, and insecurity."[30]

The fears can be seen in several ways. The newspapers, even though the most emphatic promoters of confidence, were very inconsistent. Some commonly denied a depression one week, searched for a scapegoat the next, and denied it ever existed in the third week. Having never faced such a challenge before and with no conception of what to do about it, the press groped along from day to day. The press felt the pinch of hard times. Almost all publications lost advertising revenue and were forced to reduce the size of their

(March, 1930), 3.

[27] "Letter to the Editor," Canadian *Record*, February 27, 1930; "Letters to the Times," El Paso *Times*, October 12, 1931; A. B. Weakley to R.P. Lamont, May 1, 1930, Secretary's Corres., Commerce Dept.; telegram, August 1, 1931, Herbert Hoover Presidential Library, Presidential Papers, Box 272; hereafter cited as HHPL, PP.

[28] Austin *Statesman*, July 31, 1930; Brady *Standard*, September 12, 1930; Canadian *Record*, July 31, 1930; El Paso *Times*, August 31, 1930; Hebbronville *News*, March 19, 1930; *Terry County Herald*, April 18, 1930.

[29] "Business Conditions Good," *Dallas*, IX (May, 1930), 25; "Real Estate Slow Over Nation; Good Here," *The Hub*, III (January, 1930), 7.

[30] Galbraith, *The Affluent Society*, 46.

journals; in some cases hard times forced them out of business.[31]

Articles about unemployment and welfare inadvertently revealed that problems were growing. While proclaiming prosperity, some editors admitted that times could be better and advised outsiders looking for work to go elsewhere. Second thoughts about Hoover's confidence campaigns became more common. Labor newspapers also tried to remain confident, but worsening conditions made it difficult. Even while it praised Hoover's business conferences, the Dallas *Craftsman* warned working men to stay away from Dallas because there were not enough jobs even for its own citizens. Reports of the Salvation Army's soup kitchens and protest meetings of the unemployed belied the general prosperity theme. The *Weekly Dispatch*, a labor weekly at San Antonio, was hard-pressed to exhibit confidence because of widespread unemployment that could lead to a general depression.[32] The El Paso *Times* was probably speaking for Texas farmers when it editorialized, "What the American farmer would appreciate is more cash and less optimistic conversation."[33]

Although business journals did not participate in spreading pessimistic stories, some individual businesses certainly did not see the same rosy future. Private correspondence of a company on the South Plains, for example, revealed that the firm was hard-pressed for funds, partially because customers could not pay accounts and because business was very bad.[34]

[31] Galveston *Daily News*, December 5, 1929, January 24, 1930, March 4, 1930; *Waco Farm and Labor Journal*, February 21, 1930, March 21, 1930, January 30, 1931; Electra *News*, February 20, 1930; Port Isabel *Pilot*, October 22, 1930; Austin *Statesman*, June 5, 1930.

[32] Dallas *Craftsman*, December 27, 1929, January 24, 1930, February 7, 1930; *Weekly Dispatch*, March 15, 1930.

[33] El Paso *Times*, December 11, 1929.

[34] Baker Mercantile Company, Correspondence, Southwest Collection, Texas Tech University, Lubbock, Texas, Customers Letters, A-D, 1926-31,

Some individuals in Texas also dissented from the general feeling. Newspapers were criticized as being unrealistic when they advised all people to laugh at hard times because it was difficult for a man out of work to laugh; others challenged the accuracy of unemployment figures because many groups, especially white collar workers, were not usually recorded.[35]

As the depression deepened in 1930, Texans found it more difficult to deny the existence of hard times. Although many people were aware of the depression by the spring and summer, they still did not understand its extent or severity. By March 1930, some people were willing to admit that the state had suffered a mild "recession."[36] Because they thought they could see a quick end to the trouble, it was no danger to public confidence to admit that a mild recession was underway. The El Paso *Times*, one of the first newspapers to recognize and acknowledge the crisis, was forced to admit by March that a temporary business depression existed.[37] The *Times* was the exception rather than the rule, however, since few newspapers accepted the situation before the summer. During the fall and winter numerous other papers followed the lead of the *Times*[38] even though a few did

October 21, 1930, December 13, 1930; hereafter cited as Baker Mercantile Company.

[35]"Letters From Readers," Dallas *Morning News*, February 15, 1930, March 18, 1930, October 2, 1930.

[36]Seldes, *The Years of the Locust*, 56; Fusfeld, *The Economic Thought of FDR*, 166; "Business," *Editorials of the Month for Texas*, I (March, 1930), 112-113; William Edward Montgomery, "The Depression in Houston during the Hoover Era, 1929-1932" (M.A. thesis, The University of Texas at Austin, 1966), 56.

[37]El Paso *Times*, March 30, 1930.

[38]*Terry County Herald*, September 5, 1930; Haskell *Free Press*, September 11, 1930; Austin *Statesman*, September 22, 1930; Amarillo *Daily News*, October 13, 1930; Galveston *Daily News*, October 31, 1930; Pecos *Enterprise and Gusher*, October 31, 1930; Hebbronville *News*, December 3, 1930; *Texas Spur*, December 12, 1930; Seguin *Enterprise*, January 9, 1931; Port Isabel *Pilot*, January 14, 1931.

not recognize the depression until the spring or summer of 1931.[39]

Some special interest groups also began to agree that the nation was in the midst of a depression by the beginning of 1931.[40] A professor of economics at Texas Christian University said, in July 1931, what state leaders and opinion makers should have been saying for several months.

> It is of paramount importance that we face the facts involved in the present economic situation. First we must face the fact of depression, and secondly we must face the fact of unemployment.
> We must frankly admit that we are in a depression of no small consequence; in fact, said by some to be the most severe in 100 years.
> The current depression is world wide and therefore is not simply in the United States.
> The depression is industrial and not simply financial.
> The depression is agricultural as well as financial and industrial.[41]

Even chamber of commerce journals, always the most optimistic, could not deny the depression by mid-1930, but they still refused to accept its severity. Popular magazines published in Texas concurred that no one should worry that the depression would become serious. Private citizens who spoke out generally agreed.[42]

When the state was finally forced to recognize the depression most of the publications quickly announced that it was only a temporary condition that would soon be over. There was no reason to be concerned, they believed, since

[39]Cameron *Enterprise*, April 16, 1931; Bonham *Daily Favorite*, August 26, 1931.

[40]*Weekly Dispatch*, December 6, 1930; "On the Upswing," *Southern Florist and Nurseryman*, XXIX (September 19, 1930), 14; *The Alcalde*, XIX (November, 1930), 41.

[41]Dr. Edwin A. Elliott, "Economic Depression and Unemployment," *The Texas Outlook*, XV (July, 1931), 11.

[42]"Farm Labor Division Helps Farmers," *The Hub*, IV (November, 1930), 7; "What Next?" *East Texas*, V (December, 1930), 19; "Modern Methods and the Panic," *Holland's*, September, 1930, 3; *The Texas Weekly*, November 15, 1930, 1; "Letters From Readers," Dallas *Morning News*, November 10, 1930, January 7, 1931; Jenkins, "Austin during Depression," 53-55.

the national economy was strong enough to recover quickly.[43]
American leadership, they said, had taken control of the
situation and "Old Man Gloom" would soon be on his way to
be quickly replaced by "Miss Smiling Prosperity."[44] Even
though business and popular publications concurred, some
became a bit more cautious. Still believing the depression
to be only temporary, they stopped proclaiming the complete
return to pre-crash days, declaring instead that recovery,
however difficult and slow, would come in the near future.[45]
Even one farm journal said the crisis was only temporary,
but the West Texas Chamber of Commerce proclaimed the Biblical prophecy of seven good and seven bad years meant that
hard times could not be ended by man-made solutions. It
was convinced, however, that the farmer was reaching the
end of his seven bad years.[46] A number of individuals likewise agreed that the depression would soon end and no ill
effects would result. They declared that worse crises had
been endured before, that conditions were better already,
and that good times would soon return.[47]

To reinforce the belief in the temporary nature of the
depression the state press quoted anyone considered to be a
financial expert. Roger Babson, prophet of the stock mar-

[43]Amarillo *Daily News*, November 16, 1931; Cameron *Enterprise*, November 19, 1931; Electra *News*, January 5, 1933; Port Isabel *Pilot*, November 18, 1931; Ozment, "Temple and Depression," 9; *Waco Farm and Labor
Journal*, January 30, 1931.

[44]*San Patricio County News* (Sinton), December 11, 1930; Dallas
Morning News, November 2, 1931.

[45]"Wrong Both Times," *Houston*, III (July, 1932), 15; "Prosperity
is Close By," *Hardware and Implement Journal*, XXXVII (September, 1932),
9; "What's Ahead For Business?" *East Texas*, VI (October, 1931), 11; *The
Texas Weekly*, August 27, 1932, 1-3.

[46]*The Valley Farmer*, December 5, 1930, 18; "Joseph and Surplus,"
West Texas Today, XII (August, 1931), 10.

[47]Connally Papers, January 28, 1931, Box 14; "Letters From Readers," Dallas *Morning News*, September 19, 1930, December 15, 1930, August
5, 1931.

ket crash, was probably the most widely quoted individual of national prominence. Since his stock market prediction had proved accurate, he was considered a true prophet. Even after he wrongly staked his reputation on the return of prosperity in July 1931, he was still widely quoted when he predicted the return of prosperity as late as November 1932.[48] Other individuals quoted were Assistant Secretary of Commerce Julius Klein, Secretary of Commerce Lamont, and Charles M. Schwab of Bethlehem Steel Corporation.[49]

Most of the eternal optimists, even after acknowledging the crisis, believed that a lack of self-assurance was the only thing wrong. They were only following the national leadership of Hoover, who often stated that all that was needed was a restoration of confidence.[50] Governor Ross Sterling, a businessman himself, followed the lead of the "Great Engineer" in a speech to an unemployment conference he had called in October 1931.

> Briefly I would suggest that our people themselves are in some measure wrong in their mental attitude toward this great problem that presses for solution. They seem to have lost confidence in the resourcefulness and recuperative powers of our citizenship, to have lost confidence in themselves, to have lost confidence in their State, and are about to lose confidence in their Nation. In short, our people seem to have lost faith, that quality of heart and mind so essential to the solution of those grave problems that sometimes appear to threaten the perpetuity of our institutions. We should forget all that; we should strive valiantly to restore confidence and faith in the American people.[51]

[48] Austin *Statesman*, September 22, 1930; Galveston *Daily News*, December 30, 1930; Amarillo *Daily News*, June 18, 1931; "Musings of Monty," *Monty's Monthly*, XIII (July, 1931), 18; Pecos *Enterprise and Gusher*, February 12, 1932; "Babson Says Get Ready to Meet Good Times," *Southern Florist and Nurseryman*, XXXIV (November 11, 1932), 12.

[49] El Paso *Times*, April 7, 1930, May 29, 1930; Galveston *Daily News*, October 25, 1931.

[50] Myers, *State Papers of Herbert Hoover*, I, 596, II, 47.

[51] State of Texas, Bureau of Labor Statistics, *Report of Committee on Resolutions of the Joint Conference of the Legislative and Governor's*

The conference followed the Governor's advice by resolving that the only need of the state was a restoration of faith in America.[52] Sampling of opinion shows that representatives of all areas of Texas life concurred in this feeling.[53] Even cattle raisers and a number of private citizens believed renewed confidence was the only solution.[54] During and after the presidential campaign of 1932 at least two Texans informed Franklin D. Roosevelt that the best thing he could do for the people was "to declare war on the depression" to restore lost faith.[55]

The attitude of the confidence-builders was expressed best in one verse of the theme song of the Convention of National Association of Credit Men held in Dallas in 1930.

> We're the men of industry
> Thirty thousand strong
> We can build prosperity
> By cheering when things go wrong
> Passing clouds conceal the sun
> But storms bring rainbow hues
> Show'rs are blessings good for everyone
> So "Quit a-singing 'bout the blues."[56]

Many Texans finally grew tired of the same statements without discernible progress. One farm editor, tired of advice not to talk hard times, asked why we should deny ourselves the right to talk about the conditions that were

Committee for Unemployment Relief (Austin: Von Boeckmann-Jones Co., 1931), 3. Hereafter cited as Bureau of Labor Statistics, *Committee for Unemployment Relief*.

[52] *Ibid.*, 12.

[53] "Ring Out the Old," *The Southern Pharmaceutical Journal*, XXIII (January, 1931), 302; "Looking Forward," *Southwest Water Works Journal*, XIII (January, 1932), 22; "Capital," *Lone Star Constructor*, VIII (August, 1931), 5; "Budget-Slashing Can Be Carried Too Far!" *Texas Municipalities*, XIX (March, 1932), 72.

[54] "Nineteen Thirty-Three," *The Cattleman*, XIX (January, 1933), 6; "Letters From Readers," Dallas *Morning News*, June 2, 1931, August 18, 1931.

[55] FDRL, October 24, 1932, Box 727, January 29, 1933, Box 731.

[56] As quoted in *Dallas*, IX (June, 1930), 12.

causing so much suffering. Since the confidence campaign did not improve matters, he thought open discussion might do some good.[57] Business periodicals also wondered if the state were not fooling itself and delaying recovery by refusing to admit the true nature of the situation.[58] A Catholic newspaper in San Antonio, recognizing the need for a restoration of confidence, firmly believed that it could be done only by honestly recognizing the true situation. The *Southern Messenger* declared that "The depression will go on until we stop swallowing slogans. The public official who uses catchwords to fool the public is a public enemy."[59] Some of the commercial press also began to question the validity of confidence-building attempts. It was a simple matter to say that confidence was needed, but it was not so easy to decree such a condition; if talk would alleviate conditions the United States, and Texas particularly, should have been in the lap of luxury by 1932.[60] The truth of the matter is "all the ballyhooing in the world is not going to bring back prosperity. Prosperity depends far more on what we DO than than on what we SAY."[61] Of the few individuals who criticized this attitude, two indicated that the problem was not a lack of confidence, but a lack of cash. Without an adequate money supply, all the confidence in the world would not do any good.[62]

[57] *The Valley Farmer*, November 20, 1930, 18.

[58] "Build Now," *Lone Star Constructor*, VII (November, 1930), 7; "Plain Talk," *Dallas*, XI (September, 1932), 12.

[59] *The Southern Messenger* (San Antonio), March 3, 1932, June 2, 1932, July 14, 1932.

[60] Haskell *Free Press*, October 8, 1931; Austin *Statesman*, January 8, 1932, July 9, 1932.

[61] Hebbronville *News*, June 10, 1931.

[62] Sam Rayburn Papers, Correspondence, 1932, Sam Rayburn Library, Bonham, Texas, December 30, 1932; "Public Opinion," Amarillo *Daily News*, June 18, 1931.

When the state finally admitted that a severe depression did exist, most of the press began to search for signs that it was over. So widespread and intense was this search, it appears to have been an organized statewide campaign. The commercial press was unrealistic in its unoriginal assertions day after day and week after week, even in the face of worsening conditions, that the depression was over or would be soon.[63] They were so intense in proving the end of the crisis near that such things as better retail sales on one individual Saturday or the increasing number of young people going to summer camp were used to prove the return of prosperity.[64] Even Senator Connally, long an accuser of the Republican Party for the disaster, predicted the end had come in November 1931.[65] It was only natural that the business and other special interest publications would join in the campaign,[66] but the degree to which farm journals concurred was surprising considering the long-depressed state of agriculture.[67]

The presidential campaign and the election of 1932 boosted the conviction that the depression was over. Franklin Roosevelt's speeches that promised to remember the "forgotten man" and a a "new deal for the American people" were certainly encouraging to most Texans.[68] This enthusiasm was

[63] *Ibid.*, December 26, 1930; Austin *Statesman*, January 6, 1931; Uvalde *Leader-News*, November 6, 1931; Port Isabel *Pilot*, January 14, 1931; *Devil's River News*, June 19, 1931.

[64] Electra *News*, September 29, 1932; Amarillo *Daily News*, July 17, 1931.

[65] *Ibid.*, November 6, 1931.

[66] "Prepare for Prosperity," *Dallas*, XI (November, 1932), 14; "Build Now," *County Progress*, VII (November, 1930), 10.

[67] "The Tide Has Turned," *Sheep and Goat Raisers Magazine*, XIII (September, 1932), 1; "Business Conditions Improve," *Cotton and Cotton Oil News*, XXXII (August 1, 1931), 6; *The Valley Farmer*, June 5, 1931, 8.

[68] Samuel I. Rosenman (ed.), *The Public Papers and Addresses of Franklin D. Roosevelt* (5 vols.; New York: Random House, 1938), I, 625, 659. Hereafter cited as Rosenman, *Public Papers of FDR*.

indicated when a Sunday School in San Antonio opened its
services one June Sunday by singing "Onward Christian Soldiers" in honor of Roosevelt's nomination; one class teacher
compared him to Moses leading his children out of bondage.[69]
Another congratulated him on his election victory by saying
it was the only thing needed to restore confidence and prosperity.[70] His election and inauguration seemed to give new
life to the press. Many who believed that fear had been
destroyed by the election results declared that his actions
on assuming office only proved their contentions.[71] One paper summed up the feeling of many when a headline shortly
after Roosevelt's inauguration declared, THE BOOM IS ON!
Wasn't the Depression Awful?"[72]

The great hope for the future was not shared by all the
state. Articles in the newspapers about large numbers applying for relief and a trend among farmers to prepare for
sustained depression seemed to deny the proclamations that
the end had come.[73] Among those attempting to get the people
to face the truth about the situation was former Governor
James E. Ferguson. Throughout the early part of 1931 Ferguson tried to show that the people were being deliberately
misled by the big daily papers; that it was ridiculous to
forecast prosperity when, in reality, starvation was the
major prospect Texas had to face.[74] "Governor Jim" was, however, only a voice crying in the wilderness as far as most
of the state press was concerned.

[69]FDRL, July 5, 1932, Box 723.

[70]*Ibid.*, November 9, 1932, Box 732.

[71]Fredericksburg *Standard*, November 25, 1932; Huntsville *Item*,
January 5, 1933; *San Patricio County News*, March 9, 1933; *Lulac News*,
II (January, 1933), 10.

[72]Sterling City *News-Record*, March 10, 1933.

[73]Cameron *Enterprise*, January 12, 1933; George West *Enterprise*,
February 27, 1931.

[74]*Ferguson Forum*, January 8, 1931, February 5, 1931, March 12, 1931.

Soon after the admission of a depression some of the press began a campaign to convince the public that Texas was not badly hurt. There may have been a depression in the country as a whole but Texas, or at least certain parts of it, had not really been affected;[75] at least one professional group and the usual chambers of commerce believed this to be true.[76] Despite this attitude one small girl, writing to Santa Claus, did not ask much for herself since "there are so many kids that need clothes"; she asked instead that he take care of the many who were less fortunate than she.[77] A man from Wink told Senator Connally that "any statement in the press . . . as to the good condition of Texas in the outlook for the coming winter is nothing but camaflage [sic], financial, and political deception" because unemployment was worse than anyone would admit.[78] Probably this man reflected the sentiment of many who were too afraid or too inarticulate to speak out.

When its existence could no longer be denied, the beneficial effects of the depression were emphasized. Students of the national economy, both at the time and later, insisted that the country was, even in the midst of bad times, still better off than it had ever been.[79] Although quite a

[75] Galveston *Daily News*, September 2, 1930; Dallas *Morning News*, October 20, 1930; Canadian *Record*, January 1, 1931; Port Isabel *Pilot*, January 14, 1931; Haskell *Free Press*, May 21, 1931; McAllen *Monitor*, January 2, 1931.

[76] "Proceedings Texas Bar Association," *Texas Law Review*, LI (October, 1932), 12; "Progress of the Port in 1930," *Houston Port and City*, VIII (November, 1930), 26; "Galland Seeks Jobs For the Unemployed," *The Hub*, IV (December, 1930), 8.

[77] *Terry County Herald*, December 5, 1930.

[78] Connally Papers, October 6, 1931, Box 15.

[79] Chamber of Commerce of the United States, *The American Economic System compared with Collectivism and Dictatorship* (Washington: Chamber of Commerce of the United States, 1936), 13; hereafter cited as U. S. Chamber of Commerce, *American Economic System*; Elanor Lansing Dulles, *Depression and Reconstruction* (Philadelphia: University of Pennsylvania Press, 1936), 314; H. Clyde Filley, *The Wealth of the Nation* (Lincoln: University of Nebraska Press, 1945), 2.

number of Texas periodicals agreed,[80] many began to look
deeper to find more beneficial results. Some tried to cheer
the people by explaining that we had had other depressions;[81]
that this experience would force us to solve the agricultural problems;[82] that it caused us to understand and search
for the causes of economic distress.[83]

An Amarillo newspaperman who called himself "the Jackass of the Plains" wrote a book entitled *I Like the Depression* in which he summarized most of the ideas expressed by
the state and undoubtedly helped to spur more comment of
this nature. Among the good features that he saw were that
we once again understood the value of money, we were more
considerate of others, and religion again became important
to the average citizen.[84] Certain groups of workers and farmers agreed that they had learned thrift and economy;[85] a revival of Christian faith and brotherhood was worth the cost
of economic depression.[86] Some thought the beneficial results included a return to a better life that included eating of less-rich more healthful food and the wearing of less
prententious clothing.[87]

[80] *Texas Bluebonnet,* September, 1932, 8; *The Texas Weekly,* September 6, 1930, 4.

[81] *Terry County Herald,* May 6, 1932; *Texas Spur,* May 8, 1931.

[82] Dallas *Morning News,* September 3, 1930, June 14, 1932.

[83] Austin *Statesman,* November 6, 1930; Haskell *Free Press,* January
8, 1931.

[84] Henry Ansley, *I Like the Depression* (Indianapolis: The Bobbs-
Merrill Company, 1932), 21, 28, 126, 128.

[85] Ruth Alice Allen, *Wage Earners Meet the Depression* (Austin: The
University of Texas Bulletin No. 3545, 1935), 27; "Necessity of Reducing
Cotton Costs," *Cotton and Cotton Oil News,* XXXII (May 23, 1931), 6.

[86] Amarillo *Daily News,* November 12, 1931; Electra *News,* December
18, 1930; El Paso *Times,* March 22, 1931, December 25, 1932; "Letter to
the Editor," Weatherford *Democrat,* May 8, 1931.

[87] *Live Oak County Herald* (George West), September 15, 1932; Haskell

Despite the popularity of this idea,[88] not everyone a-
greed with it. Most longshoremen could see no value to it,[89]
and Cyclone Davis disagreed with the Dallas *Morning News*.

> I am glad that The News can see a blessing in hard times.
> But the millions of jobless, homeless and hungry wage-
> earners and millions of sun-burnt, drouth-scorched,
> debt-ridden farmers and common business men can't enjoy
> those blessings.[90]

A woman from Levelland also became distressed with the "Jackass of the Plains" for his unrealistic attitude and his popularity.

> I can't see how people can say "I Love the Depression,"
> and watch others starve to death. I know they haven't
> had to take a notch in their belts when a meal was due,
> and maybe two notches for their second, and so on until
> they couldn't keep their belt on and had to discard it
> for an old pair of suspenders made from an old cotton
> sack and pinned up with nails. . . .
>   I can safely say any one who says he likes the de-
> pression has not had starvation staring him in the face.
> I don't like to see others go hungry while I have plenty,
> therefore, I DON'T LIKE THE DEPRESSION.[91]

Although urban sentiment may well have been the same,
Texas reaction to the presence of depression fits very neatly into the agrarian scheme of thinking. The first stage of
opinion, refusal to recognize the depression, is in keeping
with the optimism for which this country is famous; the intensity and frequency of these statements, however, indicate that behind the facade of prosperity and contentment
lay a deep anxiety that occasionally was voiced in opposition to the prevailing atmosphere. Even when admission was
forced upon them, Texans, particularly the press, quickly
searched for an end of the depression and tried to show how
good it really was. The continual refusal of many undoubt-

Free Press, August 27, 1931; "Pens of the People," Galveston *Daily News*,
January 24, 1932.

[88]*Texas Spur*, June 24, 1932.

[89]Allen, *Wage Earners Meet the Depression*, 57.

[90]"Letters From Readers," Dallas *Morning News*, September 6, 1930.

[91]Levelland *Herald* as quoted in *Terry County Herald*, June 24, 1932.

edly slowed any action that might have been taken to alleviate the distress. Only by the time of the inauguration of Franklin D. Roosevelt were they willing to try more drastic action.

CHAPTER IV

THE SEARCH FOR A VILLAIN

Public reaction to the depression at both the national
and state levels followed fairly definite patterns. Virtually everyone, at one time or another, tried to find a cause,
or perhaps "the" cause, for the crisis. In some respects,
the search for a villain became almost a witch hunt; the desire to blame an outside force, either human or non-human,
fits neatly into the agrarian mentality. The conspiracy theory, always present in American thought, became, after the
rise of agrarian protest in the 1890s, a permanent feature
of American ideology, more widely held than ever before. As
Professor Hofstadter stated, "There was something about the
Populist imagination that loved the secret plot and the conspiratorial meeting. There was in fact a widespread Populist
idea that all American history since the Civil War could be
understood as a sustained conspiracy of the international money power."[1] If this were correct about the 1880s and the
1890s, it was just as true of the United States and of Texas
in the 1930s. Once again Hofstadter was correct, at least
in reference to the thirties, when he explained, "Indeed,
what makes conspiracy theories so widely acceptable is that
they usually contain a germ of truth."[2]

Even though there were many causes for the depression in
the minds of the people, inherent in most of them, as described by one authority, is the conspiracy theory.

> Opinions ranged from the highly sophisticated to the bizarre
> and ignorant. A few people even blamed the calamity on sun
> spots. Others said it was fate and dug into their copies of
> Nostradamus. Still others said the depression was the inevi-
> table aftermath of the World War. A great many Puritan souls
> attributed the hardship to retribution for the good times of
> the 1920's and thought of the whole situation as a "hangover"

[1] Hofstadter, *The Age of Reform*, 70.

[2] *Ibid.*, 71.

72

or "the morning after." Marxists argued that the depression
was inherent in the nature of capitalism and that the only
cure was socialism. President Hoover believed that America's
hardship was only a part of the general world malaise, that
the United States had been dragged down by economic failure
in Europe. From his point of view this was a comforting
theory; it shifted the blame away from his administration
and those of Harding and Coolidge and relieved American business leadership from the responsibility. . . . Hard-shell
advocates of laissez faire blamed government "meddling."
Their argument was that the Federal Reserve System's action
in raising the rediscount rate in August 1929 had destroyed
"confidence," one of their favorite words, in the stock market and had thereby precipitated the crash.[3]

Examples may be found in Texas to show that most of these
ideas had a number of followers. In fact a man from Crock-
ett, Texas, named almost all of them when he listed the
following as causes of the depression: war debts, failure to
join the League of Nations, a conflict between industrial
and agricultural America, the Federal Reserve System, speculation, the protective tariff, poor agricultural profits,
and increased taxation.[4] Since most of them blamed only one
or two things for their troubles, few Texans wrote such long
letters and found so many causes. In the search for a conspirator, however, all of these causes, and more were found.
In the analysis that follows an arbitrary distinction has
been made between what some Texans thought the causes were
when, in reality, they are often interrelated. Such a de-
lineation is necessary to clarify the generally vague, con-
tradictory, and inconsistent thought of the average Texan.

The greatest portion of Texas people blamed President
Hoover and the Republican Party for the depression. Since
the administration always bears the risk of being blamed for
trouble, Republicans were doubly vulnerable because they had
been in power since 1921. Having taken credit for prosperity, they were unwilling, as seen in the wake of the stock
market crash, to accept the consequences of their business

[3]David A. Shannon, *Between the Wars: America, 1919-1941* (Boston:
Houghton Mifflin Company, 1965), 122-123.

[4]"Letters From Readers," Dallas *Morning News*, January 14, 1931.

policy. Texans, however, as well as Americans throughout the country, were quick to remind them of their responsibility.[5]

Most Texans willing to blame Hoover and the Republicans were individual citizens; most of the press refused to attack them directly. The few defenders, admitting that it was natural to blame those in power, emphasized that Republicans could not be held responsible for events beyond their control.[6]

The commercial press which did attack the administration usually did so by printing uncomplimentary articles that often included farmers' prayers or rewritten scriptures. One of the prayers ended by beseeching God to "lead us not into Republican Presidency, for Hoover has all the power, Mellon all the money, Rockefeller all the oil, and we have patched pants for ever and ever."[7] The most severe criticism was that the Republican promises of continued prosperity proved to be untrue as soon as Hoover was elected. To some the whole period of Republican rule was merely a reign of economic terror designed to impoverish the "little man" for the benefit of the rich; even if the Republicans were not to blame for the trouble, Hoover who was such a good engineer should be returned as soon as possible to that profession.[8] One citizen, convinced that Hoover had rather be President than right, declared, "The efforts of the Republican bunk dealers has only served to accentuate the beleif [sic] of us farmers that the Lord gave and the Republicans have taken away."[9]

[5]Hannah, "Urban Reaction," 35-36; Basil Rauch, *The History of the New Deal 1933-1938* (New York: Capricorn Books edition, 1963), 18; Warren, *Hoover and the Depression,* 111.

[6]Huntsville *Item,* October 29, 1931; *Live Oak County Herald,* June 30, 1932.

[7]Sterling City *News-Record,* January 15, 1932.

[8]"Letters From Readers," Dallas *Morning News,* November 12, 1930, June 8, 1932; Austin *Statesman,* August 15, 1931.

[9]FDRL, October 22, 1932, Box 727.

Since it is easier and simpler to personify evil, Hoover was more often directly blamed for the depression or for doing nothing to end it. According to one authority, political leaders, if they hope to remain in power, must respond to the current aspirations, ideals, and emotional needs of the people they represent.[10] Since Hoover and the Republicans in Congress never assumed economic leadership,[11] it was only reasonable for them, and particularly Hoover himself, to bear the brunt of public disapproval. The South, perhaps more than any other area, blamed Hoover for its troubles, particularly since some of these states, Texas included, bolted the traditional Democratic Party in 1928 to help elect him; now they had been betrayed.[12]

Hoover refused to take action that was against his own personal philosophy of government, even though it might have been popular. His prestige suffered when Arthur Woods, the big businessman chairman of the Committee on Unemployment, advocated that everyone buy two of everything--automobiles, telephones, radios--to end unemployment. When the well-known financial empire of Samuel Insull collapsed shortly before the nominating conventions in 1932, Hoover was further weakened.[13]

Hoover received many personal insults from Texans since it was much easier to put the blame on him personally. Hobo jungles became "Hoover Hotels," a jalopy car was the "Republican Prosperity Model," and jackrabbits were now "Hoover Hogs" or "Hoover ham."[14] One Texan told Governor Roosevelt

[10]Thurman W. Arnold, *The Folklore of Capitalism* (New Haven: Yale University Press, 1937), 21.

[11]Hannah, "Urban Reaction," 56.

[12]Cash, *The Mind of the South,* 378.

[13]Joslin, *Hoover Off the Record,* 11; Clement Wood, *Herbert Clark Hoover: An American Tragedy* (New York: Michael Swain, 1932), 326; Warren, *Hoover and the Depression,* 83.

[14]Ralph W. Steen, *Twentieth Century Texas* (Austin: The Steck Com-

soon after the election of 1932 that "Hoover hogs" had been praying for his election since they had suffered so much and their numbers had decreased during the Hoover administration.[15] The Big Spring *News* declared that Hoover hated poor people; one man called him a "Jellyfish"; and another paper was insulting about the extravagance evident in Hoover's secretarial staff.[16] A rural editor warned Texans to beware of electing Ross Sterling governor in 1930 because his promises of prosperity might be just as disastrous as Hoover's had been in 1928. Since "we are reduced to 'lasses and corn bread with Hoover," the editor did not wish to "forego the 'lasses" with Sterling.[17] Another Texan declared, "Truly, I have been hit hard, but I deserve no sympathy, I voted for Hoover."[18] Governor Sterling also came in for some of the blame when a farmer asked him how the nation would survive "while Hoover and you may suck your thumbs."[19]

Hoover did have his defenders in Texas although they were neither as numerous nor as vocal as his detractors.[20] They did believe, however, that if anyone could bring the

pany, 1942), 23; FDRL, July 20, 1931, Box 721; *Texas Spur*, January 30, 1931.

[15] FDRL, November 9, 1932, Box 736.

[16] Big Spring *News*, as quoted in *Terry County Herald*, April 22, 1932; letter, August 4, 1930, Gen. Corres. Re. Texas, 1929-1932, Office of the Secretary of Agricuture, Department of Agriculture, Record Group 16, National Archives, Washington, D. C.; hereafter cited as Dept. of Agriculture, Correspondence; Uvalde *Leader-News*, June 24, 1931.

[17] *Terry County Herald*, August 29, 1930.

[18] "Letters From Readers," Dallas *Morning News*, January 7, 1931.

[19] Ross S. Sterling Files as Governor of Texas, Correspondence, Texas State Archives, Austin, Texas, September 1, 1931, Box 176. Hereafter cited as Sterling Papers.

[20] See for example: FDRL, July 6, 1932, Box 724, November 7, 1932, Box 730; Connally Papers, n.d., Box 12.

nation out of the depression it would be Hoover;[21] others who did not believe that the depression was Hoover's fault thought he had done all he or any man could do.[22]

Of those who refused to attack the President personally, many were willing to blame the Republican Party and its administrations for the trouble. Most of the Texas congressional delegation, including Senator Morris Sheppard, believed that the nation was "so sick and tired of republican misrule" that it would glady turn to the Democrats in 1932. Wright Patman was convinced that Republican policies favoring the wealthy were responsible for the stock market crash and subsequent developments; Thomas L. Blanton blamed ten years of Republican extravagance.[23] Martin Dies declared that "The Republican Party has sowed the wind and now is reaping the whirlwind"[24] because of its continuing policy of aiding the wealthy and privileged classes of the country. Despite their attempt to avoid the responsibility, Republicans would be judged by history for causing the depression.[25] A number of private citizens believed that the Republican Party, acting in an un-American way, had brought dishonor upon itself and distrust for those in power. They were possibly driving the state into the hands of communism, pauperism, or autocratic socialism.[26]

[21] "Letters From Readers," Dallas *Morning News*, April 15, 1930.

[22] *Lamar County Echo* as quoted in Dallas *Morning News*, November 18, 1930; "Letters From Readers," *ibid.*, November 16, 1930, June 9, 1931; Galveston *Daily News*, March 4, 1930; Uvalde *Leader-News*, February 5, 1932; "Public Opinion," Amarillo *Daily News*, September 18, 1930; "Looking Forward," *Southwest Water Works Journal*, XIII (January, 1932), 22.

[23] Clipping from Texarkana *Press*, November 30, 1931, in Morris Sheppard Scrapbook, Morris Sheppard Papers, University of Texas Archives, Austin, Texas; Wright Patman to Sam Rayburn, June 22, 1932, Rayburn Papers; *Congressional Record*, 72d Cong., 1st Sess., 1932, LXXV, Part 5, 4962.

[24] *Ibid.*, 72d Cong., 1st Sess., 1931, LXXV, Part 1, 737.

[25] *Ibid.*, 735; *ibid.*, Part 4, 3998.

[26] FDRL, August 3, 1932, Box 727, September 6, 1932, Box 727; "Pub-

Although only a few of the state newspapers blamed Republicans, those that did were usually rather vehement about it.[27] One of the most striking attacks came from a South Texas editor who claimed that, despite the good character of many Republicans, their system of government was wrong.

> It is based upon the principle of prosperity for the upper
> lords who are supposed to let some of the prosperity per-
> colate down to the underlings. Such a policy is fallacious
> and erroneous. . . . Traced back to its original it is seen
> to be founded on the old theory of the divine right of kings--
> the right for the great and mighty to have their place in the
> sun while the toiling masses sweat and labor, starve and shiver
> to uphold a civic structure built on a foundation of shifting
> sand.[28]

The election of 1932 prompted many individuals to speak out against Republicans. Governor Roosevelt received numerous letters from Texans telling him the Democratic opportunity had arrived; that the Democratic Party could win only as long as it was the party of the people as Bryan had said it was; that defenders of the Republican Party could no longer be found in the South; that he could win if he did not step into the shoes of the old-guard Republicans.[29]

Even one physician, a member of a profession long considered conservative, succumbed to the hatred for Republicans.

> The life of the republican party is one of plunder. It has
> no principles and is ruled by policy, the cornerstone of
> which is the doctrine of protection, under which the rich
> are privileged to rob the masses. From protection they have
> never wavered but as occasion has seemed to demand, they have
> espoused in every instance the cause of the mighty against
> the weak. They are entrenched in power behind a breastwork
> of riches and maintain their position by bribery, subterfuge,

lic Opinion," Amarillo *Daily News*, February 1, 1932; Connally Papers, December 8, 1929, Box 7.

[27] Galveston *Daily News*, December 30, 1930; George West *Enterprise*, December 27, 1929.

[28] Hebbronville *News*, November 18, 1931.

[29] FDRL, November 27, 1929, Box 718, April 18, 1932, Box 721, July 11, 1932, Box 724, December 3, 1932, Box 733.

falsehood and misrepresentation. Their appeal is to avarice,
passion, prejudice and bigotry. Under republican rule we
have seen the rich grow richer and the poor grow poorer.
They have reduced the richest and happiest people in the
world to beggery and misery.[30]

Hoover and the Republican Party were the first to be attacked, but the other deities of the twenties--particularly banks and business in general--also came in for their share of the blame. Bankers of the United States were charged with causing the depression for several reasons. The major argument was that, accidentally or through design, money had been removed from circulation, resulting in deflation that caused the dollar to be worth more than normal. The people, therefore, simply did not have enough money to buy the necessities, pay their debts, and keep the economy running smoothly.[31] When banks continued to fail as the depression deepened, the press tried to stop deteriorating confidence in the banking system; individuals became concerned that the runs might continue; many businesses were crippled by the further restriction of money in circulation.[32] Many Texans, convinced that bankers were deliberately restricting circulation because of fear or because they were deliberately trying to bankrupt the country, continued to lose respect for the banking system.[33] A man from Brownsville, hoping to get a true picture of public sentiment, asked over forty people if they would deposit $10,000 (if they had it) in a bank; in each case the answer was negative, and many respon-

[30] *Ibid.*, January 14, 1931, Box 721.

[31] *Ibid.*, January 30, 1933, Box 738; Connally Papers, n.d., Box 10, February 14, 1931, Box 25; "Letters From Readers," Dallas *Morning News*, August 5, 1931.

[32] Fredericksburg *Standard*, March 4, 1932; El Paso *Times*, November 22, 1931; Connally Papers, October 6, 1931, Box 15; September 7, 1931, Baker Mercantile Company, Wholesale Letters, 1931-1935.

[33] October 3, 1932, November 29, 1929, Secretary's Corres., Commerce Dept.; March 29, 1932, December 30, 1932, Rayburn Papers; Connally Papers, October 6, 1931, Box 15; Ansley, *I Like the Depression*, 27-28.

ded with violent criticism of both national and state banks.[34]

Only a few people believed Hoover's charge that the Federal Reserve System was reponsible for the depression, but among them were Congressmen Wright Patman and Martin Dies and former Governor Jim Ferguson who believed that stricter federal regulation should be established over the Federal Reserve System to forestall such a calamity in the future.[35] An attorney from Comanche almost lost his composure when writing to Congressman Sam Rayburn about the damage caused by both the Federal Reserve System and local banks.

> And it is damn strange to me that you fellows up there in Washington cannot understand what has been done to the public! The truth about it is, we have no money to do a damn thing. . . .
> If every damn bank was sunk into the ocean and every railroad was torn up and moved away, and every God-derned public building was blown away by a cyclone, the people of this country could go right on and do business, but when you have stopped the currency from going to the people, who grow and manufacture the products which we eat and wear, and paint our faces with, as well as manicure our nails, by God, you have stopped the thing![36]

Anti-bank sentiment was also expressed by the labor press and by the official publication of the League of United Latin American Citizens. The latter group was so distressed by usurious rates charged by banks that it asked why the federal government should not abolish all privately-owned banks and establish a government-owned system that would be fair to the average citizen.[37]

Businessmen, especially Big Businessmen, were blamed for causing the depression as much, if not more, than the President and the Republican Party. Many Americans believed that

---

[34] FDRL, April 12, 1932, Box 722.

[35] Wright Patman to Rayburn, June 22, 1932, Rayburn Papers; *Congressional Record*, 72d Cong., 1st Sess., 1932, LXXV, Part 4, 3996; *Ferguson Forum*, May 21, 1931.

[36] Letter, May 31, 1932, Rayburn Papers.

[37] *Weekly Dispatch*, January 30, 1932; J. T. Canales, "Usury," *LuLac News*, I (July, 1932), 5.

businessmen who had gladly taken credit for prosperity, should bear the responsibility when the capitalist system failed to work properly.[38] In view of the actions of many industrial leaders, the anger is more easily understood. Alfred Sloan, president of General Motors, who voluntarily reduced his salary in 1932 from $500,000 a year to $340,000, accomplished very little since the cut of $160,000 was more than the individual income taxes paid annually by two million residents of Mississippi.[39] A southern factory owner reflected industrial irresponsibility when he solemnly told his workers that their salaries would be reduced by 15 percent since he could not maintain wages and support both his daughter in her Swiss school and his wife who was spending the summer in a very fashionable resort.[40] Likewise, public veneration for business was not increased with the revelation that financial leaders such as J. P. Morgan often paid little or no income taxes.[41]

Texans also became more resentful of business after giving praise--perhaps only lip service--to the business philosophy of the twenties. Although most of the criticism came from individuals, the commercial press--and occasionaly business journals--joined the chorus. An individual, a newspaper, or even a business organ that praised business might

[38] For a discussion of the lowered prestige on a nationwide scale the following would be helpful: Frederick Lewis Allen, *The Big Change* (New York: Harper & Brothers, 1952), 149-150; Arnold, *The Folklore of Capitalism*, 36-37; Filley, *The Wealth of the Nation*, x; Hannah, "Urban Reaction," 56; George Soule, *The Coming American Revolution* (New York: The Macmillan Company, 1934), 159, 202-203; Wecter, *The Great Depression*, 2-3.

[39] Cohn, *King Cotton*, 244.

[40] Cash, *The Mind of the South*, 367.

[41] Arthur M. Schlesinger, Jr., *The Crisis of the Old Order*, Vol. 1 of *The Age of Roosevelt* (3 vols.; Boston: Houghton Mifflin Company, 1957), 253. Other examples of business extravagance and tax evasion may be found in the following: Robinson, *Fantastic Interim*, 188; William E. Leuchtenburg, *Franklin D. Roosevelt and the New Deal, 1932-1940* (New York: Harper & Row Torchbooks, 1963), 21.

have to face public displeasure.

On rare occasions when the commercial press blamed business for the depression, the criticism usually was barbed. The Austin *Statesman* challenged business spokesmen who said that the solution was to leave the country in the hands of business. The editor remarked that businessmen, few of whom had made progress since the depression, had their opportunity in 1930 when Congress refused to take action; however, business had done nothing to ease conditions.[42] Another daily opposed the demand of the United States Chamber of Commerce that government be turned over to business because when it was done in the twenties, the result had been to concentrate wealth further into the hands of the few with little attendant public responsibility.[43] One South Texas editor expressed the sentiment of many when he declared, "The culprit in the case is not General D. Pression, . . . but . . . Mr. Capitalist, who is putting out nothing but holding fast to that which he has."[44] Anti-business sentiment, reflected by Congressmen Hatton Sumners and Marvin Jones, also became involved in the gubernatorial election of 1932.[45]

Organized labor in the state demanded that instead of the people trying to find other causes, the blame should be placed squarely in industry where it belonged. Business disregard for the welfare of the workers and public at large should be dealt with in a firm manner. The Dallas Chamber of Commerce, for example, should not be allowed to advertise outside the state about how good Texas conditions

---

[42] Austin *Statesman*, October 17, 1931, January 6, 1932.

[43] Bonham *Daily Favorite*, May 1, 1931, July 25, 1931.

[44] "Musings of Monty," *Monty's Monthly*, XIII (January, 1931), 34.

[45] *Congressional Record*, 72d Cong., 2d Sess., 1932, LXXVI, Part 1, 1017; Roby *Star-Record*, October 30, 1930; Seth Shepard McKay, *Texas Politics, 1906-1944* (Lubbock: Texas Tech Press, 1952), 228-229.

were when, in reality, there were not jobs at all.[46]

Various segments of the public in Texas expressed anti-business sentiment. Charges that great businesses were untaxed and that commercial interests were in control of the government were quite common.[47] As a bank employee from Roxton explained, "Our Captains of Industry, our 'head hunters' have lost their rabbit's foot and are 'all wet.'"[48]

Significantly, as criticism of industry continued, class consciousness became more pronounced among individuals. A Latin American journal declared that we were governed only for the benefit of the wealthy; others, when speaking of "our people," did not include the rich. Some believed that the wealth of the nation was created not by the few rich people but by the "masses"; that the average citizen had no voice in governmental affairs; that the wealthy were willing to use the poor for cannon fodder in wartime, but were unwilling to help them in time of trouble.[49] One man asked Congressman Rayburn, "How can your conscience allow you to squander the people's tax money on such women as Mrs. Longworth, many times a millionaire, who so far as the majority of the people are concerned is not worth ten cents?"[50]

Although not all religious groups in Texas were willing to challenge business leadership as was being done by numerous national religous figures, many, including one Catholic newspaper and some fundamentalist Baptist leaders, did become critical of it.[51]

---

[46] *Weekly Dispatch*, November 8, 1930; Dallas *Craftsman*, December 27, 1929, March 28, 1930.

[47] "Correspondence," *The Texas Outlook*, XV (March, 1931), 2; FDRL, May 24, 1932, Box 722, September 5, 1932, Box 727.

[48] Letter, March 29, 1932, Rayburn Papers.

[49] J. T. Canales, "Usury," *Lulac News*, I (July, 1932), 5; FDRL, August 23, 1931, Box 720, December 12, 1932, Box 736, February 1, 1933, Box 734; letter, October 17, 1931, Sterling Papers, Box 180.

[50] Letter, January 5, 1932, Rayburn Papers.

[51] *Southern Messenger*, May 5, 1932; FDRL, December 10, 1932, Box

The few defenders of business were mostly the small town
weekly newspapers. During the entire period under discussion
many of them continued to speak of business as if the depression never occurred. They declared that a depression was no
argument against modern corporate finance; since the government was dependent upon industry, the only way government
could correct its problems was to adopt business methods.[52]
As late as the spring and summer of 1932, papers were still
declaring that if left alone business could end the depression; one paper, believing businessmen to be greater heroes
than any military leader or political official, advocated the
establishment of a business hall of fame.[53]

On the rare occasions when individuals defended business, they were more concerned about small businesses which
were being destroyed by the giants.[54] A San Antonio resident
declared, "Business has become the forgotten man. Let our
Party espouse his cause, and want will vanish, the depression
be forgotten and prosperity again be the normal state of all
our people."[55]

Few business publications came to their own defense, but
most of those that did believed the reason for the depression
to be the upsetting of natural law by government interference
with business.[56] The West Texas Chamber of Commerce wondered
if perhaps the rights of the dollar were not being destroyed
by the overemphasis on human rights;[57] it was very happy, how-

734; undated newspaper clipping in Norris Scrapbook, Norris Papers.

[52] Sterling City *News-Record*, December 13, 1929; George West *Enter-prise*, January 24, 1930; *San Patricio County News*, June 25, 1931.

[53] Canadian *Record*, July 14, 1932; Roby *Star-Record*, March 25, 1932.

[54] FDRL, November 4, 1932, Box 735; Connally Papers, n.d., Box 12.

[55] FDRL, November 1, 1932, Box 734.

[56] W. L. Clayton, "The World's Economic Tangle," *Acco Press*, IX (April, 1931), 22.

[57] "The Rights of the Dollar," *West Texas Today*, XII (February, 1932), 8.

ever when Governor Sterling, himself a businessman, selected the regional chambers of commerce to help distribute relief funds because "in each case the personnel of the committees reveals that the foremost business and professional men and women of West Texas have been selected."[58]

Perhaps the resentment against business and Republican leadership can best be illustrated by the actions taken by Congressman Wright Patman against Secretary of the Treasury Andrew Mellon. Mellon, long considered the best Secretary of the Treasury since Alexander Hamilton, increasingly came in for more virulent attacks as the depression deepened.[59] On January 6, 1932, Patman astonished his colleagues and the nation when he stated on the floor of the House of Representatives, "Mr. Speaker, I rise to a question of constitutional privilege. On my own responsibility as a member of the House, I impeach Andrew William Mellon . . . for high crimes and misdemeanors." He based the charges on a law of 1789 that forbade any person directly or indirectly involved in trade or commerce from holding the office of Secretary of the Treasury.[60] Although the action received little public attention,[61] Hoover, according to one student of the period, was so frightened by it that he appointed Mellon to the vacant post of Ambassador to the Court of St. James.[62] One of Hoover's personal aides, without mention of the Patman incident, said that Mellon was appointed to the London post be-

[58] "Behind the Relief," *ibid.*, XIII (December, 1932), 8.

[59] Dallas *Morning News*, February 5, 1932; Ben F. Miller, *A Presidential Survey From Washington to Hoover Inclusive* (Slaton, Texas: Privately Printed, 1932), 120-121; hereafter cited as Miller, *Presidential Survey*; Davis, *Memoir*, 84.

[60] *Congressional Record*, 72d Cong., 1st Sess., 1932, LXXV, Part 2, 1400.

[61] Edwin C. Hill, *The American Scene* (New York: Witmark Educational Publications, 1933), 34.

[62] Robinson, *Fantastic Interim*, 224.

cause his financial abilities would be helpful in the war
debts controversy. [63] Another aide reported in his diary
that Hoover was especially concerned about the political impact impeachment and trial would have on the 1932 presidential election. This aide viewed the appointment to London as
a shrewd political move. [64] Whatever the reasons may have
been the event did not receive much attention in Texas. The
few papers commenting editorially were astounded that such
an unqualified man as Mellon should be appointed to a very
sensitive diplomatic post. As for Patman's role, Texans were
not certain that he had been instrumental; however, since he
might have been, they were willing to let him take the credit. [65]

Obviously, the most highly respected people in the twen-
ties--the Republican Party and big business--were the most
criticized for having brought on the depression, but they
were not the only causes that Texans found. Some of the
other beliefs were quite serious and were widely held, while
others were much less significant.

Overproduction was considered a cause of the depression
by such groups as a Senate subcommittee of which Morris Sheppard was a member, the daily, weekly, and special interest
press, and professional economists. [66] A rather meaningless
distinction was made by a number of citizens, including Congressman Wright Patman, who declared that underconsumption
rather than overproduction was the cause. [67] A few even ar-

[63] Joslin, *Hoover Off the Record*, 182-183.

[64] Diary, January, 1932, MacLafferty Papers, Box 1, HHPL.

[65] Dallas *Morning News*, February 5, 1932; Galveston *Daily News*,
February 5, 1932.

[66] U. S., Congress, Senate, Subcommittee of the Committee on Manufactures, *Hearings, Establishment of National Economic Council*, 71st
Cong., 3d Sess., 1931, 183; Austin *Statesman*, May 25, 1931; *Devil's
River News*, November 7, 1930; *Weekly Dispatch*, August 6, 1930; Dr. Edwin A. Elliott, "Economic Depression and Unemployment," *The Texas Outlook*, XV (July, 1931), 11.

[67] FDRL, April 22, 1932, Box 722; Connally Papers, n.d., Box 20;

gued that neither overproduction nor underconsumption could be blamed since the real cause was underdistribution. Conditions were such that food and goods produced in one area were not available to those in other areas that desperately need them.[68] Whatever the cause, Texans were correct to assume that in some parts of the country and state large surpluses existed while in other areas people could not get the things they needed even if they had the money with which to purchase them.

Another cause of the depression to many Texans was the hoarding of money by individuals. Since such a development had not been encountered in previous depressions Hoover did not know what, if anything, he could or should do about it. He, therefore, continued his unimaginative and unoriginal approach by trying to convince the hoarders to spend their money or deposit it in banks. Although a number of Texas newspaper editors believed he was partially correct,[69] a few individuals disagreed with him.[70] Since most people recognized the problem to be one of confidence more than anything else,[71] the solutions proposed included taxing hoarded money, guaranteeing bank deposits to restore confidence, and lowering the salaries of hoarders until all their reserves were spent.[72]

Wright Patman to Herbert Hoover, August 19, 1930, Dept. of Agriculture, Correspondence.

[68] "Letters From Readers," Dallas *Morning News,* March 14, 1930; Amarillo *Sunday Globe-News,* November 30, 1930.

[69] Leonard P. Ayres, *The Economics of Recovery* (New York: The Macmillan Company, 1934), 43-44; Amarillo *Daily News,* February 5, 1932; Galveston *Daily News,* February 6, 1932; Dallas *Morning News,* February 5, 1932.

[70] *Terry County Herald,* October 23, 1931; Miller, *Presidential Survey,* 209.

[71] *Ibid.,* 211; FDRL, January 29, 1933, Box 731; Bonham *Daily Favorite,* October 12, 1931; "In Our Opinion," *Editorials of the Month for Texas,* I (November, 1930), 555.

[72] FDRL, January 4, 1933, Box 735, November 9, 1932, Box 735; "Letters From Readers," Dallas *Morning News,* June 3, 1932.

Although Hoover during the campaign of 1928 envisioned
a nation where the wealth was spread evenly among the people,
many Americans, by the thirties, complained of its concentration in a few hands.[73] Most Texans agreed that the wealth
was not evenly distributed;[74] estimates of twenty, fifty, or
one hundred men controlling 75 or 80 percent of the wealth,
and thus the nation, were common.[75] Even though a number of
the people believed that the holders of great wealth had a
responsibility to the public to use it wisely, one Dallas
citizen disagreed when he wrote to the Hebbronville *News*.

> One who has accumulated wealth owes nothing to his fellow
> man other than to attend strictly to his own business and
> vote to set up equal rights for all to use the earth. He
> served his fellow man when he accumulated his wealth, and
> his accumulation is nothing more than his reward for serv-
> ice rendered.[76]

The editor was undoubtedly correct when he replied that this
attitude was responsible for much of the disrespect for the
wealthy.

> Such thoughts . . . is[*sic*] in harmony with the thoughts
> and beliefs held by the high-jacker, the gangster, the
> highway man and all those who believe they have the right
> to take whatever they can by might, or strategy, or dupli-
> city, or chicanery. It is this thought . . . that is rush-
> ing to destruction the present capitalistic system and is
> going to create such antagonism to wealthy men that they
> will become victims of an enraged and outraged populace.[77]

Solutions for this problem included limiting the amount a
person or business might own, higher progressive taxation,
and inheritance taxes to limit the passing of huge fortunes

[73] Wilbur, *The New Day*, 176; Charles A. and Mary R. Beard, *America in Midpassage*, Vol. III *The Rise of American Civilization* (3 vols.; New York: The Macmillan Company, 1946), 105.

[74] FDRL, January 26, 1933, Box 732, September 12, 1932, Box 730; *Southern Messenger*, May 5, 1932.

[75] FDRL, May 12, 1932, Box 721; "Public Opinion," Amarillo *Daily News*, January 20, 1931; "Letters From Readers," Dallas *Morning News*, September 12, 1931.

[76] Hebbronville *News*, June 17, 1931.

[77] *Ibid.*

to others.[78]

The protective tariff, long an issue in American history, was heavily criticized during the depression. Since most people believed the agricutural segment of society suffered most from high tariffs Hoover, soon after he became President, called Congress into special session for the purpose of revising tariff schedules to aid the farmer. The final bill, the Hawley-Smoot Tariff, raised the rates on so many items that it was one of the highest in history. Republican leaders who thought the revision would end the depression within a month or two were surprised and disturbed when about the only reaction was that other nations passed retaliatory increases of their own duties.[79]

Although many Texans believed high tariff policies were the root of all economic problems,[80] others were a bit more sophisticated about the matter. They believed that the tariff was just as harmful in the long run to business interests as it was to farmers and consumers because it tended to stagnate international trade.[81] This attitude was best expressed by a dentist from Dublin.

> The "rich" and factory oporators [*sic*] have acted very foolish in having a Tariff that oporates [*sic*] to their advantage & against the common people & thereby killing their buying power & now they have no buyers for what they make.[82]

[78]"Letters From Readers," Dallas *Morning News*, April 15, 1930; Amarillo *Daily News*, June 16, 1932; D. A. Bandeen, "Don't Try to Tinker with Fundamentals," *West Texas Today*, XIII (February, 1933), 19.

[79]Connally, *My Name is Tom Connally*, 135; Carroll Kilpatrick (ed.), *Roosevelt and Daniels* (Chapel Hill: The University of North Carolina Press, 1952), 105-106; Sidney Ratner, *American Taxation* (New York: W. W. Norton & Company, Inc., 1942), 442.

[80]FDRL, January 23, 1932, Box 721, September 6, 1932,. Box 727; "Letters From Readers," Dallas *Morning News*, June 12, 1931.

[81]Hebbronville *News*, June 24, 1931; Huntsville *Item*, August 20, 1931; "Free Trade," *The Common Herd*, XV (March, 1930), 14-15; letter, September 2, 1931, Unemployment, Box 272, HHPL, PP.

[82]FDRL, April 19, 1932, Box 722.

By and large, farming interests in Texas were most opposed to the tariff policy of the previous ten years. Some
newspapers demanded a reduction or even the elimination of
the tariff to ease the farmer's condition.[83] Texas political
leaders were quite vocal in charging that the tariff was the
cause of the depression and of the farmers' serious plight.
Governor Sterling told a mass meeting of farmers in 1931
that the tariff was the main cause of low prices and State
Senator Pink L. Parrish of Lubbock made it an issue in his
campaign for congressman-at-large in 1932. Congressmen Jones
and Garner both declared that the return of prosperity could
only come when the price of their purchases was reduced.[84]
Congressmen Box, Dies, and Lanham believed that the tariff
which had restricted international trade, hurt unprotected
agricultural products the most. These men believed we had
been so favorable to special business interests that we had
legislated ourselves into a depression.[85] Congressman Sumners, in a statement very reminiscent of Bryan's Cross of
Gold Speech, spoke the feeling of many Texans.

> If somebody looks wise and proposes . . . an absurd thing
> for these farmers he is classed as a profound economist.
> Yet we know that these producers of exportable surpluses
> have no share in the tariff system. I am not speaking in
> prejudice here. I come from no mean city myself, but we
> city people have to recognize that if we would put our idle
> men to work, we have to give these farmers a chance to buy.
> That is all there is to it. The city people who manufacture
> do not seem to realize that they are living off the bounty
> which this Government forces these farmers and others to pay.
> What is the tariff but a bounty; and what is the tariff
> boost in the sale price but a sales tax which people have
> to pay.[86]

[83] Greenville *Messenger* as quoted in *Ferguson Forum*, January 29,
1931; Bonham *Daily Favorite*, August 26, 1931; Weatherford *Democrat*, June
12, 1931; letter, April 11, 1932, Cotton, Box 106, HHPL, PP.

[84] Fredericksburg *Standard*, September 11, 1931; Amarillo *Daily News*,
June 16, 1932; Roby *Star-Record*, October 30, 1930; Warren, *Hoover and
the Depression*, 88.

[85] *Congressional Record*, 71st Cong., 3d Sess., 1931, LXXIV, Part 4,
4384; *ibid.*, 72d Cong., 1st Sess., 1931, LXXV, Part 1, 733; *ibid.*, 72d
Cong., 2d Sess., 1932, LXXVI, Part 1, 991.

[86] *Ibid.*, 72d Cong., 2d Sess., 1932, LXXVI, Part 1, 1017.

A number of farm journals and businesses directly dependent upon agriculture were constant attackers of the high tariff policies that benefitted only industrial groups.[87]

A sampling of opinion among individuals indicates that Texans were opposed to the tariff mainly because the farmer was not protected. They, therefore, advocated the passage of tariff bills that would protect agricultural products, in some cases, to the exclusion of all others.[88] One man told Franklin Roosevelt that he could be elected if only he would:

> put on a number 9 pair of brass toed shoes and kick
> down that damnable wall of high tariff, that was built
> on a rotten foundation--built especially for the rich--
> and place a tariff on what the farmer raises on the
> farm and garden and nothing else. . . .[89]

A sampling of other public opinion including newspapers, congressmen, cattle raisers, and the Texas Bar Association, shows that they agreed with the idea of placing tariffs on imported agricultural products.[90]

Another cause in the eyes of many was excessive taxation; if not the cause it was, at least, prolonging the depression. Since high taxes stifled industrial development, no improvement could be made in the general economic situation until they were reduced. Therefore, high taxes were responsible for unemployment and the other evils of the depression.[91] Since so few people were heavily taxed, some-

[87]*The Valley Farmer*, May 20, 1931, 6; "An Open Letter to Our Friends," *Acco Press*, X (July, 1932), 4-5.

[88]FDRL, January 7, 1929, Box 719; Connally Papers, October 25, 1929, Box 6; U.S. State Department Decimal File, 1910-1929, Record Group 59, National Archives, Washington, D. C., March 21, 1929, Box 6228.

[89]FDRL, April 5, 1932, Box 718.

[90]Sterling City *News-Record*, December 6, 1929; *Congressional Record*, 71st Cong., 2d Sess., 1930, LXXII, Part 11, 12246; "Of Things that Concern Cattle Raisers," *The Cattleman*, XVIII (September, 1931), 5-6; "What's the Matter with Texas," *Texas Law Review*, L (October, 1931), 85-101.

[91]Secretary's Correspondence, Individual Case File, 1929-1933, Department of the Treasury, Record Group 56, National Archives, Washington, D. C., November 4, 1931, Box 2; hereafter cited as Sec. Corres.,

thing had to be done to prevent chaos that would result when they could no longer pay.[92] One man very cearly stated the problem when he replied to a creditor's demand for payment, "You dont no how hard I live. had to sell my milk goat to pay my Tax & done with out my coffee & many other things."[93] At least one woman was concerned that Franklin Roosevelt might not win the presidency because poor people in Texas could not pay the poll tax.[94] Even A. S. Burleson, Post-master-General under Woodrow Wilson, spoke from his retire-ment home in Austin against oppressive taxes.[95]

A manifestation of the discontent was shown by the grow-ing number of people advocating "tax strikes" or "tax holi-days."[96] This revolt, led by the State Taxpayers Association of Texas, was an attempt to organize sections of the state to advocate reduction. If reduced taxes were not forthcom-ing, the next step was to refuse to pay them altogether.[97] There were those, however, who believed American taxation not to be oppressive when compared with other countries. Some Texans believed a danger to the government was inherent in indiscriminate reduction; particularly hurt would be educa-tion.[98]

Treasury Dept.; Ansley, *I Like the Depression*, 57; McAllen *Monitor*, Octo-ber 7, 1932; Huntsville *Item*, November 24, 1932; Pecos *Enterprise and Gusher*, January 6, 1933.

[92]"Letters From Readers," Dallas *Morning News*, September 12, 1931.

[93]Baker Mercantile Company, April 25, 1932, Customer's Letters, 1931-33.

[94]FDRL, November 4, 1932, Box 724.

[95]*Ibid.*, December 2, 1932, Box 731.

[96]Dallas *Morning News*, March 26, 1932; Hebbronville *News*, April 15, 1931; Canadian *Record*, May 26, 1932.

[97]"In Our Opinion," *Editorials of the Month for Texas*, III (January, 1932), 11; Austin *Statesman*, April 5, 1932; Roby *Star-Record*, January 22, 1932.

[98]"Musings of Monty," *Monty's Monthly*, XIII (October, 1931), 33-34; *The Texas Weekly*, February 14, 1931, 6; *The Alcalde*, XXI (November, 1932), 37.

Since the United States was predominantly Protestant
and, to a degree, fundamentalist, many of the poeple believed the depression to be merely the fulfillment of the
scriptural prophecy of seven good and seven bad years. This
attitude was particularly strong in the rural areas where
fundamentalism flourished.[99] Quite a large number of Texans
concurred in this theory. The depression had occurred because of the lack of honesty, the competitive economic system that caused people to be immoral, or the abdication of
spiritual leadership by the ministers in the twenties.[100] Regardless of the truth of the charges against religious leadership, the churches tried quickly to take moral leadership
during the depression. The Catholic press did not attribute
the cause solely to immorality, but it did believe the only
real solution to the problem was the return to a more moral
life.[101] Protestant groups, much more outspoken, thought that
the depression could be ended only by a religious revival.
It was not unusual for them to require unfortunate transients
to endure sermons about how their evil ways had caused the
depression before they were fed.[102] The most outspoken of the
group, J. Frank Norris, preached that the depression was a
sign of the end of the world and that the "New Deal" of
Franklin D. Roosevelt was a sure indication that Christ would
soon return. He believed the depression had come because the
nation had turned away from fundamentalism to the "social
gospel" which had little to do with man's salvation.[103]

[99]Galbraith, *The Great Crash*, 174; Cash, *The Mind of the South*, 371.

[100]FDRL, July 2, 1932, Box 723, February 23, 1933, Box 738; "Public Opinion," Amarillo *Daily News*, February 17, 1932.

[101]*Southern Messenger*, March 3, 1932.

[102]Austin *Statesman*, June 3, 1932; Merton L. Dillon, "Religion in
Lubbock," *A History of Lubbock*, 482; Maury Maverick, *A Maverick American*
(New York: Covici, Friede, 1937), 157.

[103]E. Ray Tatum, "Conquest or Failure: a biographical study in the
life of J. Frank Norris" (unpublished manuscript in the possession of
the author at the University Baptist Church, Lubbock, Texas), 237, 239,
243.

Many Americans agreed with Hoover and the Republican
Party that the real cause of the depression was international. This involved the restriction of international trade
caused by world tariffs, heavy international indebtedness,
and the collapse of European credit institutions.[104] Texas
newspapers that concurred tried to persuade Texans that American prosperity was dependent on world conditions, that all
the world must prosper or none would, and that international
commerce was the key to world prosperity.[105]

The most serious question of a foreign nature involved
the cancellation, reduction, or postponement of war debts
and reparations payments. In keeping with his desire to restore confidence, Hoover began in the summer of 1931 to propose a one-year moratorium on war debts payments. Emphasiz-
ing that this did not in any way imply cancellation, he did
believe, however, that it would be the stimulation the world
needed. Immediate world and national reaction was immensely
favorable.[106]

Texas press reaction to Hoover's action was generally
favorable. War debts which had hindered world trade since
the end of the war would probably never be collected anyway.
Therefore, Hoover's action would show our good faith to the
rest of the world and might help to restore confidence.[107]
A few papers, moreover, believed that the partial or complete
cancellation of the uncollectable debts would be a greater

[104]Roy V. Peel and Thomas C. Donnelly, *The 1932 Campaign: An Analysis* (New York: Farrar & Rinehart, Inc., 1935), 134; Ayres, *The Economics
of Recovery*, 2-3; The Brookings Institution, *The Recovery Problem in the
United States*, 37, 43, 49.

[105]Amarillo *Daily News*, August 19, 1931; Hebbronville *News*, July
30, 1930; Huntsville *Item*, October 22, 1931; *San Patricio County News*,
July 31, 1930; "Isolation Not Possible," *Dallas*, XI (August, 1932), 12.

[106]Myers, *State Papers of Herbert Hoover*, I, 592-596; Joslin, *Hoover
Off the Record*, 102-103; Seldes, *The Years of the Locust*, 129, 138.

[107]Tahoka *News* as quoted in *Terry County Herald*, July 17, 1931;
Uvalde *Leader-News*, June 26, 1931; Galveston *Daily News*, July 2, 1931;
The Texas Weekly, August 27, 1932, 1; F. A. Buechel, "Is the Curve Turn-
ing Upward?" *West Texas Today*, XIII (October, 1932), 4.

stimulant to world prosperity than merely a one-year moratorium.[108]

Strangely enough, Texas political leadership did not agree with public opinion. Those congressmen who commented on the moratorium--Blanton, Patman, Lanham, Garner--were all opposed to it because it would probably lead to cancellation. The two Texas senators disagreed; Sheppard supported the bill in the Senate while Connally voted against it.[110]

One of the most serious issues during the depression was national prohibition. During the twenties prohibition had caused an increase in crime and a health problem; the economic conditions of the thirties made some people believe that it caused the depression. Prominent individuals, including former Governors Jim Ferguson and Will Hobby, were convinced that repeal would eliminate many of the social problems, would decrease the cost of government for police protection, and would help end the depression because of the number of people that would be employed and because of the increased governmental revenue available from taxation of liquor.[111] In Dallas, for example, several organizations supported repeal on the grounds that it would do away with the speakeasy and taxes would be reduced because of less need for law enforcement. The Dallas Chamber of Commerce believed control of liquor should be a local matter. National prohibition should be repealed since it was a national failure

[108] Amarillo *Daily News*, December 29, 1932; Dallas *Morning News*, October 1, 1931; Galveston *Daily News*, November 12, 1930.

[109] *Congressional Record*, 72d Cong., 1st Sess., 1931, LXXV, Part 1, 352; *ibid.*, Part 2, 4963; *ibid.*, 72d Cong., 2d Sess., 1932, LXXVI, Part 1, 991; Bascom M. Timmons, *Garner of Texas* (New York: Harper & Brothers, 1948), 132-133; Galveston *Daily News*, December 23, 1931.

[110] FDRL, July 13, 1931, Box 718; *Ferguson Forum*, June 25, 1931; FDRL, October 23, 1931, Box 719, August 10, 1931, Box 718.

[111] *Ferguson Forum*, February 26, 1931; James A. Clark and Weldon Hart, *The Tactful Texan: A Biography of Governor Will Hobby* (New York: Random House, 1958), 171; FDRL, April 8, 1932, Box 721, July 4, 1932, Box 726; "Letters From Readers," Dallas *Morning News*, January 15, 1932.

and a disgrace.[112] There were those, however, who opposed repeal on both moral grounds and with the argument that it would not really help the economic situation because it would create more problems than it would solve. Efforts of ministers such as those in Dallas to fight for the retention of prohibition existed throughout Texas.[113]

Prohibition was an issue in Texas politics from the time it was enacted and continued to be until it was finally repealed. For example, repeal was one of the issues in a special election in Houston in January 1933 to fill the congressional seat of the late Daniel E. Garrett. The repeal candidate, Joe H. Eagle, won the election.[114]

Antagonism toward foreign groups, particularly Mexicans, increased in Texas as rising unemployment caused the depression to worsen. A movement to restrict Mexican immigration or to eliminate it completely was strong; many people demanded that 90 percent of all workers be "red-blooded Americans" and not foreigners would could not even speak English.[115] Most editorial comment, made during 1930 before the depression became very severe, stated that the number of aliens in Texas exactly equally the number of people unemployed. The fact that Mexicans would work for less wages and would accept lower living standards was responsible for much of the trouble.[116] Efforts to control immigration will be discussed in the next chapter.

Quite a number of Texans believed the cause, or at least

[112] DeMoss, "Dallas during Depression," 139.

[113] Uvalde *Leader-News*, February 26, 1932; "Letters From Readers," Dallas *Morning News*, June 24, 1932, December 1, 1932; DeMoss, "Dallas during Depression," 139.

[114] Montgomery, "Depression in Houston," 142.

[115] April 17, 1932, Rayburn Papers; FDRL, October 8, 1932, Box 728, November 6, 1932, Box 731; "Letters From Readers," Dallas *Morning News*, July 14, 1930.

[116] Dallas *Morning News*, April 11, 1930; Galveston *Daily News*, June 25, 1930; Fredericksburg *Standard*, March 15, 1930.

the continuation, of the depression was due to the number of married women who worked outside the home. This caused unemployment to be more severe and brought suffering to many families whose fathers and husbands could not work because some married women were holding jobs they should have.[117] Most of the defense for working wives came from the big city dailies who argued that in most cases wives were working because they were forced to do so to feed their families. They did not condone women being employed when no need existed, but employers should be careful not to discharge a worker just because she was a woman.[118]

Texans found many other causes of the depression. Because we had become fat, lazy, stupid, and selfish we had over-indulged in too much installment buying that caused too much indebtedness.[119] Increased automation or particularly the "machine" was blamed by many for the trouble. Even Ross Sterling said as much in a speech at Huntsville during the 1930 gubernatorial campaign. The automobile, some believed, was the most vicious machine because it was designed to cost more money to operate than the average citizen could afford.[120] Other causes included price cutting forced by the proliferation of chain stores, government interference with private business, the lack of purchasing power, and the low price of silver.[121]

[117] FDRL, January 17, 1933, Box 735; Connally Papers, February 2, 1931, Box 24; Sterling Papers, September 26, 1931, Box 180; Nordeman, "Midland during Depression," 145; Madeline Jaffe, "Rural Women in Unskilled Labor" (M.A. thesis, The University of Texas at Austin, 1931), 84-86; *Waco Farm and Labor Journal*, December 5, 1930.

[118] Austin *Statesman*, May 30, 1932; El Paso *Times*, June 26, 1932; Galveston *Daily News*, September 2, 1930.

[119] Haskell *Free Press*, August 27, 1931; *Holland's*, March, 1931, 5; Hebbronville *News*, November 19, 1930.

[120] FDRL, December 16, 1932, Box 735; *Waco Farm and Labor Journal*, February 28, 1930; as quoted in Montgomery, "Depression in Houston," 65; "Letters From Readers," Dallas *Morning News*, August 8, 1931.

[121] *Devil's River News*, April 8, 1932; Connally Papers, n.d., 1930,

Many of the causes in the minds of Texans were superficial; quite often they mistook symptoms of the conditions as the real cause. Conversely, in some instances, they were very astute at uncovering more realistic explanations. Whatever the reason for the trouble, the Texan of the thirties was true to his agrarian background. The dislike and, in some cases, the intense hatred of all things not rural were almost psychopathic. The hatred for the "East," Republicans, the wealthy, and bankers were all manifestations of the agrarian mentality.

Box 12; January 5, 1932, Rayburn Papers; *Austin Labor Journal*, October 3, 1930; *Waco Farm and Labor Journal*, May 22, 1931.

CHAPTER V

VERY FEW ESCAPED

The depression was so pervasive that virtually no as-
pect of American life was spared. Earlier depressions had
been serious, but none had been so deep or so long. Texans
were bewildered by economic dislocation that most of them
could not understand, much less do anything about. Society
seemed to be crumbling before their eyes. Nearly all groups
and institutions felt the sting.

The depression was so traumatic that many Americans
were unable to withstand the strain. From 1930 to 1932 mental patients in public institutions tripled in number as compared to the 1922 to 1930 period; suicides were on the increase; Governor Sterling reported to Senator Hiram Bingham
that, by February 1932, probably a hundred thousand people
in the state were destitute. These few examples show that
the health of the state, both physical and mental, was seriously impaired, perhaps for generations to come, by the serious consequences of unemployment, undernourishment, malnutri-
tion, pneumonia, and tuberculosis.[1] Although studies are
limited, some evidence exists to show that a hidden fear
gripped Texans. Mental breakdowns and suicides increased,
at least in such cities as Houston and San Antonio. Although
not many did so, a few of the suicides left notes blaming depressed conditions for their actions.[2]

Another concept that weakened relief resources and created additional social problems was the widely-held belief
in the balanced budget and reduced governmental spending.

[1] Wecter, *The Great Depression*, 141; Houston *Labor Journal* as quoted
in *Ferguson Forum*, July 3, 1931; Ross Sterling to Hiram Bingham, February 29, 1932, Sterling Papers, Box 180; Maverick, *A Maverick American*,
160-161; Dallas *Craftsman*, September 9, 1932.

[2] McMillan, "San Antonio during Depression," 99; Montgomery, Depression in Houston," 136-137.

To achieve these goals government salaries and services had
to be reduced; rather than solving the problem, however, it
only accentuated it. According to John Kenneth Galbraith,
"it would be hard to imagine a better design for reducing
both the private and the public demand for goods, aggravat-
ing deflation, increasing unemployment, and adding to the
general suffering."[3] Presidents Hoover and Roosevelt continued to support the concept of a balanced budget achieved by
reduced expenditures and higher taxes. It was not until 1936
that John Maynard Keynes launched a formal attack on the concept in *The General Theory of Employment, Interest and Money.*
As he advocated an unbalanced budget and deficit financing in
times of economic crisis, more and more Americans began to
agree with him, hoping to find a solution for the depression.
In the period under discussion, however, the desire for a
balanced budget remained paramount.[4]

In Texas sentiment was almost unanimous in supporting
the balanced budget and a reduction in governmental expenditures. Almost all the press agreed that the government
operated much as did a family unit. Therefore, the only
solution to a financial problem was to retrench spending until it came into line with income.[5] Since such a demand for
tax reduction came from Texas, most of the press believed
the only sane way to do so was to reduce expenditures enough
so that taxes could be reduced while still maintaining a
balanced budget.[6] Only rarely did the press believe that
budget-cutting could be carried too far. Essential govern-

[3]Galbraith, *The Affluent Society*, 24.

[4]*Ibid.*, 24-25.

[5]The sentiment was so widespread that only a few examples can be
given here. See: Amarillo *Daily News*, February 5, 1932; Bonham *Daily
Favorite*, January 19, 1933; Brady *Standard*, January 3, 1932; Hebbronville *News*, September 30, 1931; *Terry County Herald*, July 8, 1932;
Uvalde *Leader-News*, May 13, 1931.

[6]"The Facts About Taxes," *Texas Opinion*, I (March 19, 1932), 9;
"Overbalanced," *Dallas*, XI (August, 1932), 12; R. M. Farrar, "The Way
Out," *Acco Press*, XI (March, 1933), 6.

ment services might be curtailed to the point of hurting society more than it would be helped.[7] So popular was the idea of budget-balancing and government economy that the administration of Governor Sterling advocated the reduction of state expenses by eliminating unnecessary offices and reducing salaries throughout the state. Despite his hopes, most of the retrenchments were never made.[8]

A number of attempts at economy were made on the local level. Austin eliminated such expenditures as travel allowances for city officials, furniture and equipment for city offices, and appropriations for municipal concerts. Haskell County abolished the offices of county agent and county home demonstrator and looked for other ways to reduce expenditures.[9] San Antonio reduced funding for the homes for the aged and paupers, county assessor, district attorney's office, and the Joske Memorial Home. Funding was totally eliminated for the Sanitary Inspector, the county nurse, and for doctors who served the poor. In Dallas the positions of superintendent and bookkeeper at the Municipal Garage were combined into one position.[10]

Occasionally an economy program such as the consolidation of counties, which had some merit, ran into serious opposition because of local pride despite the benefits possible.[11] Within the Texas congressional delegation Speaker

[7]Austin *Statesman*, June 14, 1932; *Live Oak County Herald*, July 21, 1932; "Budget Slashing Can Be Carried Too Far!" *Texas Municipalities*, XIX (March, 1932), 72.

[8]Seth S. McKay and Odie B. Faulk, *Texas After Spindletop*, Vol. VI of *The Saga of Texas*, ed. Seymour V. Connor (6 vols.; Austin: The Steck-Vaughn Company, 1965), 125; McKay, *Texas Politics, 1906-1944*, 226, 230.

[9]"First Things First," *West Texas Today*, XIII (July, 1932), 8; Jenkins, "Austin during Depression," 87; R. E. Sherrill, *Haskell County History* (Haskell, Texas: Haskell County Historical Society, 1965), 133.

[10]Harold Arthur Shapiro, "The Workers of San Antonio, Texas, 1900-1940" (Ph.D. dissertation, The University of Texas at Austin, 1952), 230-232; McMillan, "San Antonio during Depression," 101, DeMoss, "Dallas during Depression," 31.

[11]*Live Oak County Herald*, February 16, 1933.

John Garner and Senator Morris Sheppard believed in the balanced budget. [12] An exception was Senator Connally who believed the only solution was "to reduce taxes drastically and inaugurate federal borrowing for direct relief." He became very distressed with President-elect Roosevelt for his unrealistic insistence upon a balanced budget and an economy program. [13]

A large number of individuals also agreed with the economy program. Most of them believed that since prosperity could not be restored through public spending, a balanced budget was necessary; to do this, federal salaries should be reduced. [14] As one East Texan explained, "The most decussed [sic] topic in my District is taxation. The high cost of vorement [sic] or the high cost of being governed. We believe there is too much graft. We know there is too much money being spent. WE know we have it to pay." [15] Proportionately more individuals opposed the economy program than did businessmen or newspaper editors who believed that if the economy program were carried too far, it would ruin the country instead of helping it. [16] In fact, "This thing of cutting salaries and laying off employes, is one of the main things that has brought on this depression era." [17]

The people most affected by the economy moves were the persons who lost their jobs. In most places, those caught

[12]Timmons, *Garner of Texas*, 128-129; Hill, *The American Scene*, 32-33; clipping from Texarkana *Press*, November 30, 1931, Sheppard Papers.

[13]Connally, *My Name is Tom Connally*, 147-148.

[14]FDRL, December 31, 1932, Box 733, September 16, 1932, Box 725; letter, May 31, 1932, Rayburn Papers; "Letters From Readers," Dallas *Morning News*, March 28, 1932.

[15]FDRL, September 12, 1932, Box 723.

[16]Connally Papers, October 8, 1931, Box 21; FDRL, February 2, 1933, Box 737; "Public Opinion," Amarillo *Daily News*, January 28, 1931; "Letters to the Times," El Paso *Times*, May 21, 1932.

[17]Letter, March 28, 1932, Rayburn Papers.

in such a situation had no alternative except to join the
ranks of the unemployed. There is no way to know how many
people actually lost their jobs due to economy measures; in
total numbers it probably was not high. Even so, those so
affected were hurt by the actions while the benefit to the
larger public was negligible.

Public education was one of the governmental services
most seriously affected by the depression and the concern
about spending and one about which more information is available. Many states reduced appropriations for universities
and public schools to the point that the systems were severely weakened. This was especially true in the South
where the educational system had never been strong. Its
large school-age population had never been educated as
soundly as the rest of the country.[18] Although the level
of education in Texas was also poor, it was better than in
most parts of the South. In a study of a representative
working group in Texas the poor educational level was evident. Most of the men did not finish high school and had
begun to support themselves during their teenage years.[19]

As the depression deepened in Texas the threat to education both at the public and the university levels became
very real. In Electra a danger existed that the public
schools would have to close for a lack of funds. In all
areas the demand for expenditure reduction usually resulted
in the lowering of teachers' salaries and the elimination of
"unnecessary" school employees.[20]

In Houston the level of public education funding continued through 1930, but by 1932 employees, both teachers
and custodial, were asked to donate three days pay so that

[18] Kilpatrick, *Roosevelt and Daniels*, 132-133; Cohn, *King Cotton*, 244.

[19] Allen, *Wage Earners Meet the Depression*, 49.

[20] Electra *News*, November 17, 1932; "The Depression in Public Education," *The Texas Outlook*, XVI (June, 1932), 36; B. H. Miller, "The
Depression and the Schools," *ibid.*, XVI (July, 1932), 36.

the budget could be balanced. Salaries were eventually cut. In San Antonio, cuts in teachers' salaries were so severe that the city fell to eleventh among the twelve largest cities in Texas. Teachers in San Antonio, as was true in many communities, were paid in scrip rather than cash. Although teachers' salaries were reduced by 22 percent, the Midland school district never had to resort to scrip.[21]

The issue of working married women was a special issue in public education. Concern that women might be earning a second income for a family caused consternation among some local school boards. In August 1931 the San Antonio Board of Education officially stated that no married women would be hired and the marriage of a woman teacher would be considered a resignation. In Midland, the action was not so drastic. Women teachers already married were not dismissed, but no married women would be hired in the future. When salary cuts were made the martial status of a woman teacher and the employment status of her husband were considered. Some women teachers found their salaries cut more severely than single women or men.[22]

In related educational functions such as public libraries, the depression caused a decline in budgets, salaries, and book purchases. Cities such as Lubbock, Dallas, El Paso, and Corsicana reported that they were forced to revise their budgets for 1932. The Harlingen Public Library, with an income of only $100 per month, paid its staff twenty cents per hour and bought only three books for its depleted shelves from November 1931 to April 1932.[23] Although some of the

[21]Montgomery, "Depression in Houston," 103-111; McMillan, San Antonio during Depression," 54-55; Nordeman, "Midland during Depression," 145-152.

[22]McMillan, "San Antonio during Depression," 49; Nordeman, "Midland during Depression," 145.

[23]"Texas Libraries and the Depression," *Bulletin of the Texas Library Association*, VIII (April, 1932), 3-5.

press demanded that educational costs be cut as much as possible,[24] other papers occasionally pleaded that "we must not take a backward step in the matter of education of children. . . . Ignorance is the dearest luxury we have."[25] The state teachers' journal tried to relate educational standards to recovery from the depression.

> Big business when it does not give attention to the education of the people is failing in the first essential of continued business prosperity. Ignorance cannot compete with intelligence in the production of wealth. Ignorance, disease, and poverty are coordinate facts. Intelligent, educated nations rule the world. Intelligent, educated states and communities are outstanding. They produce and control the wealth of the land. Educational leaders should never apologize to any group of business men when asking for adequate support for the schools of Texas and in their respective communities.[26]

A number of people were disturbed that higher education might also suffer.[27] One of the beneficial results, however, was that public school, and to a larger degree, higher education attendance increased during the depression.[28] The University of Texas in Austin fared better than most colleges with its enrollment gradually increasing during the depression years. This was due to the high unemployment rate and to the lower tuition costs at state colleges and universities.[29] Other colleges in Texas did not fare as well.

A major threat to the future of higher education developed in late 1932. With the economic situation so serious by this time, the maintenance of several colleges throughout the state appeared as an unnecessary extravagance. The

[24] Amarillo *Daily News*, June 23, 1932; Galveston *Daily News*, December 30, 1930.

[25] Sterling City *News-Record*, January 6, 1933.

[26] "Editorials," *The Texas Outlook*, XIV (December, 1930), 22.

[27] "Editorial," *The Alcalde*, XIX (May, 1931), 261.

[28] Hannah, "Urban Reaction," 140-141; Canadian *Record*, December 10, 1931.

[29] Jenkins, "Austin during Depression," 144-148.

Legislative Efficiency and Economy Committee saw the cost
of higher education as a place where the burden on taxpayers
could be reduced.

College administrators and teachers were concerned for
their future; communities where colleges were located were
especially concerned because of the economic impact college
closings would have on them. The state teachers colleges--
the "normal" schools--came in for special consideration.
One proposal called for the closing of the teachers colleges
at Alpine, Nacogdoches, Canyon, San Marcos, and Kingsville.
Consolidation of the two colleges in Denton--the College of
Industrial Arts (now Texas Woman's University) and North Texas State Teachers College--seemed a real possibility. Reduction of Sam Houston State Teachers College at Huntsville ar
Texas Technological College at Lubbock to junior college statu
was widely discussed. The possibility of these changes became a threat in early 1933 when several bills were introduced in the Texas Legislature to carry out one or more of
the proposals.

College leaders and threatened communities around the
state mounted a campaign to keep the colleges open. Especially vocal were local newspapers. Eventually, the Legislature refused to change the status of any of the colleges even
though it did reduce appropriations for higher education.
The threat to the colleges of Texas had passed.[30]

Public education was only one of the public responsibi-
lities that suffered because of the depression. It is, however, a good example of how Texans reacted to the crisis.
The threat to the future of education in Texas did not destroy the system as some feared it might. Just as education
was threatened by public opinion and potential government
action, so too was the status of other groups brought into
question.

[30] For an excellent summary of this issue, especially as it affected
San Marcos, see: Merry K. Fitzpatrick, "Local Solutions Not Adequate:
San Marcos, 1932-1933" in Robert C. Cotner, *et al.*, *Texas Cities and
the Great Depression* (Austin: Texas Memorial Museum, 1973), 47-49.

Antagonism toward foreign groups, particularly Mexicans, increased in Texas as rising unemployment caused the depression to worsen. A movement to restrict Mexican immigration or to eliminate it completely was strong; many people demanded that 90 percent of all workers be "red-blooded Americans" and not foreigners who could not even speak English.[31] Most editorial comment, made during 1930 before the depression became very severe, stated that the number of aliens in Texas exactly equalled the number of people unemployed. The fact that Mexicans would work for less wages and would accept lower living standards was responsible for much of the trouble.[32] Texas political leadership was also concerned about the number of jobs taken by Mexican aliens. The unemployment commission called by Governor Sterling in 1931 recommended that immigration be restricted and that American workers be given preference wherever possible.[33]

Congressman Thomas Blanton, long an advocate of restriction, continued his demands on the floor of Congress and by the introduction of immigration bills.[34] Congressman Dies, from the beginning of his service, hoped for a seat on the Committee on Immigration and Naturalization. Through the years his bills restricting immigration were usually for a complete five-year restriction and an increased time limitation for becoming naturalized. Perhaps his concern is partly explained by his later interest in un-American activities.[35]

[31] April 17, 1932, Rayburn Papers; FDRL, October 8, 1932, Box 728, November 6, 1932, Box 731; "Letters From Readers," Dallas *Morning News*, July 14, 1930.

[32] Dallas *Morning News*, April 11, 1930; Galveston *Daily News*, June 25, 1930; Fredericksburg *Standard*, March 15, 1930.

[33] Bureau of Labor Statistics, *Committee for Unemployment Relief*, 9, 12.

[34] *Congressional Record*, 71st Cong., 2d Sess., 1930, LXXII, Part 11, 12247; *ibid.*, 72d Cong., 1st Sess., 1931, LXXV, Part 1, 159.

[35] Allan A. Michie and Frank Ryhlick, *Dixie Demagogues* (New York:

The most serious attempt to limit the number of aliens
was made by John Box of Texas who wanted to apply the quota
laws to all countries of Latin America. To support his bill
he placed numerous letters in the *Congressional Record*. Most
Texans agreed that Mexicans were displacing Texas workers;
that they accepted lower wages and living standards; that
they might become a majority in the state; and that they
were mongrelizing the population.[36] Generally organized labor, both in the nation and in Texas, and a number of individuals supported the Box bill.[37] There were farmers, however, who opposed the measure on the grounds that it would
limit the number of workers available for agriculture since
most native Americans would not do such menial tasks.[38]

Apparently, most Texans were too concerned about survival to become actively involved in the restriction movement. After 1933 relief measures of the New Deal reduced
the pressure, and interest in immigration restriction declined.

Just as teachers' salaries were reduced and Mexican immigrants were opposed because they would work for less, members of organized labor felt themselves threatened. Texas
had never been overly receptive to labor unions; in the economic crisis the trade unions found themselves faced with a
declining membership and less control over their members.
Records of Texas labor unions are filled with examples of
discipline of members for working below the stated union
scale or for working for non-union employers.[39]

The Vanguard Press, 1939), 62; *Congressional Record*, 72d Cong., 1st
Sess., 1931-1932, LXXV, Part 1, 159, 736, Part 4, 4407.

[36]*Ibid.*, 71st Cong., 3d Sess., 1931, LXXIV, Part 4, 4381-4387.

[37]Austin *Statesman*, October 20, 1929; *Weekly Dispatch*, May 24,
1930; "Letters From Readers," Dallas *Morning News*, February 8, 1930.

[38]*Ibid.*, January 31, 1930.

[39]Painters, Decorators, and Paperhangers of America of Tyler, Texas,
local 855, minutes, March 10, 1931, December 22, 1931; International
Longshoremen of Houston, local 1273, February 18, 1931, Texas Labor Archives, The University of Texas at Arlington; hereafter cited as TLA,UTA.

As the depression became more serious, unions grappled with the issue of wage scales. Some workers wanted to reduce the daily or hourly rate in order to compete with non-union workers. Others felt, however, that a reduction would weaken the trade union movement without providing any more work. Eventually most unions had to face reality and reduce their rates. Sometimes this was done at the request of employers and sometimes by the union members. Unions were so hard-pressed that they had to reduce the salaries of union officials. They also reduced initiation fees and union dues. This was a bitter pill for proud union men to accept, but all segments of society were hurt bad enough that they had to accept things never dreamed of before. [40]

One of the major movements of the early thirties by a group that felt itself dispossessed was for the so-called veterans "bonus." Throughout American history, but especially in the twentieth century, the veteran has been of social, economic, and political importance. At the end of the First World War a movement began to pay the veteran a "bonus" for his military service that would make his income comparable to that of the civilian worker during the war. After a great deal of debate, a bill was passed in 1924 to provide "adjusted compensation" for the veteran equal to $1.00 per day of domestic service and $1.25 for each day served overseas. Instead of paying the money immediately, the bill provided for endowment insurance policies to be paid on January 1, 1945, with added interest. As the depression deepened, Congress passed a bill in February 1931, over Hoover's veto, providing that veterans might borrow from the government up to one-half the face value of the certificates. Shortly thereafter, a movement began, led by Wright Patman

[40]Austin Typographical Union Collection, minutes, February 7, 1932, March 6, 1932; Fort Worth Carpenters Union, local 208, minutes, July 20, 1932, December 9, 1931, November 9, 1932; Painters, Decorators, and Paperhangers of America of Tyler, Texas, local 855, minutes, November 2, 1931; San Antonio Carpenters' Union No. 14 Collection, minutes, January 3, 1933, TLA,UTA; *Waco Farm and Labor Journal*, February 12, 1932.

of Texas, to pay the balance of the certificates immediately.[41] Among the veterans' groups there was some difference of opinion about the advisability of this proposal. Patman stated that his bill was supported by such organizations as the Veterans of Foreign Wars and the Disabled American Veterans, but the largest group, the American Legion, after a speech by Hoover to its convention, passed a resolution opposing the bill.[42]

The adjusted compensation bills fathered by Patman had very controversial and confusing lives. The first bill (H. R. 1), introduced on the first day of the first session of the Seventy-Second Congress, December 8, 1931, provided simply for the full payment of the certificates without any mention of the source of the money. Later, other bills were introduced to provide for the printing of Treasury notes that would serve the double purpose of expanding the currency and aiding the veteran.[43]

The arguments in Congress for and against the proposal were of some significance. Patman warned the House that the country was facing a very grave situation brought on by the depression. He demanded that Congress aid the veterans as a stop-gap measure to prevent the outbreak of violence. This would do more to restore confidence than all the talk for the past two years. Thomas Blanton said that the President's opposition only reflected the Republican policy of aiding industry and the wealthy and letting the people shift for themselves. Other proponents of the bill declared that payment would show the good faith of Congress in dealing with its constituents. It would, likewise, bring relief to thousands or perhaps millions of people by putting more money into cir-

[41] Mitchell, *Depression Decade*, 109; Wecter, *The Great Depression*, 37; *Congressional Record*, 72d Cong., 1st Sess., 1931, LXXV, Part 1, 1144-1145.

[42] *Ibid.*, 1144; Myers, *State Papers of Herbert Hoover*, II, 151.

[43] *Congressional Record*, 72d Cong., 1st Sess., 1932, LXXV, Part 12, 13044.

culation. It might, in fact, be the thing required to bring the nation out of the depression. Opponents, on the other hand, believed it would not solve the problem, that it would destroy faith in American currency, and that it would only foster demands by other groups for federal aid.[44]

The attitude of Texans toward the payment of the bonus revealed a fairly strong class-consciousness. About the only groups to oppose the bill were the big city dailies and an occasional business journal. By and large, however, business stayed out of the controversy. The Galveston *Daily News*, one of the most outspoken opponents, believed it to be merely class legislation designed to aid the veterans at the expense of the other segments of the economy. It also questioned whether the nation really had any moral obligation to the veteran and if the veteran himself really wanted the payment or whether it was merely election year politics that motivated it.[45] Other opponents declared that the payment of the bonus would do no good. One paper was unhappy because the bill would hurt the veteran more than it would help him since the original idea had been to provide aid for his old-age. If the certificates were redeemed ahead of schedule, he would be left without any resources at retirement.[46] Obviously, to this editor, the depression was not serious enough to merit immediate payment.

By far, most Texans supported the payment of the bonus. The Texas State Senate and organized groups from such places as Crowell, Blum, and Bonham petitioned Congress to pass the bill to alleviate distressed conditions.[47] Maury Maverick

[44] *Ibid.*, Part 14, 15496; *ibid.*, 71st Cong., 2d Sess., 1930, LXXII, Part 11, 12246; *ibid.*, 72d Cong., 1st Sess., 1932, LXXV, Part 11, 12395. A very full debate on the issue may be found in *ibid.*, Part 12, 12911-12938.

[45] Galveston *Daily News*, April 14, 1932, September 2, 1931, April 27, 1931.

[46] "The A.G.C. Recommends . . . ," *Lone Star Constructor*, VIII (October, 1931), 5; Austin *Statesman*, December 13, 1930.

[47] *Congressional Record*, 71st Cong., 3rd Sess., 1931, LXXIV, Part

reported that most of the transients in the state, although they knew little about it, had the vague idea that it might help conditions. Of the few newspapers that supported the bonus, the *Ferguson Forum* and the Big Spring *News* were the most outspoken.[48] Most of the individuals who supported the measure believed that it and other relief measures were the only things that would offer true relief and really make a dent in the depression.[49] As the controversy continued the sentiment, particularly among the veterans and the poor, became very class-conscious. Perhaps a letter written to Governor Sterling, despite its length and the near-illiteracy of its author, best represents the trend of public opinion.

> I served in the Texas National Guards in the year of (1918) nineteen hundred and eighteen and I have not received one penny in payment for the services of same. If you and your class and Senators and etc. are so interested in helping the unemployed why the state should pay us boys for this service which they are about 90 percent of us boys out of work and about 50 percent as like myself with nothing to eat and no place to stay. In the year of 1917 and 1918 your class was hollowing *patriotic* to your country that us boys was fine boys during that time but now we are nothing. You and your Senators and so on says it is hard to get a bill through corporating money. They can stay in Session all the year drawing from five dollars to ten dollars a day, they can vote a bill mighty easy and quick to pay themselves, but you and no other of the state's representatives are in favor of voting a bill to help us boys, I am more patriotic now than I ever was because I am hungry and out of work. But I do not intend to let this country make a numbskull out of me anymore. . . .[50]

As the controversy over the bonus became more serious, a group of Oregon veterans under the leadership of Walter W. Waters, an unemployed thirty-five year-old veteran, decided to go to Washington to present their petitions to

4, 4000-4001; *ibid.*, 72d Cong., 1st Sess., 1932, LXXV, Part 11, 12655; *ibid.*, Part 10, 10744; letter, December 16, 1931, Rayburn Papers.

[48] Maverick, *A Maverick American*, 155-156; *Ferguson Forum*, March 12, 1931; Big Spring *News* as quoted in *Terry County Herald*, April 22, 1932.

[49]"Pens of the People," Galveston *Daily News*, April 4, 1932; "Letters From Readers," Dallas *Morning News*, November 8, 1930; Connally Papers, February 14, 1931, Box 25, FDRL, January 4, 1933, Box 733.

[50]Sterling Papers, October 17, 1931, Box 180.

Congress in person. The movement began as only an attempt
of a few veterans to obtain what they believed was right-
fully theirs. As the group moved eastward, however, living
as best they could, others began to join them and other
groups began to leave from other parts of the country. By
the time the Bonus Expeditionary Force (B.E.F.) reached
Washington it appeared to be a group of unemployed persons
more than a group of veterans.[51] The movement, quite popular among Texans, acquired a sizeable following. Estimates
of Texans marching to Washington ran as high as three or
four thousand. Of a total of over 28,000 men in Washington,
according to Waters, Texas had almost 1300. Texas was
eighth in rank with four percent of the total number.[54] Despite warnings that the march revealed a dangerous state of
mind in the country, the editor of the Austin *Statesman* believed it was really encouraging. He said that the very
fact that a peaceful movement of such a large group of people could take place without the rest of the country going
into panic was a sure sign of the strength of American democracy. To buttress his argument, he asked what the reaction
would have been if as large a group of German war-veterans
had marched on the German government.[55]

After the B.E.F. had been in Washington a short time
the pension bill finally passed the House by a vote of 211
to 176 with all but two of the Texas delegation voting for

[51] Schlesinger, *The Crisis of the Old Order*, 256-259; Dumond, *Roosevelt to Roosevelt*, 388-389; Warren, *Hoover and the Depression*, 235-236;
Soule, *The Coming American Revolution*, 185.

[52] Austin *Statesman*, June 3, 1932; Galveston *Daily News*, June 3,
1932; W. W. Waters as told to William C. White, *B.E.F.: The Whole
Story of the Bonus Army* (New York: The John Day Company, 1933), 307;
hereafter cited as Waters, *B.E.F.*

[53] Austin *Statesman*, June 10, 1932.

[54] Haskell *Free Press*, June 23, 1932; Sterling City *News-Record*,
June 10, 1932; Amarillo *Sunday Globe-News*, June 5, 1932; Ozment, "Temple
and Depression," 112-113.

[55] *Weekly Dispatch*, June 25, 1932; Austin *Statesman*, June 10, 1932.

it. The bill was defeated, however, in the Senate, perhaps because of the threat of a presidential veto. The two Texas Senators disagreed; Sheppard supported the bill but Connally, surprisingly, voted against it. Connally, obviously concerned about how his vote would be viewed at home, issued a lengthy statement explaining why he voted the way he did. The Galveston *Daily News* believed it to be to the Senate's credit that it rejected the bill in the face of public opinion and in an election year.[56]

When it became apparent that the bill was dead, some of the veterans began to leave Washington. When the majority refused to leave, however, Congress proposed several bills to provide funds for them to return to their homes. Perhaps they would have accepted had Congress not stipulated that the transportation funds would eventually be deducted from the money owed to them. Public sentiment, however, believed that they should have accepted the offer.[57]

As a last resort, Hoover ordered a contingent of the United States army to disperse the remaining veterans. This was done by burning the shacks and tents where the veterans, many with their families, lived. The sight of heavily armed soldiers driving out helpless starving people aroused increased sympathy for the veterans and further tarnished Hoover's image as the Great Humanitarian.[58]

Texans reacted very bitterly to the manner in which the veterans were ejected from Washington. The newspapers, even

[56]*Congressional Record*, 72d Cong., 1st Sess., 1932, LXXV, Part 12, 13053-13054, 13274; *Waco Farm and Labor Journal*, July 15, 1932; Galveston *Daily News*, June 20, 1932.

[57]*Congressional Record*, 72d Cong., 1st Sess., 1932, LXXV, Part 13, 13957, 14725, Part 14, 15747; Sidney Lens, *Left, Right & Center: Conflicting Forces in American Labor* (Hinsdale, Illinois: Henry Regnery Company, 1949), 264; hereafter cited as Lens, *Left, Right & Center;* Hill, *The American Scene,* 140; Galveston *Daily News,* July 10, 1932.

[58]Schlesinger, *The Crisis of the Old Order,* 261-264; Alfred B. Rollins, Jr., *Roosevelt and Howe* (New York: Alfred A. Knopf, 1962), 355; Mitchell, *Depression Decade,* 110; Karl Schriftgiesser, *This Was Normalcy* (Boston: Little, Brown and Company, 1948), 278.

those that had opposed the bonus from the beginning, believed it to be a pitiful and sorry spectacle and declared
it to be the worst mistake Hoover ever made.[59]   Individuals,
also distressed, informed Franklin Roosevelt that the event
only guaranteed his election to the presidency.[60]

Hoover, at the time and later, defended his actions as
necessary because the B.E.F. represented a threat to the
government because it had been infiltrated by Communists who
were using it as a foundation for a violent revolution. General Douglas MacArthur who was in charge of the military forces agreed fully with the President. He declared that only
a small portion of the men were actually veterans; the larger number, by far, were criminals and Communists. Waters
emphasized, however, that the marchers presented no radical
threat whatever. He had been constantly on the alert to keep
Communists out of the B.E.F., a task in which he succeeded
very well.[61]   Despite the charges and whatever truth there
may have been to them, the net effect was to destroy most of
the President's remaining prestige without any improvement
in the situation of the veterans.[62]

Just as the veterans failed in their objective, so too
did most efforts of other groups before the New Deal came in
1933. There were, without question, many Texans who did not
suffer seriously from the depression, but not very many ele-
ments of society were spared the agony. This economic crisis was so deep and prolonged that everyone felt it in one
way or another. One of the most serious aspects of the depression was the homeless people it created.

[59] Austin *Statesman*, July 30, 1932; Dallas *Morning News*, August 5,
1932; Galveston *Daily News*, July 31, 1932.

[60] FDRL, August 6, 1932, Box 724, September 15, 1932, Box 724.

[61] Myers, *State Papers of Herbert Hoover*, II, 242; Hoover, *The Great
Depression*, 225-230; Douglas MacArthur, *Reminiscences* (New York: McGraw-
Hill Book Company, 1964), 92-94; Waters, *B.E.F.*, 2, 102.

[62] Mauritz A. Hallgren, *Seeds of Revolt* (New York: Alfred A. Knopf,
1933), 188; Hill, *The American Scene*, 143.

CHAPTER VI

HOMELESS PEOPLE

One of the most striking developments of the early depression years was the emergence of a growing number of
transients throughout the United States. Just who these
people were is difficult to ascertain; yet, we can get a
general impression. They were a group of people truly
homeless in every sense of the word. The existence of a
class of "bums" or "hoboes" was nothing new in America;
nor was the continual migration of people from one place
to another unusual.[1] The unique feature of the thirties
was the number of people involved, an indication that something was basically wrong in society. Most migrants were
unable to find a new place to live because the same problems that expelled them from their homes existed almost
everywhere in the country.[2] The fear was strong a permanent migrant class might develop that would wander aimlessly
"on the cold crust of a cold earth."[3] A New Dealer and a
prominent leader in relief measures, Harry Hopkins, probably best described who these people were and the frustrat-
ing conditions they faced.

> They were industrial workers, artisans, laborers who after
> years of settled life, were forced by necessity to seek em-
> ployment in new places. They were dispossessed farmers,
> travelling westward with their families as their fathers

[1] In fact, Stephan Thernstrom says: "The bottom layer of the social
order in the nineteenth century American city was thus a group of families who appear to have been permanent transients, buffeted about from
place to place, never quite able to sink roots." Stephan Thernstrom, "Urbanization, Migration, and Social Mobility," in Barton J. Bernstein, ed.,
Towards a New Past: Dissenting Essays in American History (New York: Random House Vintage Books edition, 1969), 169. Probably there was also a
somewhat permanent migrant or transient class in the rural areas in the
nineteenth century.

[2] Hannah, "Urban Reaction," 120; Hopkins, *Spending to Save*, 126-128;
Steen, *Twentieth Century Texas*, 22-23.

[3] Cohn, *King Cotton*, 253.

had done before them. They were young men who had never had
a chance to work, and who could no longer remain in dependence on their burdened parents. They were country people
looking for work in the city and city people looking for
security in the country. They were negroes, following the
usual road of opportunity northward. They were the aged,
the tuberculous and otherwise infirm, moving to the widely
touted climates of Florida, California and the Southwest
in the hope that a favorable climate would somehow miti-
gate the rigors of poverty.[4]

The transients are usually classified into two cate-
gories. One group included the adults--men, women, and
even whole families--who were trying to find a new place
for themselves. The other group was composed of younger
people, ranging in age from around thirty to as low as five
or six years of age who seemed to have little direction.
People of both types made their presence felt in Texas as
they wandered, desperately and often hopelessly, over their
native land.

To determine how many people were homeless in the
thirties at either the national or the local level is difficult. Though official estimates are not entirely reliable, an estimate of the total number of migrants was
from 1,500,000 to 2,000,000.[5] Of this number, the Children's Bureau of the Department of Labor estimated in August 1932 that 200,000 were children.[6] One month earlier
the Austin *Statesman*, citing an unnamed Washington source,
said there were 300,000.[7]

For obvious reasons the number of transients within the
state at any given time is difficult to estimate. Moreover,
the number constantly fluctuated. A West Texas banker informed Senator Tom Connally that if agricultural relief did

[4] Hopkins, *Spending to Save*, 126.

[5] Soule, *The Coming American Revolution*, 186; Steen, *Twentieth Century Texas*, 22-23; Hannah, "Urban Reaction," 120; Ozment, "Temple and
Depression," 34; the papers of Herbert Hoover are filled with documents
of this sort; see for example Boxes 6,7,8, HHPL,PP.

[6] Seldes, *The Years of the Locust*, 288.

[7] Austin *Statesman*, July 1, 1932.

not come immediately, farmers would be forced upon the road. He explained that farmers in Jones County had sold everything possible just to subsist and that their condition had not improved. He informed the Senator that an estimate of one-half to two-thirds of the land lying idle was conservative. Already, he reported, many heads of families had left home to find work and others with their families would soon follow if relief were not forthcoming.[8]

Communities in the southern and southwestern parts of the state and those located on major railroads had the most serious problem, but it is safe to assume that relatively few towns and cities escaped the influx of transients. In one period of six months, an estimated 45,000 transients moved through El Paso.[9] A labor newspaper in Dallas complained in 1930 that city officials refused to recognize the urgency created by homeless people. In 1933 the same paper reported that 300 transient men were living in unbearable conditions in Dallas.[10] Even smaller cities had the same problem; in February 1932 the Texas and Pacific Railroad ejected from its train two hundred tramps in the small town of Weatherford.[11] Cities throughout the nation, including several from Texas, responding to the survey made by Senator Robert M. LaFollette of Wisconsin on matters of unemployment and relief, reported that transients were creating serious problems for them and overburdening their relief facilities.[12] The Houston Chamber of Commerce inadvertently gave an indication of the seriousness of the situation in that city. In one of the optimistic statements so common at that time, the Chamber declared that

[8] Letter, n.d., Department of Agriculture, Correspondence.

[9] Seldes, *The Years of the Locust*, 288; Nordeman, "Midland during Depression," 106-107.

[10] Dallas *Craftsman*, January 24, 1930, January 20, 1933.

[11] Weatherford *Democrat*, February 26, 1932.

[12] *Congressional Record*, 72d Cong., 1st Sess., 1932, LXXV, 3087, 3235-3241.

unemployment was not really severe in Houston since 90 percent of those without jobs were non-resident itinerants and thus should not be counted in determining Houston's unemployment rate.[13] San Antonio also attracted its share of transients. Every train arriving there from New Orleans in 1932 had from fifty to one hundred tramps on board; on big nights the number might rise to 250. Trains arriving from the west through El Paso usually had as many as those from the east.[14]

Obviously, any attempt to enumerate the number of transients is impossible. However, it is possible to draw definite conclusions from this social phenomenon. The number of transients and the hardships of such a life indicate the severity of the depression. The attitude of the migrants was, to some extent, a reflection of the thinking of the nation as a whole. The conditions under which they lived affected their health for years to come and provided ammunition for those who argued that the economic system had failed. Texas reaction to and treatment of the transient population probably revealed basic state and regional characteristics.

Available information about the effects of the depression on the transient and the general public is scarce. Two very good studies made at the time, however, are excellent sources. Thomas Minehan, a professor at the University of Minnesota, made a number of trips throughout the country where he lived among the youthful transients and later recorded their thoughts and actions. Among those he studied were many Texans. The other study was made by Maury Maverick, later a Congressman from San Antonio, among the adult transients within Texas. These two fine studies, and other less important ones, give at least an indication of the daily life of the transient.

---

[13] "Prosperity Now," *Houston*, I (March, 1930), 16; Montgomery, "Depression in Houston," 119-120.

[14] Maverick, *A Maverick American*, 152-153.

Physically, the transients lived in very undesirable conditions. Standards of nutrition, housing, sanitation, and personal hygiene were most difficult to maintain. The birth of a child on the road was not at all uncommon. For example, "'Hobo Bill,' five-day old knight of the box car" was born in Dalhart, Texas, in June 1933, when his mother was found in a freight car and taken to the local hospital. His mother was on her way from Bolinger, Alabama, to visit her sister in Clovis, New Mexico. Apparently after the child's birth his mother resumed her travel in the previous manner since "Hobo Bill" rode on three freight trains during the first five days of his life. Reportedly, the baby suffered no ill effects from the experience;[15] others were probably not so lucky.

Certain traditions and values were challenged by the depression as much among the transients as among the general population. For example, religious faith was challenged particularly among the young.[16] Minehan reported that loyalty to a church was uncommon; the one religious organization that maintained a small degree of loyalty was the Catholic Church, probably because of the intense religious training of children.[17] Maverick reported that among Texas transients, both young and old, adherence to traditional values was stronger. He concluded, however, that the pious and condescending manner in which many religious bodies treated the men caused a resentment against organized religion.[18]

A significant social change, if Maverick is to be believed, was the breaking-down of racial barriers. He declared that among the transients in Texas racial distinc-

[15] Santa Fe *New Mexican*, July 1, 1933.

[16] Maxine Davis, *The Lost Generation* (New York: The Macmillan Company, 1936), 68-69.

[17] Thomas Minehan, *Boy and Girl Tramps of America* (New York: Farrar and Rinehart, Inc., 1934), 165.

[18] Maverick, *A Maverick American*, 152-159.

tions were completely erased. "There was no race feeling, very little suspicion, and considerable amount of good will."[19] He explained that anyone who did not ride freight trains would not, or could not, understand this. Conditions were such that men and women of both races were thrown together and lived together without a feeling of race prejudice. Their mutual problems created a fraternal bond that overshadowed their suspicion of one another. This was, of course, even more amazing in Texas than in other sections of the country. Had the general public been aware of this racial mingling that Maverick reported, the reaction might have been stronger than it already was against the migrants.[20]

Nelson Algren, a writer of distinction who spent some time as a young man in Texas in the early thirties, indicates in one of his novels that race prejudice was not completely erased and that a transient could find himself in more trouble than normal by associating with Negroes. Such an association would be resisted by both townspeople and fellow transients.[21] One example was found in Waco where the Austin Avenue Methodist Church sponsored a soup kitchen where "all white people whether residents or transients" were welcome.[22] Christian charity apparently applied only to whites. Algren also indicated that segregation and discrimination against Mexican-Americans continued to be the rule.[23] Algren

[19]*Ibid.*, 156, 165.

[20]*Ibid.*, 156.

[21]Nelson Algren, *Somebody in Boots* (New York: Farrar, Straus & Giroux, Inc., 1935, reprinted in Berkley Medallion paperback, 1965), 115-129. This book, of course, is fiction and might be considered an unreliable source for this study. However, from Algren's own comments about his style of writing and his comments about his personal experiences in Texas during the depression one can conclude that although the characters in the book are fictional, the conditions are real. See H.E.F. Donohue, *Conversations With Nelson Algren* (New York: Hill and Wang, 1964).

[22]*Waco Farm and Labor Journal*, December 19, 1930.

[23]Algren, *Somebody in Boots*, 40.

was probably more accurate on this matter. Maverick may have been exaggerating the extent of racial harmony in an attempt to prove the solidarity of the dispossessed.

Another significant development was the extensive radicalization of many of the transients. According to Minehan, communism was strong enough among the youthful tramps that every group had at least one Bolshevik, if not more. Of the youngsters who believed that capitalism had failed, some embraced communism while others, unwilling to go that far, became socialists. Most of them, more concerned with restoring economic prosperity by any means, did not have an ideological basis for their ideas. They were particularly critical of an economic system that allowed food to rot in the fields while people went hungry. Perhaps a boy identified only as "Texas" best summed up the feeling when he said, "It's the duty of the President to see that nobody starves."[24]

Despite the cautious attitude expressed by many of them, Minehan stressed that the growth of communism among the young was significant. He said communists were among the few who would speak in defense of the moneyless man and the young tramps. To young people communism offered hope for the future, an improvement in economic conditions, and a chance for education. The only reason why the growth of communism had been slow, he believed, was because so many of the communists were personally offensive. That was changing, however, as more of the spokesmen were American-born persons who better understood how to deal with young people.[25] Minehan indicated that conversion to radical thought was less common among the older men because they had a "mental holdover of war psychology, the anti-Red drives of Palmer, and a belief in the American success story, which will not let

[24] Minehan, *Boy and Girl Tramps*, 162.

[25] Ironically enough he reported a statement common among the young transients of the thirties that would (with a few changes) become common after the development of nuclear power: "I'd rather be Red than starving and dead." *Ibid.*, 164. Perhaps the young were prophetic.

them accept the new doctrines."[26]

The bitterness and disillusionment of the youngsters could also be seen in their loss of patriotism and their belief and desire that a revolution was imminent in this country. Minehan reported that many of them indicated that they would never serve in the armed forces; they would go to jail first. He also said that when an attempted assassination of President-elect Franklin D. Roosevelt in 1932 failed, the boys were very disappointed. When this event proved not to be the beginning of the long-awaited revolution, they began to lose hope. Yet, despite their common beliefs, there was little class solidarity among them.[27] Once again, "Texas" summed up the difficulty in creating a revolution when he said, "the workers could do it, but they won't. They're too damn dumb. You never saw a working stiff who wouldn't cut another working stiff's throat for a nickel."[28]

Maverick's work among the transients did not show significant political radicalism, possibly due to the differences between the group he studied with that of Minehan. He said the adult transients were average people who had been forced into this situation and often did not understand it. Political sophistication was almost non-existent.[29] In late 1932 Maverick attempted to alleviate conditions somewhat by establishing a community near San Antonio to provide relief for transients. Political and economic knowledge was limited among those who lived there. Socialism was only a word that reflected something "bad"; communism was Russian, unpatriotic, and sinful. Collectivism was unknown to most of them.[30] He said they did not really un-

[26] *Ibid.*, 164.

[27] *Ibid.*, 165-171.

[28] *Ibid.*, 171. This whole question is discussed at length in *Ibid.*, 161-171.

[29] Maverick, *A Maverick American*, 155-156.

[30] Maverick's attempts at colonization are described in *ibid.*, 167-

derstand ideological differences because to most of them capitalism was "a state of society in which you can be hungry for awhile, but you will finally get a good job, and possibly have others than can either go hungry or work for you."[31] Maverick said their radicalism was really more a form of pragmatism. They were willing to espouse virtually any cause if it would provide relief; thereafter, they became capitalists. He was so disgusted by the lack of understanding of the situation and the unfeeling attitude that he declared, "what sickens me is that some men who rode the rods and have gotten jobs are now as reactionary as Du Ponts."[32] Obviously, radicalism among transients in Texas was mostly of the pragmatic variety.

Nelson Algren's description of conditions tends to support Maverick. He did indicate that a class consciousness of a sort developed among the men, but that it usually had little or no ideological basis. In some cases the men formed friendships, but, by and large, the transient was a lonely man. There was, however, the comradely feeling among them as being a group set apart from the rest of society; many of them would probably never return to the normal relationships that the average person enjoyed.[33]

Stefan Thernstrom, although discussing the nineteenth century, may have found the reason why radicalization and the development of a permanent proletariat did not occur on a large scale in the thirties when he said that "few Americans have stayed in one place, one workplace, or even one city long enough to discover a sense of common identity and common grievance."[34] This is particularly true of the trans-

176, and in Donald W. Whisenhunt, "Maury Maverick and the Diga Relief Colony, 1932-1933," *Texana*, IX (Summer, 1971), 249-259.

[31] Maverick, *A Maverick American*, 170.

[32] *Ibid.*, 163.

[33] Algren, *Somebody in Boots*, 18-19, 55.

[34] Thernstrom, "Urbanization, Migration, and Social Mobility," 168.

ient population of the thirties.

The depression also had its impact on the moral standards among the drifters. Obviously, people cast adrift would have a tendency to loosen their standards in the face of such a catastrophe. As mentioned before, one of the striking things about the depression was the large number of children without homes. Harvey Ferguson of the United Press called them a "hungry horde" and said they were comparable on to the so-called "wild children" of Russia.[35] Under conditions such as these, children without parental guidance would and did become involved in moral and sexual practices not in keeping with normal standards. Patterns of behavior changed, however, among almost all the transients. Maverick reported that many erstwhile women of high moral standards turned to prostitution to survive. Yet, many others were promiscuous simply because of existing conditions and their own desires. Depravity, homosexuality, and other perversions were common. Certainly this was to be expected with living conditions as they were. According to Maverick, "there was promiscuity, filth, degradation."[36]

The migrants were often accused of responsibility for the growing crime rate. The extent to which they were responsible for local petty crimes is debatable, but certainly when faced by a hostile community the transient was undoubtedly tempted to steal anything necessary for survival. As the national crime rate increased, the larger number of youthful offenders was alarming. The depression, in general, and specifically the lower moral standards, were blamed for this increase. The editor of the Amarillo *Daily News* lamented the fact that no stigma seemed to be attached to lawbreaking any longer since so many young people were happy to boast of their crimes.[37] Probably he was exaggerating the

[35] Seldes, *The Years of the Locust*, 288.

[36] Maverick, *A Maverick American*, 165-166.

[37] Ozment, "Temple and Depression," 33-34; Amarillo *Daily News*, April 23, 1932.

situation, but it is true that local small crimes were on the
increase. Another Texas editor was convinced that migrants
were responsible for much of the increase, but at the same
time he warned his readers not to be too anxious to blame
the transients for all of it. Undoubtedly, much of the property loss attributed to the drifters was actually the work
of local citizens who hoped that the outsiders would be blamed
Since the chance of arrests was slight, this editor advised
his readers that the best protection was to "lock up and watch
out."[38] Maverick, denying the existence of a large criminal
element among the transients, said they were honest men willing to work if they could only get a job.[39]

    Nelson Algren described very well the attitudes of local
communities toward the transients. Local law enforcement officials were often zealous (or over-zealous) in their attempts
to keep transients out of the towns. He characterized the
small-town Texas sheriffs and the railroad policemen as people who wear boots. "There were only two kinds of men where-
ever you went--the men who wore boots, and the men who ran."[40]
The transient grapevine was always active to warn the men
about the dangers of the law. Uvalde, Texas, the home of
Speaker of the House of Representatives and later Vice President John Nance Garner, was especially feared by those on
the road. "The homeless had a special fear of this place.
It was here . . . that the hungriest jailhouse and the cruel-
est bulls in all southern Texas were located. There had
been an epidemic in the place, and its fame had spread among
the transients far and wide as a place sedulously to be avoided."[41]

    The misunderstanding of the migrants, partly the result

[38] Brady *Standard*, August 15, 1930.

[39] Maverick, *A Maverick American*, 155.

[40] Algren, *Somebody in Boots*, 55.

[41] *Ibid.*, 111.

126

of unfair publicity, was a major reason for the unrealistic attitude taken toward them. According to Harry Hopkins, the migrant "appeared at once glamorous and reprehensible." This lack of understanding made it difficult to deal with the basic problem. "So long as he was popularly regarded as a cross between a carefree gypsy and a fugitive from justice, a reasonable approach to his quandry was impossible."[42]

The Texas attitude concerning the migrants was expressed mostly in the press; local citizens did not speak out as often on this matter as they did on other issues of the depression. Letters-to-the-editor occasionally came from a displaced person needing help or from someone who deplored the whole situation;[43] however, the great mass of the public apparently remained silent.

This was not true of the press. In fact, the general public might have been unaware that transiency was so widespread had the press not made such an issue of it. On the other hand, small-town and country editors undoubtedly reflected the sentiment expressed in their conversations with local citizens. Particularly in those cities most affected was the press vocal. Port Isabel, whose local editor obviously considered it the garden spot of America and the promised land to every unemployed person in the country, was constantly on guard against intrusion from unwanted outsiders. He continually declared that the city was unable to care for all the nation's unemployed; in 1932 he applauded the efforts made by local authorities to keep them out altogether.[44] Other papers from around the state were also alarmed about the increasing number of transients and the problems they brought to Texas.[45]

[42] Hopkins, *Spending to Save,* 127-128.

[43] "Letters to the Times," El Paso *Times,* August 31, 1932, May 5, 1931.

[44] Port Isabel *Pilot,* October 22, 1930, December 24, 1930, February 24, 1932.

[45] Galveston *Daily News,* January 10, 1931, Hebbronville *News,* December 3, 1930.

A number of newspapers believed that most tramps and beggars were not really destitute but were only taking advantage of the sympathetic and generous nature of the public.[46] Brownfield merchants who contributed to the Associated Charities were given large cardboard signs to place in their windows showing that they had already donated to discourage "professional bums and beggars."[47] Likewise, towns such as Uvalde and Sinton felt they were being imposed upon by people without a real need. As in the case of Sinton, part of the hostility resulted from the competition provided for local merchants by the transients who sold items from door-to-door.[48]

Bitterness against the transients was certainly strong by the time Senator LaFollette dispatched his questionaire to city mayors. Officials from Huntsville and Smithville were both outspoken against migrants. Sam McKinney of Huntsville, after stating that his city did not have a relief problem, hastily added, "However, we are not advertising this fact, as we do not want those from other sections to come to us to be taken care of."[49] C. F. Bastain, secretary of the Smithville Chamber of Commerce, was even more outspoken when he declared that the nation's distress came "more from . . . the viciousness of the unscrupulous beggar, vag, and bum than from any other source."[50] Attitudes such as this resulted in the West Texas Chamber of Commerce reporting in 1933, with obvious pleasure, that "Deadbeats, loafers, and professional bums are having a difficult time getting any of the R.F.C. funds in West Texas."[51]

[46] Pecos *Enterprise and Gusher*, January 23, 1931; Hebbronville *News*, November 12, 1930.

[47] *Terry County Herald*, December 5, 1930.

[48] Uvalde *Leader-News*, December 12, 1930; *San Patricio County News*, December 11, 1930.

[49] *Congressional Record*, LXXV, 3238.

[50] *Ibid.*, 3240.

[51] "Facts About Distribution of R.F.C. Relief Funds," *West Texas Today*, XIII (February, 1933), 21.

Many suggestions were made to eliminate the transient problem and to deal with it effectively if it could not be eliminated entirely. The Austin *Statesman* wanted some national action to keep the unemployed from taking to the highways since the communities where they went were no more able to care for them than were their own home towns.[52] Since this was difficult to do, the state Bureau of Labor Statistics recommended that each city take care of its own citizens first, discourage outsiders from moving in, and encourage its own people to stay at home.[53] This sentiment was reflected by various other groups in the state as well.[54] In fact, the "stay-at-home" sentiment probably had the most statewide support.[55] Suggestions for solving the problem included the drafting of transients[56] and the intervention of the federal government to remove the relief burden from local communities.[57] The Austin *Statesman*, shortly before the Civilian Conservation Corps was established, suggested that young men be employed in national forests.[58]

A prevalent view throughout the state was that migrants actually did not want to work and would not do so even if jobs were offered to them; thus, they should either be made to work for relief or forced to move on.[59] The Hebbronville

[52] Austin *Statesman*, August 16, 1931.

[53] Bureau of Labor Statistics, *Committee for Unemployment Relief*, 6.

[54] *Devil's River News*, October 31, 1930; "Penalty Lifted from Texas Road Contractors," *Lone Star Constructor*, IX (May, 1932), 3.

[55] Letter, October 1, 1931, Sterling Papers, Box 180; Beeville *Bee-Picayune*, September 17, 1931; Austin *Statesman*, July 1, 1932; Painters, Decorators, and Paperhangers of America of Tyler, Texas, local 855, minutes, March 10, 1931; Fort Worth Carpenters Union, local 208, minutes, April 1, 1931, February 2, 1932, TLA,UTA.

[56] FDRL, January 6, 1933, Box 733.

[57] Weatherford *Democrat*, February 26, 1932.

[58] Austin *Statesman*, February 20, 1933.

[59] Uvalde *Leader-News*, November 25, 1932; *Waco Farm and Labor Jour-*

editor, an outstanding spokesman of this viewpoint, believed there were too many deadbeats and dishonest persons among the transients. He declared, "The time has probably arrived when a judicious use of the old fashioned chain gang on that class who refuses to work and roam from place to place fattening off the sympathising [*sic*] public may be required."[60] Despite his tortured prose he probably represented the thinking of many people.

Despite the general public hostility, there were occasional expression of support for the homeless men. One individual told Governor Roosevelt that the depression and the transients had developed all "because a few money grabbers didn't want to live and let live."[61] The Electra *News*, arguing that keeping people at home was right "and backed by Holy Writ," questioned what was to be done with and for those who truly had no homes.[62] Another editor asked if it was not a responsibility of local communities to extend all available aid to these people. The editor told his readers, "Caring for this class of people is just as much a moral obligation as though there were a severe law providing it."[63] The editor of the Austin *Statesman*, a humanitarian with a conscience, described the migrants as "simply pioneers in a land that needs pioneers no longer."[64]

Although the attitude of Texans varied, sincere attempts were made, despite major problems, to provide some relief. The New York *Times* was probably correct, however, when it

nal, September 5, 1930; telephone message from city manager of Fort Worth to White House, October 17, 1932, Cotton, Box 106, HHPL, PP; Dianne Treadaway Ozment, "Galveston during the Hoover Era, 1929-1933" (M.A. thesis, The University of Texas at Austin, 1968), 165; Montgomery, "Depression in Houston," 135.

60
Hebbronville *News*, November 12, 1930.

61
FDRL, August 2, 1931, Box 721.

62
Electra *News*, December 4, 1930.

63
Pecos *Enterprise and Gusher*, September 18, 1931.

64
Austin *Statesman*, October 17, 1931.

said that "Texas relief agencies have more Western breeziness than Southern hospitality."[65] Maury Maverick's experiences as an amateur bum are the best descriptions we have of the conditions under which the migrant lived and how he was treated in Texas.[66]

Treatment of the transients left much to be desired. Many religious organizations, particularly the Salvation Army, attempted to aid the unfortunate. Despite the high motives of most groups, Maverick rendered a severe indictment of their actions partly because of the poor quality of employees. He constantly referred to the "four-flushing racketeers who called themselves preachers, men who were a disgrace to any religion" who constantly insulted the men by their pious and condescending manners.[67] Most of the missions formed by religious groups insisted that transients hear a sermon and show signs of conversion before meals would be served. At the "Star of Hope" mission in Houston, Maverick listened to "the most ignorant, brutal, cowardly, cur that ever delivered a 'sermon' to me in my whole life." He emphasized to the unfortunate men that the cause of their misfortune was their own personal sin. "He assured us that if we were not sinners, we would not be in such shape. Return to Jesus, he said, and everything would work out."[68] Maverick may have been overly critical, but the treatment he experienced (and he quickly explained that his experiences were only a sample of the life of the men who lived this way for months and even years) was a major cause of the demoralization of the transient. As already indicated, the major concern of most cities was to provide one or two meals and perhaps a night's lodging for the transients with the under-

[65]New York *Times*, December 25, 1932.

[66]Maverick discusses his experiences at length in Maverick, *A Maverick American*, 150-166.

[67]*Ibid.*, 153.

[68]*Ibid.*, 157.

standing that they would leave town as soon as possible.[69]
In some instances abandoned buildings were provided for the
homeless, but the more common sleeping places for people of
all ages and sexes were "jails, hot railraod urinals, cellars,
dugouts, tumble-down shacks."[70] Maverick was convinced that
the problems created were more than just local in nature;
the depression was a national crisis. Even when people were
fed the food was often inedible. In his own experience with
mission food, Maverick was only able to keep it down until
he got outside the building into an alley where, as he said,
"In this secluded spot I fed the fish."[71]

Algren's description of transient conditions in Texas
tend once again to support Maverick's experiences. Algren
spent some time in a Texas jail and riding the rails throughout the state. His descriptions of conditions in Texas con-
cur with most other reports.[72] For example, although the food
was almost inedible the number of homeless men seeking the
food was always large. Many Texas cities made a practice of
spraying oil or other noxious liquids on all garbage cans
and other refuse to keep the hungry from eating. To the
homeless men this seemed to be an even greater insult than
the general unwelcome attitude of the state.[73]

One of the effects of the depression that concerned Maverick most was the health of the people who lived under such
poor conditions for long periods of time. He said the impact of the depression on the health of the nation was similar to the aftermath of a war and would be felt for gene-

[69]Weatherford *Democrat*, February 26, 1932; Uvalde *Leader-News*, No-
vember 25, 1932; Hebbronville *News*, November 12, 1930; Steen, *Twentieth
Century Texas*, 22-23; Nordeman, "Midland during Depression," 106-107;
Ozment, "Galveston during Hoover Era," 165.

[70]Maverick, *A Maverick American*, 166.

[71]*Ibid.*, 154.

[72]Donohue, *Conversations With Nelson Algren*, 32-61 *passim*.

[73]Algren, *Somebody in Boots*, 104-105.

rations. He concluded, "The depression has marred the race."[74]
His predictions were borne out when such a large percentage of
young men were found physically unfit for military service in
World War II, apparently due to the dietary deficiencies and
health problems resulting from the privations of the depression years.[75]

Undoubtedly, one of the nation's most serious problems
during the depression was the transient population. Since
the depression was so severe, many people probably did not
pay much attention to the transient. It might be said that
the migrant was an invisible part of society; his presence
was known but ignored as much as possible. As a part of the
inarticulate mass, he was unable dramatically to make his
plight known and to demand aid. Thernstrom's description of
the poor of the nineteenth century is applicable to the transients of the thirties. They "were tossed helplessly from city
to city, from state to state, alienated but invisible and
impotent."[76]

[74] Maverick, *A Maverick American*, 160-161.

[75] Richard N. Current, T. Harry Williams, Frank Freidel, *American History: A Survey* (New York: Alfred A. Knopf, 1967), 783.

[76] Thernstrom, "Urbanization, Migration, and Social Mobility," 173.

CHAPTER VII

DEBATE OVER RELIEF

As the depression intensified human suffering could be relieved only when those in power became convinced that a serious problem truly existed. President Hoover, his advisors and others close to him had begun, shortly after the stock market crash, a campaign to build public confidence. One element of this campaign was to deny that any serious weakness existed within the economy or that anyone was suffering unusually from the upheaval. Hoover and his supporters maintained throughout that relief was a private matter and should not be shifted to public agencies. They stated over and over that there was no depression, that the crisis was temporary, and that very few people were in actual need.

In Texas many public officials and a wide sprectrum of the press were in complete agreement with Hoover. Letters from newspaper readers also indicated that at least a segment of the public believed that he was correct. However, for the media and others to have continued to ignore the increased number of relief applicants, the pressures on charitable organizations and the general suffering would have been foolish.[1] Nonetheless, there were those who continued to refuse to see the problem for many years.[2]

Once the problem was recognized the Texans' first reaction was to provide relief by reliance on friends, neighbors, relatives, private charity groups, and local or state governments. The myth of self-help and rugged individualism was so prominent in Texas that dependence upon the federal government, an unthinkable alternative to many Texans, was a

[1]Canadian *Record*, July 24, 1930; *Terry County Herald*, May 22, 1931; El Paso *Times*, March 21, 1931; *Weekly Dispatch*, October 24, 1931; Dallas *Craftsman*, March 21, 1932.

[2]"Theoretically Independent," *Acco Press*, VIII (July, 1930), 8; "Public Opinion," Amarillo *Daily News*, March 30, 1932.

fate worse than starving to death. However, a relatively large segment of Texans steeped in the agrarian myth and with neopopulist ideas quickly demanded that the national government assume its proper role by providing for the physical needs of its citizens. To these people, particularly in rural and agricultural Texas, it was easy to forsake old myths when actually confronted with hunger and lowered living standards. Even so, the laissez faire philosophy so prominent in the twenties died a rather slow and painful death.

Before any coordinated effort could be made by any level of government, an understanding of the root cause of relief needs--unemployment--was necessary. At first only a problem in the industrial centers of the nation, unemployment became serious even in the rural villages of Texas as economic indicators continued to worsen month after month with little sign of improvement.[3]

Unemployment statistics during the first years of the depression are unreliable since no state agency was equipped or capable of compiling such figures. The Dallas *Morning News*, deploring the lack of information and public concern, was correct when it warned that very little could be done to alleviate conditions until the authorities understood the true situation.[4] The Bureau of Business Research at the University of Texas, in a rather primitive statistical way, revealed that the total number of unemployed was on a constant increase during the early stages of the depression. Governor Sterling estimated in February 1932 that at least 300,000 persons were unemployed in Texas.[5] Various labor groups reported increasing

[3] Seguin *Enterprise*, June 27, 1930; Connally Papers, March 4, 1931, Box 25; "The President's Address," *Texas Law Review*, LI (October, 1932), 12; "Unemployment Returns by States: April, 1930," unemployment, Box 273, HHPL, PP.

[4] Dallas *Morning News*, October 26, 1930.

[5] Houston Labor Council, minutes, February 18, 1930, May 6, 1930, March 15, 1932, May 17, 1932; Austin Typographical Union Collection, minutes, October 4, 1931, TLA,UTA; *Austin Labor Journal*, April 1, 1932.

unemployment among their members, as well as pressure from some employers for workers to return to ten and twelve hour work days.[6]

Unemployment had become so serious by the spring of 1930 that mass meetings of protest were held by displaced workers throughout the state in such divergent places as Shamrock, Houston, and Dallas. The very limited press coverage perhaps revealed that newspaper editors were reluctant to report the discontent that contradicted their optimism.[7]

As the rate of unemployment and demands for relief became more acute, Senator LaFollette of Wisconsin on February 2, 1932, placed into the *Congressional Record* replies he had received from telegrams sent to mayors of cities across the country. Twenty-eight Texas communities, including such small towns as Goose Creek, as well as major cities like Austin, Dallas, and Houston, responded to this questionnaire.

Replies from Texas officials did not give a comprehensive or meaningful picture of the situation. For example, the mayor of Electra reported that the number of unemployed had increased 200 percent since 1929, but most of the cities had an increase of only 10 to 15 percent on relief. Only a few city officials, including those of Galveston and Lockhart, stated that the number of people unemployed or on relief had actually decreased. Houston officials replied that in November 1929 only 670 families had been aided, and one year later the number had risen to only 789. However, by November 1931, 2,231 familes were partially or wholly cared for by the city. Likewise, almost all the municipal officials predicted that the number applying for relief in the winter of 1932 would

[6] El Paso *Times*, April 18, 1930; Lionel V. Patenaude, "The New Deal and Texas" (Ph.D. dissertation, The University of Texas at Austin, 1952), 341; Sterling to Hiram Bingham, February 29, 1932, Sterling Papers, Box 180.

[7] Bonham *Daily Favorite*, April 19, 1930; Galveston *Daily News*, March 7, 1930; "The Dallas Mob," *The Common Herd*, XVI (June, 1931), 3-4; Montgomery, "Depression in Houston," 28-31.

increase above previous years.[8]

The problems of unemployment and resulting needs for relief were not limited to the poor or the unskilled in the early stage of the depression; highly skilled and professional people also found themselves facing destitution. A San Antonio resident told Congressman Rayburn that most architects and structural engineers were without clients because increasing unemployment and depression had decreased the demand for their services. A pharmacist, complaining about how unemployment had wrecked his business, asked Rayburn to use his influence to find him a job.[9]

Although almost everyone in Texas was affected by unemployment, minority groups, especially blacks, were the most hard-hit. Blacks, most of whom were unskilled and poorly educated, constituted the largest single group of the unemployed. Since they performed manual labor or worked as domestic servants, they were the first to be discharged in a depression. Mayor W. E. Monteith said that Negroes and Mexicans constituted the major portion of the relief problem in Houston. There is also evidence that minority groups, including Negroes and Mexicans, suffered discrimination in the distribution of relief funds.[10]

In San Antonio there were many more blacks and Mexican-Americans applying for relief work. The conditions of Mexican Americans was so bad that the Mexican Blue Cross of San Antonio reported in April 1932 that it had served 33,763 meals. With the exception of San Antonio, most Texas cities reported that salaries of black teachers were significantly less than for whites in comparable positions. After 1933 studies show that blacks often fared better than other

[8]*Congressional Record*, 72d Cong., 1st Sess., 1932, LXXV, Part 3, 3235-3241.

[9]Letters, September 19, 1932, July 9, 1932, Rayburn Papers.

[10]McKay and Faulk, *Texas After Spindletop*, 118; Dallas *Morning News*, June 20, 1931; "Pens of the People," Galveston *Daily News*, April 7, 1930; *Congressional Record*, 72d Cong., 1932, LXXV, Part 3, 3238.

groups.[11]

Unemployment was intensified by the hiring of women and children at lower rates than would have been paid to men for the same jobs. The conditions under which these people worked were so bad, according to the Fredericksburg *Standard* that "instances have been found . . . where unscrupulous employers have taken advantage of the glutted labor market to exploit defenseless . . . women and children." In fact, "cases have been found where young girls and women have received pay checks for as low as 49 cents for two weeks work in a department store in one of the larger cities of Texas." The *Standard* was so concerned that, if the charges were true, it was willing to support a minimum wage law for women.[12]

One of the most obvious indicators of increasing unemployment was the appearance of large numbers of transients on the national scene. As the number of transients arriving in Texas increased, the Texan's lack of understanding of the entire problem of unemployment and relief was obvious.[13] (See Chapter VI for a discussion of the transient problem.)

Congressman Thomas Blanton of Abilene echoed the sentiments of many and that of the State when he declared, "Some of them [the unemployed] are too lazy, and they would not work long if there were plenty of jobs available."[14] Dr. Edwin A. Elliott, head of the Department of Economics at Texas Christian University, deplored the attitude of Blanton and others when he said, "Too many of our people feel the jobless

[11] Ozment, "Temple and Depression," 28; Montgomery, "Depression in Houston," 103-109; McMillan, "San Antonio during Depression," 65-69; William J. Brophy, "Black Texans and the New Deal," in Donald W. Whisenhunt, ed., *The Depression in the Southwest* (Port Washington, New York: Kennikat Press, 1980), 117-133.

[12] Fredericksburg *Standard,* June 24, 1932.

[13] *Terry County Herald,* December 5, 1930; Dallas *Morning News,* December 11, 1931.

[14] *Congressional Record,* 71st Cong., 2d Sess., 1930, LXXII, Part 11, 12247.

man could get work if he really wanted to." He attributed this outlook to "the philosophy of abundance which character- izes many of our self-made American businessmen." He in- sisted that when seven million or more were without work as they were at this time (July, 1931), it was not the indivi- dual worker's fault.[15] Elliott's sympathetic attitude was echoed when the Electra *News* told its readers that they had a responsibility to the unfortunate, especially after a fam- ily in Electra had been "obliged to butcher the family dog and were found devouring the beast."[16] Unfortunately, most people were not well enough informed to have a clear picture of the situation.

Most Texans believed that unemployment could be ended only by finding the cause and proposing a solution. Among those who thought they knew the solution was a woman from Denison who suggested to Governor Roosevelt that he should, on assuming the presidency, "Dismiss people who have had work regularly for, say, ten years or more and give the un- employed a chance to get a few days work."[17] Other citizens with more insight believed it to be the responsibility of both the state and national governments to perform their pub- lic duty by finding the cause of unemployment and depression. Some believed the solution was the establishment of a na- tional pension program.[18] Others who did not believe in go- vernment intervention or who thought that it would not help, placed the responsibility for unemployment and its solution directly on the shoulders of industry.[19] Unfortunately, most

[15] Edwin A. Elliott, "Economic Depression and Unemployment," *The Texas Outlook*, XV (July, 1931), 11.

[16] Electra *News*, February 5, 1931.

[17] FDRL, January 12, 1933, Box 718.

[18] Sterling City *News-Record*, January 2, 1931; letter, n.d. Rayburn Papers.

[19] *Weekly Dispatch*, May 14, 1932; "When Will Business Come Back?" *Hardware and Implement Journal*, XXXVI (July, 1931), 40.

of the proposed solutions were simplistic and unrealistic.

Even after the existence of a problem was admitted, it took some time before a serious and well-directed effort was made to provide the necessary relief. All through the Hoover administration and to a lesser extent, through the New Deal period, those in need suffered while others debated how and by whom the destitute should be aided.

To an apparently small group, the responsibility for aid rested only with the individual himself. Organized charity of any kind would be insignificant anyway, but, moreover, it would be harmful to the individual's character. One Texas farmer, who told Governor Sterling he was the largest planter in Texas, said that the individual farmer had overplanted and no one else was to blame. In fact, the "farmer knew when he planted cotton exactly what he was doing, and there's only one way to break him from sucking eggs--just let him go hungry."[20] Therefore, if any improvement in the situation was to be made, it would have to be done by the individual who brought trouble on himself by his unwise actions.

Even many of those who admitted that help was needed-- that in such a situation an individual could not help himself--were willing only to resort to private charitable groups In this attitude, Texans were merely following the lead of Hoover and Roosevelt. Most of the municipal officials responding to Senator LaFollette's questionnaire replied that almost all relief activity was conducted by private agencies; rare city aid usually took the form of public works. Private agencies most often responsible included the Red Cross, the Salvation Army, and the Community Chest. Within a relatively short time, however, the funds of private groups and the limited resources of the local communities were exhausted.[21] The effectiveness of local efforts was also hin-

[20]"Public Opinion," Amarillo *Daily News*, October 21, 1931; Sterling Papers, September 2, 1931, Box 176.

[21]*Congressional Record*, 72d Cong., 1st Sess., 1932, LXXV, Part 3, 3235-3241; Lawrence L. Graves, "Education, Welfare, and Recreation," *A*

dered by other considerations. For example, the Citizen's
Emergency Relief Committee of Dallas had refused a private
donation of $350 because it had been raised by the presenta-
tion of a dramatic performance on a Sunday night. Likewise,
Scurry County decided to cancel a $600,000 road bond election
because its promoters suddenly realized that a successful
election would probably raise their own taxes.[22] Probably
the poor questioned the sincerity of such people.

Attitudes and actions of this type meant that it would
be only a matter of time before much of the public would demand that the state or federal governments take over the
handling of relief. A Jewish newspaper in Houston became so
disgusted with the bumbling local efforts that it advocated
state operation of relief agencies.

> It is a reflection upon civilization to permit welfare
> institutions to be supported by private purses. It is
> the duty of the State to impose a tax so that the care
> of the orphan, of the aged, of infirm, the sick, the
> unemployed, the poverty-stricken shall be the responsi-
> bility of the State. . . . No self-respecting nation
> should permit such an intolerable condition to exist.
> And the same thing applies to other charities. One
> might just as well ask that public schools be supported
> from private pocketbooks![23]

Governor Sterling, reluctant to provide direct individual
relief, believed that state government had a larger responsibility than it had yet assumed. Despite the support of such
prominent men as former Governor Hobby, his proposed road-
bond issue to provide relief received very little support.
Sterling also appointed a committee for the relief of unemployment and later called a special session of the legislature
to deal with the problem. The inexperience of local and state
officials who were overburdened by the demands made on their
resources precluded any truly effective state action.[24]

History of Lubbock, 547-549; letter, n.d., Department of Agriculture,
Correspondence; Richardson, *Texas the Lone Star State*, 326.

[22]
New York *Times*, January 3, 1932, III, 6; *Terry County Herald*,
October 31, 1930.

[23]
Texas Jewish Herald, January 9, 1930.

[24]
Lenora Nickels, "Public Services of Dan Moody" (M.A. thesis,

As the depression intensified more and more people concluded that action by the federal government was the only realistic answer, but this shift in public opinion did not occur overnight. Many people agreed with Hoover when he said that federal relief would "impair something valuable in the life of the American people" and that "the basis of successful relief in national distress is to mobilize and organize the infinite number of agencies of self help in the community."[25] However, by the time of the election of 1932, after Hoover's feeble attempts at relief had failed, many Texans were ready to agree with Roosevelt's idea "that we are facing an emergency today more grave than war." Roosevelt abandoned his earlier dependence on local relief when he realized that depression-inspired fear caused people "with more or less unity . . . to turn to our common Government at Washington."[26]

Although Roosevelt's change was partly a practical politician's response to the public will, it also reflected a realization of the inadequacy of local relief. Much anti-Hoover and anti-Republican sentiment developed throughout the nation for the simple reason that Hoover was not able to adjust and adapt his own concept of government to changing public sentiment. His insistence that aid to individuals might demoralize them, but that it would not harm big business, long the recipient of government aid, did not raise his prestige with the average citizen. The favorable position of business was reflected by Secretary Mellon's conviction that tax refunds for corporations would contribute to

Texas Technological College, Lubbock, Texas, 1948), 98; Clark and Hart, *The Tactful Texan*, 171; Richardson, *Texas the Lone Star State*, 326; Austin *Statesman*, August 16, 1932.

[25] President's Research Committee on Social Trends, *Recent Social Trends in the United States* (New York: McGraw-Hill Book Company, Inc., 1933), 1270-1271; hereafter cited as President's Committee, *Recent Social Trends*; Dwight Lowell Dumond, *Roosevelt to Roosevelt* (New York: Henry Holt and Company, 1937), 421; Rexford G. Tugwell, *The Battle for Democracy* (New York: Columbia University Press, 1935), 79-80; as quoted in Schriftgiesser, *This Was Normalcy*, 277; Hoover, *The Great Depression*, 56.

[26] Rosenman, *Public Papers of FDR*, I, 631.

the public welfare and by Hoover's appointment of a big businessman committee for unemployment relief. Although both
actions received favorable comment in the larger Texas dailies,[27] there was a conspicious lack of comment from most
Texas citizens.

One example will show Hoover's lack of understanding of
the situation and his inability to deal with economic and
political realities. In 1931, in the face of a severe drought
that was turning the plains states into a dust bowl, Hoover
finally recommended the extension of aid to distressed farmers in the form of business loans. When the provisions proved unclear, the Director of Extension Services of Texas A &
M College wanted to know if loans would be made for food.
The Secretary of Agriculture, replying to his inquiry, stated
that loans would be made for seed, fertilizer, feed for work
animals, and fuel and oil for tractors. His statement that
no loans would be made for food since he "did not interpret
food as an item incident to crop production," caused one dis-
traught Texan to complain bitterly, "Feed for cattle in the
Northwest, but not a single pound of wheat for the starving
South seems to be the motto of President Hoover." [28]

Some federal functions such as the activities of the
Children's Bureau of the Department of Labor,[29] had been un-
disputed for some time; the new debate involved the total
concept of the federal government. The serious nature of
the crisis caused many Texans to express a belief, perhaps

[27] Schlesinger, *The Crisis of the Old Order*, 252-253; Hofstadter,
American Political Tradition, 308; Rexford G. Tugwell, *The Democratic
Roosevelt* (Garden City, New York: Doubleday & Company, Inc., 1957), 198-
199; Dallas *Morning News*, December 20, 1930; Austin *Statesman*, December
29, 1930.

[28] Rauch, *The History of the New Deal*, 17; letters, December 23,
1930, December 29, 1930, Dept. of Agriculture, Correspondence; Miller,
Presidential Survey, 201.

[29] U.S. Department of Labor, Children's Bureau, *Nineteenth Annual
Report of the Chief of the Children's Bureau* (Washington: Government
Printing Office, 1931), 6-42.

latent during prosperity, that the government had the responsibility for extending aid when all else failed.[30] Senator Connally was informed that the government had a moral
obligation to help its citizens because:

> In the beginning God created earth, man and everything
> hereon. Man holds the high position as God's super-
> visor here on earth and man has organized governments
> for the protection of the human being. . . . We also
> believe that government should sponsor and protect
> everything that is good for its own people and abo-
> lish everything that is bad according to known facts
> as we know them.[31]

This may have been an extreme view, but variations of it
were expressed by people of all sorts. The President of Texas Presbyterian College believed that since Hoover and the
national administration had taken credit for national prosperity, they had a moral responsibility for alleviating depressed conditions. Fundamentalist minister J. Frank Norris,
among other religious leaders, did not take a stand on the
validity of federal aid; instead, he and some others saw
government intervention in economic affairs as a fulfillment
of the Biblical prophecy of the end of the world.[32]

Members of the Texas congressional delegation also had
a concept of federal responsibility. John Garner said that
he would use federal funds before he would see Americans
starve. His sponsorship of a two billion dollar Public Works
Bill gave him a radical tinge, made him more well-known, and
undoubtedly boosted his chances for the presidential nomination in 1932. In truth, he was not the liberal that many believed; he was, instead, willing to use federal funds in a
serious emergency. On the Senate side of the capitol, Morris
Sheppard, without stating his own opinion, told a Texas audience that increasing demands would probably force Congress

---

[30] Galveston *Daily News*, January 2, 1932; FDRL, January 17, 1933, Box 735.

[31] Connally Papers, December 14, 1929, Box 9.

[32] *Ibid.*, September 16, 1931, Box 15; J. Frank Norris, *The Gospel of Dynamite* (no city, no publisher, n.d.), 21.

to pass a relief measure. Connally, on the other hand, openly worked with liberal Democrats and insurgent Republicans
to pass a public works bill only to have it vetoed by the
President.[33]

Texas groups of all types concurred, to a degree, in the
belief in federal responsibility. Organized labor demanded
that Washington perform its proper function and duty by taking action to eliminate unemployment. Farmers of Haskell
County quickly demanded federal help. One major business,
Anderson-Clayton Corporation of Houston, not sure of the
federal role, wanted equal treatment for all by the government.[34] This meant that it wanted its share if the federal
government began handing out money. Among the more official
groups, the County Judges and Commissioners' Association desired increased federal spending, but the Texas Municipal
League was more insistent when it proclaimed the imminence
of bankruptcy for many Texas cities without federal action.[35]

A philosophical justification for aid from Washington
was unnecessary to many Texans. Bankers, strong defenders
of laissez faire in the twenties, deluged the office of Senator Connally with petitions and delegations demanding help.
They were so desperate that they swallowed their pride by
appealing to the hated Fergusons for help.[36] After Mrs.
Miriam Ferguson's second inauguration as governor in 1933,
her daughter said that it would have been easier to mention
the few bankers who did not come to Austin than to list those

---

[33] Timmons, *Garner of Texas*, 128; Patenaude, "The New Deal and Texas,"
41; clipping from Naples *Monitor*, December 4, 1931, in Morris Sheppard
Scrapbook, Morris Sheppard Papers; Rauch, *The History of the New Deal*,
17; Connally, *My Name is Tom Connally*, 136.

[34] *Weekly Dispatch*, March 29, 1930; Sherrill, *Haskell County History*,
132; "An Open Letter to Our Friends," *Acco Press*, X (July, 1932), 5.

[35] *Congressional Record*, 72d Cong., 1st Sess., 1931, LXXV, Part 1,
180; "Is Federal Government Encroaching Upon Rights of Cities?" *Texas
Municipalities*, XIX (December, 1932), 262.

[36] DeMoss, "Dallas during Depression," 75.

who did.[37] In essence, the favorable or unfavorable attitude toward federal aid depended upon who received help. Only six of the twenty-eight mayors and city managers responding to Senator LaFollette's questionnaire favored a federal appropriation to the cities to help them over the difficulty.[38] A cynic might conclude that they would only desire the aid when it would help them personally. Perhaps a resident of McAllen best expressed public opinion when he declared, "Write and phone if you hear of any relief coming down my way. I am willing to be either a Democrat or a Republican for a few weeks if that will help any."[39]

Despite the increasingly favorable attitude toward it, there were still many who opposed federal aid. To a great number the solution of economic ills was really the responsibility of industry. Others, although they never cited specific instances, thought that the crisis had been caused and prolonged by the government going too deeply into business in competition with private enterprise.[40] This group was convinced that "the people are sick and disgusted with the Government being in business" because it was an invasion of the "rights of the private citizen" and because it was "Socialistic and of [a] vicious nature." Congressman Sterling P. Strong uttered the phrase that most appealed to them: "More business in government and less government in business."[41]

Others believed that government aid, as in the case of

[37] Connally, *My Name is Tom Connally*, 149; Ouida Nalle, *The Fergusons of Texas* (San Antonio: The Naylor Company, 1946), 224.

[38] *Congressional Record*, 72d Cong., 1st Sess., 1932, LXXV, Part 3, 3235-3241.

[39] As quoted in McAllen *Monitor*, December 11, 1931.

[40] FDRL, August 24, 1932, Box 723; Dallas *Morning News*, June 14, 1932; Fredericksburg *Standard*, October 23, 1931; Haskell *Free Press*, March 24, 1932.

[41] FDRL, September 5, 1932, Box 723; "Government Then and Now," *West Texas Today*, XIII (June, 1932), 8; FDRL, December 19, 1932, Box 731; "Letters From Readers," Dallas *Morning News*, April 27, 1932.

agriculture, simply would not do any good; that we should
rely on God more than Washington; that government aid had the
effect of destroying the individual's future potential. [42]   An
Abilenian declared that the demands for government aid reminded him of the "head of a family [who] wanted a cow that would
give enough milk to furnish plenty for his family of sixteen,
raise a large calf, and live by sucking herself." [43]   Other
opponents of government aid believed it was predicated on a
basis not in keeping with American governmental philosophy.
It would destroy the federal system by consolidation of local
and state rights in the hands of the national government and
would probably lead Americans into "the same condition as the
Russians with all individual initiative and opportunity
gone." [44]

One of the best examples of public ambivalence in Texas
was the reaction to the Reconstruction Finance Corporation
(RFC). Called into being by Hoover in the fall of 1931 to
provide loans for the assistance of banking, insurance,
transportation, and agriculture, it appeared to many people
as only an example of Hoover's class favoritism.[45]   A number
of Texans agreed that if Hoover were truly interested in
ending the depression he would make loans available to individuals to buy food as well as to produce jobs and crops.[46]
To them, relief should go to the place where the depression
began--the individual producers. Relief would have to come

[42]"Trade Associations," *Lone Star Constructor*, VIII (July, 1931),
7; Uvalde *Leader-News*, February 17, 1933; "Letters From Readers," Dallas
Morning News, August 18, 1931.

[43]*Ibid.*, January 14, 1930.

[44]*Ibid.*, January 27, 1932; "Let's Pass a Law," *Dallas*, X (October,
1931), 14.

[45]Peel and Donnelly, *The 1932 Campaign*, 14; Bernard Sternsher, *Rexford Tugwell and the New Deal* (New Brunswick, New Jersey: Rutgers University Press, 1964), 36.

[46]Austin *Sunday American-Statesman*, October 16, 1932; Amarillo
Daily News, June 3, 1932.

to these people first if permanent recovery was to be expected.[47] Tom Connally said that the chief trouble with Hoover's
theory was that he did not understand "that millions of workers and farmers were in dire need of immediate help if they
were not to starve and lose their farms."[48]

Despite the opposition and the troubles it had in getting
started (as described by its administrator, Jesse Jones of
Houston), the RFC managed, by April 1933 to loan approximately
seven million dollars to various Texas agencies.[49] Most Texans, very happy about the establishment of the RFC, believed
that it was exactly what was needed to start industrial
wheels to turning again. If there were a danger to American
initiative, it was slight because the RFC was more of a stimulus to industrial development than to its retardation.[50] As
a Dallas citizen expressed it, the government

> has at last hit upon a plan that is beginning to put
> motivative power behind the industrial, agricultural
> and financial institutions of our people. The govern-
> ment move has . . . been the one tangible step that
> has halted the downward trend of morale of our people
> in whatever endeavor they might have been engaged.[51]

The Austin *Statesman* was one of the few papers to question if the actions of the RFC were not encroaching upon the
rights of the states and the localities. To most Texans, however, the depression had become so serious that they were willing to modify or silence their objections if some type of aid
would be forthcoming. The *Statesman* was just about as incon-

[47] FDRL, April 16, 1932, Box 718.

[48] Connally, *My Name is Tom Connally*, 135.

[49] Jesse H. Jones with Edward Angly, *Fifty Billion Dollars* (New
York: The Macmillan Company, 1951), 16; Richardson, *Texas the Lone Star
State*, 326-327; Wilson Elbert Dolman, "Odessa, Texas During the Depression, 1932-1936" (M.A. thesis, The University of Texas at Austin, 1968),
24.

[50] FDRL, December 22, 1932, Box 735; Baker Mercantile Company, July
30, 1932, Wholesale Letters, 1931-33; "Letters From Readers," Dallas
Morning News, June 8, 1932; El Paso *Times*, November 23, 1932.

[51] "Letters From Readers," Dallas *Morning News*, May 9, 1932.

sistent as the rest of the state because about a year earlier it had been so proud of the RFC that it thought future historians would take its establishment as a turning point in American history.[52]

While the debate continued throughout the depression years about whether relief should be provided and who should be responsible for it, the minor efforts that were made proved weak and unenlightened. Direct personal aid was opposed almost universally, at least at first.

Because of England's discouraging experience, many Americans opposed the use of the word "dole" or the providing of that type aid. Prominent leaders, including Governor Roosevelt who would later have to resort to it, thought that direct aid of any type would destroy a man's character if employed for very long.[53] In keeping with the national attitude, many county newspapers in Texas printed "canned" or syndicated editorials proclaiming that direct aid would only bring about the pauperization of the nation without solving the basic problem.[54] Many individuals, denying any desire for direct relief payments, declared that they only wanted an opportunity to work their way out of the crisis.[55] The belief that it was a disgrace to accept charity from whatever source is readily apparent. Public officials, including Governor Sterling and members of the congressional delegation, also believed the best solution was to provide work rather than to give direct aid.[56] The El Paso-*Times* very clearly expoun-

[52] Austin *Statesman*, January 16, 1933, February 1, 1932.

[53] Hannah, "Urban Reaction," 105-107; Wecter, *The Great Depression*, 19; Rosenman, *Public Papers of FDR*, I, 456.

[54] Sterling City *News-Record*, October 2, 1931; Canadian *Record*, October 1, 1931; Beeville *Bee-Picayune*, February 20, 1931; Cameron *Enterprise*, August 13, 1931.

[55] Connally Papers, February 5, 1931, Box 13; FDRL, January 26, 1933, Box 733; letter, June 1, 1930, Secretary's Corres., Commerce Dept.

[56] Bureau of Labor Statistic, *Committee for Unemployment Relief*, 4; *Congressional Record*, 72d Cong., 1st Sess., 1932, LXXV, Part 11, 12223.

ded most of the opposition to the dole. Such a practice, it said, had no place in the American economic system; in fact, Rome had been destroyed, and maybe England would be also, because it had supported a large group of idle people. The use of direct relief was an admission of a nation's failure. "The dole, though well intended, works out to be a governmental concession to laziness and an acknowledgement by the government that it is unable to cope with adverse economic conditions." [57] Individuals agreed.

> Doles, scattered unwisely, do more harm than good; it should be remembered help given without discrimination hurts and is injurious to the one who receives it and the one who gives.
> The charity that gives aid to the idle class, the sort that would rather be idle than at work, is a mistaken charity and one the consequences of which will be for evil, rather than for good. [58]

To the unemployed workers, the philsophical discussion must have seemed rather academic. They undoubtedly agreed with the editor of the Austin *Statesman* who stated, "That little word 'dole' is no doubt a fairly horrifying word. It is not, however, quite so horrifying as that other word, 'starvation'." [59] In the face of such an emergency, the nation should not argue about who is responsible for relief. The question to be answered is how to aid the distressed; the effects on morale and moral fibre should be discussed under normal conditions. "Why use the word 'dole' as if it were poison? Why federal relief a 'dole' and local relief not a 'dole'?" [60]

When relief activities finally began, the methods used by Texans were unoriginal and uninspiring. In order to avoid a "dole," made-work of some sort was suggested by many people, including the block-aid plan started originally in Buffalo, New York, where residents took the responsibility of provid-

[57] El Paso *Times*, November 2, 1930.

[58] "Letters From Readers," Dallas *Morning News*, September 3, 1931.

[59] Austin *Statesman*, January 5, 1932.

[60] *Southern Messenger*, July 14, 1932.

ing aid and employment for the unemployed on their own block. Some believed the answer was to encourage people to hire someone for any sort of job, even if for only a few hours.[61] Solutions such as "character loans" for professional people or the exemption of widows from taxation were also suggested.[62] All of these reveal the Texan's lack of understanding of the seriousness of the crisis. The proposed solutions were only primitive stop-gap measures that might or might not provide relief temporarily. Only rarely did Texans, or Americans as a whole, delve deeper into the situation and understand the broader implications of the crisis.

One proposal that received widespread support and had some merit was the use of surplus wheat to feed the destitute. It was only a small step from this to the idea of using whatever surplus commodities available for helping the unfortunate.[63] Another of the more serious discussions involved the growing sentiment in Texas, and in the nation, for a system of unemployment insurance and a type of social security for old age.[64]

The actual management of relief was disgraceful. Most localities were so determined to avoid public relief that they relied heavily on such agencies as the Red Cross and Salvation Army, but the load proved very heavy. For example, in the spring of 1931 in Dickens County, with a total population of only 8,601, the Red Cross aided over 3,000 people. When the demands became so great with approaching winter in

[61] Austin *Statesman*, February 15, 1933; Amarillo *Daily News*, February 16, 1932; Dallas *Morning News*, April 19, 1931; "Letters to the Times," El Paso *Times*, December 26, 1931.

[62] FDRL, October 29, 1932, Box 728, October 14, 1932, Box 725.

[63] "Public Opinion," Amarillo *Daily News*, July 31, 1931; "Letters From Readers," Dallas *Morning News*, December 17, 1930; Haskell *Free Press*, January 21, 1932; Huntsville *Item*, November 13, 1930.

[64] John T. Flynn, *Country Squire in the White House* (New York: Doubleday, Doran and Company, Inc., 1940), 40; Hannah, "Urban Reaction," 72-74; *Congressional Record*, 71st Cong., 2d Sess., 1929, LXXII, Part 1, 433.

1931, the Red Cross announced that it could no longer feed
the destitute.[65] When the federal government began to provide
surplus flour to the needy, the Red Cross was used in many
areas as the distribution agency.[66] As the private agencies
began to collapse, some cities tried other means to provide
relief without using public money. Stop-gap measures included public drives to obtain clothing and to preserve food for
use in winter months.[67] The community of Big Spring staged
a rodeo to aid the unemployed and Lubbock leaders conducted
a huge rabbit hunt to provide for the needy.[68]

Inherent in most public activities was a determination
to aid the needy at the lowest possible cost. Unfortunately,
reasonable concern for frugality sometimes led to some rather
ridiculous actions and some that were very humiliating to
those forced to rely on charity. For example, the Plainview
American Legion Post proudly announced it had been able to
feed fifty people for only 28 cents. The meal, however, was
nothing to boast about since it "consisted of hot porridge
made from cracked wheat seasoned with butter and sugar."[69]
A citizen from Galvestion complained that to get relief or
work on public projects one had to undergo a barrage of very
personal and humiliating questions from public authorities.
To make matters even worse, they were paid with a bag of commodities that "contain the line of such wholesome and bulky
dainties as broken rice, the cheapest coffee, a dab of sugar,
a little flour, sour [sic] belly and red beans and such."[70]

[65] The Texas Almanac--1931, 136; Texas Spur, February 27, 1931,
August 21, 1931.

[66] Canadian Record, May 5, 1932.

[67] Haskell Free Press, January 29, 1931; Austin Statesman, July 8,
1932.

[68] Sterling City News-Record, September 25, 1931; Pecos Enterprise
and Gusher, January 23, 1931.

[69] Austin Statesman, September 17, 1932.

[70] "Pens of the People," Galveston Daily News, December 13, 1931.

In the fall of 1931 the Salvation Army in Galveston devised
a plan where three men could be fed at the cost of feeding
one the year before.[71] Before a child would be fed in the
public schools of El Paso a complete check was made on the
financial status of his family. The officials in charge
were so proud that nothing was being wasted that, undoubtedly,
many suffered needlessly.[72]

Maury Maverick in his tour across the state was appalled
to discover that most of the state did absolutely nothing of
a public nature. Even where aid was available the unfortunate had to endure a very insulting and condescending manner
and often a sermon from officials in charge to get a meal
that was barely edible.[73] In addition, discrimination in the
distribution of aid did exist, since Houston announced that
Negroes and Mexicans could not apply for relief and they
would have to shift for themselves;[74] just how widely this
sort of thing was practiced cannot be determined with accuracy. One example, as mentioned earlier, was a church in Waco
that opened a soup kitchen for whites only.[75] Among Texas cities
that responded to Senator LaFollette's unemployment questionnaire, most reported that they provided from two to four dollars per week in cash or commodities for a family of two ad-
ults and two children. That amounted to only about two to
four cents per person per meal.[76] Obviously, Texans were
either rather callous about the degree of destitution or they
were financially incapable of taking care of the poor. In
either case, it became apparent as the depression worsened

[71] Ozment, "Galveston during Hoover Era," 165.

[72] "Letters to the Times," El Paso *Times*, May 12, 1932.

[73] Maverick, *A Maverick American*, 153-154.

[74] Mitchell, *Depression Decade*, 103-104.

[75] *Waco Farm and Labor Journal*, December 19, 1930.

[76] *Congressional Record*, 72d Cong., 1st Sess., 1932, LXXV, Part 3,
3235-3241.

that a more massive and comprehensive program had to be devised quickly to save many of the poor from starving to death.

The tragedy of the depression in Texas, as in most of the nation, was the inaction of the states and localities in providing relief. By the time Texas overcame its aversion to organized relief, the situation was so serious that the state, already in difficulty, could do little about it. Thus, the only agency with the resources to handle the problem was the federal government. Texans learned to accept federal intervention although many continued to grumble about how it would destroy initiative, states rights, and the American way of life. The seriousness of the situation, however, caused them to abandon their philosophy for the time being when the New Deal of Franklin Roosevelt began to take more direct action.

CHAPTER VIII

"THE SALT OF THE EARTH"

American agriculture had suffered economically since
the end of World War I, and in the depression it was the
first segment of the economy to be affected. Its two-decade-
long depression lasted until World War II when war demands
absorbed the surpluses that the American farmer was able to
produce. These surpluses had driven farm prices downward
and despite the McNary-Haugen movement of the twenties, very
little improvement was made. By the time of the inauguration
of President Hoover in 1929, farmers were in an almost desperate condition.[1]

Rural America suffered from the depression, and the
South was as desperate as any section. Its continued reliance upon a one-crop economy meant that any fluctuation in
cotton prices seriously affected living standards. The depression was intensified by 1930 and 1931 when record crops
increased the surplus and caused the collapse of cotton prices.[2] Also contributing to Southern susceptibility to market
fluctuations was the large number of tenants and sharecrop-
pers who lived a tenuous existence and were the first to be
affected by price changes. A difference of one or two cents
per pound in the price of cotton might determine if the tenant family would go hungry. Southern tenant farms had increased significantly since 1880 when they constituted 36.2
percent of the total. By 1920 49.6 percent were tenant-
operated, and by 1930 the percentage had increased to 55.5.[3]

---

[1]Rauch, *The History of the New Deal*, 8-9; Tugwell, *The Battle for
Democracy*, 227; Gilbert C. Fite, *George N. Peek and the Fight for Farm
Parity* (Norman: University of Oklahoma Press, 1954), 220; hereafter
cited as Fite, *George N. Peek*; Filley, *The Wealth of the Nation*, 111-114.

[2]Cash, *The Mind of the South*, 369; Cohn, *King Cotton*, 241.

[3]*Ibid.*, 247.

Although exact figures are not available for Texas, it is
certain that, in the Southern tradition, tenancy was widespread. An example of the condition of farmers in general
and tenants in particular was provided by a resident of Corsicana. He reported that, on one farm, two tenant families
with a total of twelve adult workers received only $945 for
1931, an annual income of $79.75 per person.[4]

Further evidence of the extent of the farm depression
was shown by reports from various parts of the state. Drought
conditions in 1931 resulted in the starvation of much live-
stock, particularly horses and mules in North Texas. Causes
included the absence of pasture grass and the inability of
owners to buy feed. By 1932 prices had fallen so low that
farmers resorted to the burning of corn and other produce
for fuel. "In our youth, we were taught that to burn anything
of food value was sin and waste, but circumstances alter all
cases. . . . There is no waste in burning something that has
a heating capacity and is hardly worth hauling to town."[5]

As the farmer's plight worsened, the state as a whole
reacted in a typically rural fashion--in the tradition of
the agrarian myth. To the Texan who believed the agrarian
way of life was best, the farmer was truly the "salt of the
earth." Although this exact expression was rarely used,
newspapers often referred to the farmer as "the keystone of
the arch upon which our republic is founded," and Governor
Moody's Drought Committee informed the Agriculture Department that farmers "are the bone and sinew of the country."[6]
Individuals agreed that "the producer is the foundation of
the world" and that the farmer was "the backbone of our coun-

[4]"Letters From Readers," Dallas *Morning News*, October 5, 1931.

[5]El Paso *Times*, January 31, 1931; *Terry County Herald*, December 23, 1932.

[6]Fredericksburg *Standard*, November 18, 1932; Committee on Drought
Relief to Arthur M. Hyde, August 29, 1930, Department of Agriculture,
Correspondence; Moody to Hoover, September 1, 1930, Drought, HHPL, PP.

try."[7] The business press was convinced that the only thing
needed to restore prosperity was to restore the purchasing
power of the farmer. Since he was the most important single
factor in the economy, his well-being would assure the prosperity of society at large. Governor Roosevelt endeared himself to Texans, and probably increased his chances of carry-
ing Texas in the presidential election, when he declared that
one of the essential parts of his program would be "to restore purchasing power to the farming half of the country.
Without this the wheels of railroads and of factories will
not turn."[8]

Numerous causes of the farmer's distress were discovered. High taxes and the control of farming by capitalists
instead of by farmers were blamed for the trouble.[9] A Texas
magazine was convinced, however, that the real cause of the
agricultural depression in Texas was the farmer himself.
Despite the increasing utilization of substitute fibers and
increasing world production of cotton, Texas farmers refused to face reality and continued to increase cotton acreage
until the already glutted market was even more overburdened.
Instead of diversifying, the Texas farmer insisted on remaining with the traditional staple, cotton. He should have
concentrated more on the production of food to sell to the
available market in the growing urban centers of the state.
As far as this editor was concerned, "Many of the ills of
Texas Agriculture appear to be self-inflicted."[10]

Texas farmers were among the first to overcome whatever
reservations they may have had about the intervention of the

[7] "Public Opinion," Amarillo *Daily News,* November 7, 1931; letter,
January 5, 1933, Rayburn Papers.

[8] "Theoretically Independent," *Acco Press,* VIII (July, 1930), 8;
"Ford Leads the Way to Chaos," *Hardware and Implement Journal,* XXXVII
(February, 1932), 32; Rosenman, *Public Papers of FDR,* I, 626.

[9] Amarillo *Daily News,* January 2, 1933; *Congressional Record,* 71st
Cong., 1st Sess., 1929, LXXI, Part 1, 478.

[10] "Ills of Texas Agriculture," *Texas Opinion,* I (March 19, 1932), 9.

federal government in economic matters. Governor Moody and
the state Committee on Drought Relief both appealed to the
federal government for aid by describing the desperate condition of farmers in Texas.[11] Although they began quickly to
demand government aid, some Texans were pessimistic about the
extent to which Washington would help the farmers and the
benefits to be derived from it. Bitterness was clear in
comments about how the government rushed quickly to aid foreign governments and wealthy Americans while neglecting poor
farmers.[12] As one farmer told Governor Roosevelt, the farmer
did not want preferential treatment, but only to be given a
status of equality with the other segments of the economy,
particularly big business.[13]

Hoover, when he assumed the presidency, partially understood the extent of the farm problem. Having been disturbed
by the rising farm discontent during the campaign of 1928 he
promised a responsible farm program to stabilize prices and
to balance agriculture with industry. Soon after he took office, Congress, in special session, passed the Agricultural
Marketing Act. It created a Federal Farm Board with a fund
of $500 million to be loaned to cooperatives for the purpose
of stabilizing prices by holding products if necessary until
market prices rose. Corporations were also formed by the
Farm Board to stabilize prices through direct intervention in
the market. This was the most ambitious program ever undertaken by the federal government. Hoover had been forced to
modify or at least ignore his philosophy temporarily to justi-
fy the program. In many respects this agency was the direct
antecedent of the much more ambitious and extensive agricultural program instituted by Roosevelt's New Deal in 1933.

[11]Dan Moody to Herbert Hoover, August 19, 1930, Committee on Drought
Relief to Arthur M. Hyde, August 29, 1930, Dept. of Agriculture, Corres.

[12]*Terry County Herald*, October 10, 1930; "Letters From Readers,"
Dallas *Morning News*, November 5, 1929, January 17, 1930; Miller, *Presidential Survey*, 128.

[13]FDRL, September 27, 1932, Box 723.

The Farm Board was able to maintain domestic prices slightly above world levels until the European financial crisis of 1931. With the shrinking of American overseas markets and the dumping of competitive products in this country by Russia, Argentina, and Australia, American prices were driven to new lows. By the end of 1931 the major farm organizations realized that the Farm Board was incapable of coping with the crisis. But, when the Grange, the Farm Bureau, and the Farmer's Union met in Washington in 1932 they were unable to agree on an alternate program satisfactory to each group.

Three major factors caused the failure of Hoover's program. The financial crisis in Europe and its effects in this country limited United States foreign markets; the Farm Board did not have enough funds for the massive intervention necessary; the program was unrealistic in that it attempted to control prices without any power to control production. The last was perhaps most important since production control was absolutely necessary to any program of this type.[14]

Public opinion in Texas was almost unanimously opposed to the Farm Board. The most serious criticism was the discriminatory policy of making loans only through farm organizations.[15] The Texas Cotton Association declared, however, that the Board discriminated against cotton farmers in particular.[16] Senator Connally was informed that, since only ten percent of them belonged to the Farm Bureau, most Texas farmers would not qualify for federal loans. Connally later expanded this idea when he told a Dallas audience that the

[14]Arthur S. Link, *American Epoch* (2d ed. rev.; New York: Alfred A. Knopf, 1963), 375-377; Theodore Saloutos and John D. Hicks, *Agricultural Discontent in the Middle West, 1900-1939* (Madison: University of Wisconsin Press, 1951), 407, 433; hereafter cited as Saloutos and Hicks, *Agricultural Discontent;* Warren, *Hoover and the Depression,* 46, 184; Robinson, *Fantastic Interim,* 176.

[15]"Letters From Readers," Dallas *Morning News,* December 17, 1930; "Letters to the Times," El Paso *Times,* May 21, 1932.

[16]*Waco Farm and Labor Journal,* March 28, 1930.

whole concept of agricultural relief and recovery had been
destroyed by the reliance upon farm organizations instead of
dealing directly with the farmer.[17]   A special interest publication believed that the restriction of funds was a deliberate deception of the farmers. The editor also stated
that the Farm Board was entirely too expensive; in fact, it
would have been more efficient and economical if it had been
a part of the Department of Agriculture rather than a sepa-
rate agency.[18] Others opposed it because they did not want
any type of legislation or because it simply would not work.[19]
An opponent of the Farm Board advised Tom Connally and Congress to "Get on them and get on them hard." Another man
asked him, "Could you find out from the Dept. of Agri. why
cream, hogs & cattle & cotton has gone down so this fall &
why the F. Board does not function for the farmer; as intended or is such Depts. just outright Bunk & ingorance." He
apparently took this advice since Connally wrote Hoover in
1930 urging Farm Board action to raise cotton prices.[20] After the failure of the program became apparent, the Anderson-
Clayton Company believed that, if nothing else, farmers had
learned a very valuable lesson. In the future they would
not be so eager to get involved in such a program.[21]

     To the few defenders of the Board, the major benefit
was that it encouraged cooperation and organization, characteristics that farmers had long needed. If nothing more
than a spirit of cooperation were to result, the money would
be well-spent.[22] Others believed that the Farm Board could

[17]Connally Papers, November 12, 1929, Box 7; Dallas *Morning News*,
January 2, 1930.

[18]"Fooling the Farmers," *The Common Herd*, XV (March, 1930), 11-12.

[19]Bonham *Daily Favorite*, August 25, 1931; FDRL, December 20, 1932,
Box 731.

[20]Connally Papers, October 1, 1929, Box 7, November 10, 1929, Box 6;
Connally to Hoover, August 21, 1930, Cotton, Box 106, HHPL, PP.

[21]"Farm Board Finale," *Acco Press*, XI (March, 1933), 7.

[22]George West *Enterprise*, January 24, 1930; Beeville *Bee-Picayune*,

work if it were left alone and if its members were really sincere about the stated desire to help farmers.[23]

As the general depression intensified the farm problem several schemes, some good and some rather strange, were proposed as either partial or complete solutions. A popular idea was to devise new uses for cotton; a campaign to encourage people to use cotton rather than some substitute fiber was begun throughout the state. Martin Dies urged Congress to aid research to discover more uses for cotton; the chamber of commerce of West, Texas, petitioned Congress to require ginners and feed millers to use cotton bagging and sacks rather than jute, an imported fiber from India.[24] Numerous individuals, including public figures, encouraged the use of cotton as a substitute for wood pulp in the manufacture of paper. Quite a few people began to use stationary made from cotton paper and encouraged national leaders to use and promote it.[25] The Mortar Board, an honor society for women at the University of Texas, encouraged coeds to wear cotton clothing "to show their devotion to [one of] the leading products of the State." Likewise, the sheep men inaugurated an "Eat More Lamb" campaign.[26]

Another proposal was the "Buy a Bale" movement started by Governor Moody. Since overproduction was the major problem, the governor urged citizens to buy a bale of cotton to diminish the surplus. Although he was somewhat vague about what the average family would do with it, one man suggested that, with so great a surplus, people would be entire-

December 5, 1929.

[23] Connally Papers, October 14, 1931, Box 21; "Public Opinion," Amarillo *Daily News*, May 3, 1932.

[24] *Congressional Record*, 72d Cong., 1st Sess., 1932, LXXV, Part 4, 3998; Connally Papers, February 5, 1931, Box 25.

[25] Sheppard to Hoover, September 16, 1931, Talbot to Richey, September 16, 1931, Cotton, Box 106, HHPL, PP.

[26] New York *Times*, February 22, 1931, III, 5; "The Sheep Situation in Texas," *Sheep and Goat Raisers' Magazine*, XI (April, 1931), 241.

ly justified if they bought the cotton and burned it. Quite a number of citizens agreed with the governor that it would be, at least, a temporary solution.[27] One Texan, at least, was so convinced of the value of the plan that he telegraphed Hoover asking him to buy a bale to help the cause. The telegram was referred to Alexander Legge, chairman of the Farm Board, who reported that the Board was "not keen about Governor Moody's 'buy-a-bale' movement." He believed it would not do any good and might cause harm.[28]

Many farmers and newspapers continued to demand throughout the depression that the farmer's only salvation was organization. This involved the traditional groups such as the Grange, the Farm Bureau, and the Farmers' Union, but there were some who hinted at political activity as a last resort.[29] Others believed that Texas farmers had relied entirely too long on a single-crop economy. Therefore, the only solution was to diversify production. The farmer should abandon cotton and raise crops for which there was a demand; he should also raise large vegetable gardens to provide for his own table and to decrease his outside expenses. One man even suggested that if the legislature would legalize horse-racing in Texas, the farmer's problem would be solved because he could then raise and sell race horses, an enterprise that would be much more profitable than cotton production.[30]

A more popular remedy suggested by the cotton farmer was the fixing of agricultural prices by law either at the state or national level.[31] The laws should guarantee the

[27] "Letters From Readers," Dallas *Morning News*, September 6, 1930, September 9, 1930, October 6, 1931; Amarillo *Daily News*, September 15, 1931.

[28] Metcalfe to Hoover, August 31, 1930, Legge to Richey, September 18, 1930, Cotton, Box 106, HHPL, PP.

[29] "Letters From Readers," Dallas *Morning News*, September 25, 1930; Roby *Star-Record*, January 8, 1931.

[30] *San Patricio County News*, July 3, 1930; "Letters From Readers," Dallas *Morning News*, August 5, 1931, July 2, 1931, September 12, 1931.

[31] *Texas Spur*, December 13, 1929; FDRL, April 28, 1932, Box 721; Con-

farmer a certain price or a percentage of the selling price of the finished cotton product. Despite the popularity of the measure, some people had reservations that it was only a temporary solution. The basic problem of overproduction would remain despite the arbitrary fixing of prices.[32]

Since the basic problem was recognized by most people as being overproduction, the most serious measure considered was reduction of cotton acreage, voluntarily at first, to decrease production. The campaign for voluntary reduction, begun by the Farm Board, was taken up and echoed by people throughout the state. State leaders such as Dan Moody, the business and commercial press, and farm journals believed it to be sound advice.[33] Although the idea was generally popular, some individuals did not believe that the farmer should voluntarily reduce his production, and thus his income, while business continued to increase production. This was just another example of the Republican attitude of favoring the wealthy and the industrialists at the expense of the farmer.[34] Others who believed the idea to be sound questioned whether voluntary production controls could ever be successful. Legislation by either the state or federal government seemed to be the only solution.[35] By 1931, as will be shown later, most Texas farmers were willing to support legislative action designed to limit production. Most of those who had reservations about government interference in the economy remained

nally Papers, October 1, 1929, Box 7.

[32]"Domestic Allotment Plan," *The Cattleman*, XIX (January, 1933), 7; "Letters From Readers," Dallas *Morning News*, November 20, 1930, September 3, 1931, September 6, 1930.

[33]Fite, *George N. Peek*, 227; Electra *News*, November 6, 1930; "Acreage Reduction and Improvement of Staple," *Acco Press*, VIII (February, 1930), 8; Brady *Standard*, March 14, 1930; Beeville *Bee-Picayune*, January 27, 1931; *The Valley Farmer*, January 20, 1930.

[34]"Letters From Readers," Dallas *Morning News*, April 12, 1930, April 20, 1931.

[35]Brady *Standard*, March 25, 1930; Huntsville *Item*, April 10, 1930; "Letters From Readers," Dallas *Morning News*, September 5, 1931.

silent or tempered their objections.

The most extreme form of farmer protest in the thirties was the Farm Holiday Association centered chiefly in the Middle West. Led by Milo Reno, the militant president of the Iowa Farmers' Union, the Holiday Association was designed to force an increase in agricultural prices by withholding farm products from the market. The idea had been considered for some time although actual organization did not begin until 1932.[36] The movement was long considered to be purely a midwestern manifestation of discontent, but later scholarship revealed that Holiday Associations were formed in the southwestern and mountain states, including Texas, New Mexico, and Montana. The Texas association, formed at a Waco convention in April 1933, was led by Judge L. Gough of Amarillo who was the chairman of the board of directors. George Armstrong, president of the Texas Steel Company of Fort Worth was also president of the association. Despite its early promise the Texas association, along with most state units, ceased to exist by 1934.[37] In retrospect the high hopes of its leaders and goals of the Holiday movement made little economic sense. Whatever price increases might be obtained by withholding products, would be destroyed when the stored goods were released upon the market. Moreover, most farmers were not willing to obligate themselves by joining the Association. Many farmers, especially tenants, whose subsistence farming required immediate income could not afford to participate. The major accomplishment of the movement was the publicity it gave to the farm situation.[38]

Although non-farmers were critical of it, the Holiday movement received a generally favorable reaction from the farm states. Agricultural journals and newspapers admired

[36]Saloutos and Hicks, *Agricultural Discontent*, 435-443.

[37]John L. Shover, *Cornbelt Rebellion* (Urbana: The University of Illinois Press, 1965), 93, 172.

[38]Schlesinger, *The Crisis of the Old Order*, 268.

its goal, but some questioned if picketing and the possibility of violence were the proper methods to be used. Some of them thought a better policy was cooperative withholding rather than loosely organized individual action.[39] Criticism of the movement came from many sources. Liberal journals such as the *Nation* believed it was made up of "rebels without ideas." Conservative critics declared that the movement merely revealed the naivete of the farmer. To them farmers did not understand that other factors, including the tariff and the money question, were just as important in determining farm prices as was the scarcity of products. The movement also lost support from those who might have favored it because it raised the spectre of political and social disorder and its apparent cruel disregard of people in need.[40]

Texas reaction to the Holiday Association was very favorable. The small-town newspapers agreed that although farmers were difficult to organize, the goal was admirable.[41] The Fredericksburg *Standard*, believing that since the farmers could not expect any political help for their just cause, "there then remains nothing left for the farming element of our population to do but take the bit in their teeth and act collectively for their own preservation."[42] Most of the daily press were also favorable to the goals but were doubtful about its chances of success.[43] The most outspoken critic was the Dallas *Morning News*. Its editor declared that such a move-

[39] William R. Johnson, "Farm Policy in Transition: 1932, Year of Crisis" (Ph.D. dissertation, University of Oklahoma, 1963), 125-126; hereafter cited as Johnson, "Farm Policy in Transition.

[40] Saloutos and Hicks, *Agricultural Discontent*, 444; Hill, *The American Scene*, 147-148.

[41] Haskell *Free Press*, August 25, 1932; Weatherford *Democrat*, September 9, 1932.

[42] Fredericksburg *Standard*, September 30, 1932.

[43] Amarillo *Sunday Globe-News*, August 7, 1932; Austin *Statesman*, August 16, 1932; Galveston *Daily News*, February 7, 1933.

ment was just as lawless as the veterans' bonus march had been and its results would be the same. Such an action only brought discredit upon the participants by making it appear that they were forcing the unemployed to bow to the farmer's will. This charge, however, was answered by the editor of the Uvalde paper when he said, "It might cause suffering among many people if food supplies were cut off but the farmer has been victimized so long that he cannot be blamed for using any stringent means to get his rights."[44]

Even before the national Holiday Association was organized, manifestations of the idea were apparent in Texas. In February 1932 violence erupted in Houston when dairies reduced the price paid to milk producers from 20 cents to 16.6 cents per gallon. In protest, the producers, led by the South Texas Producers Association, poured 1500 gallons of milk into the sewers. The Association then decided to ship all milk to its own plant where it would be bottled and sold directly to the consumer at five cents per quart, one-half the regular price. Shortly thereafter milk producers who were not members of the Association were stopped on country roads and their milk was poured into ditches. Likewise, the Association tried, usually unsuccessfully, to stop the importation of milk from other areas. The local dairies had resorted to this method of providing for the urban market of Houston.[45] The milk war which soon ended did not receive much publicity since few people or newspapers commented on it. One paper that did, the Galveston *Daily News*, sympathized with the grievances of the milk producers, but opposed their methods. To the editor, the destruction of food in the midst of hunger was morally wrong. He believed the reaction of the citizenry at large to be moral indignation at such waste.[46] The *Daily News* continued to fear

[44] Dallas *Morning News*, August 20, 1932; Uvalde *Leader-News*, September 2, 1932.

[45] Galveston *Daily News*, February 15, 1932, February 17, 1932.

[46] *Ibid.*, February 17, 1932.

that the war might spread to Galveston and to other areas of South and East Texas.[47] It did, in fact, come to Galveston for about two weeks in late July 1932 before the Galveston City Commission passed an ordinance to control the situation.[48]

In August of that year the milk producers of the El Paso vicinity considered picketing the highways into the city until the processing plants paid them a fair price for their product.[49] Although it is difficult to prove, there were probably other actions of this type throughout the state. The lack of proof may be due to reluctance of newspapers to report such events; more likely, however, inability of farmers to organize effectively probably resulted in fewer incidents of this type than one would expect. The fact that many people burned wheat, cotton, and corn, or allowed fruit to rot on the trees may have been due to the futility of marketing farm products or it may have been an attempt to force an increase in prices.

Texas farmers became more desperate as the years wore on. The most ambitious action attempted, despite its ultimate failure, was the plan to prevent the planting of cotton in 1932.

[47] *Ibid.*, April 15, 1932.

[48] Ozment, "Galveston during Hoover Era," 77-78.

[49] El Paso *Times*, August 31, 1932.

CHAPTER IX

NO COTTON IN '32

One of the most radical and far-reaching schemes for
solving the farm problem during the depression in the South
was the so-called "Long Plan." Announced in 1931 by Huey
Long, governor of Louisiana, the plan proposed that all the
cotton states of the South prohibit the planting of cotton
in 1932. Since Texas compliance was crucial to the success
of the plan, the attention of the South was focused on Texas
during the summer and fall of 1931. In addition, Huey Long's
attempts to influence the governor and legislature of Texas
became quite controversial and may well have had an impact
on the ultimate decision of the Texas legislature to reject
the Long Plan. Additionally, public sentiment in Texas obviously played a decisive role in the legislature's action.

The idea of production controls did not originate with
Long. In fact, acreage reduction ideas had originated in
antebellum days. As the agricultural condition deteriorated
after the First World War, the idea of limiting production
through acreage controls became more attractive and acceptable. The last McNary-Haugen bill, while not controlling
production, did propose advisory councils for the aid of farmers wishing to reduce production.[1] Some Texans had also
accepted the idea of acreage control during the twenties.
The Waco Cotton Exchange was the most vocal advocate, but by
1929 and 1930 various individuals had decided, despite rather general newspaper opposition, that it was their only
salvation.[2]

[1]Ryllis Alexander Goslin and Omar Pancoast Goslin, *Rich Man, Poor Man* (New York: Harper & Brothers, 1935), 76; Theodore Saloutos, *Farmer Movements in the South, 1865-1933* (Berkeley: University of California Press, 1960), 284-285; Fite, *George N. Peek*, 222.

[2]Saloutos, *Farmer Movements*, 278-279; "Letters From Readers," Dallas *Morning News*, November 22, 1929, October 20, 1930; Galveston *Daily News*, October 5, 1930.

The issue came to a head in 1931 with the proposed Long plan. Long, the bombastic governor of Louisiana, embraced a very daring and simple approach formulated by a group of North Louisiana planters. The idea was deceptively simple: all the cotton growing states would enact legislation prohibiting the planting of cotton in 1932.

To those supporting the plan, this was the answer to the farmers' problems. They believed that if one year could pass without producing "a single bale," all surplus cotton would be consumed and the market price would rise to a decent level. In future years, acreage control might be necessary to prevent accumulation of new surpluses, but returning prosperity would probably make such controls unnecessary. Long believed that his plan was a better solution than the withholding of cotton from the market or by artificially supporting price levels because the prohibition of cotton planting for one year would create a true scarcity rather than an artificial one.[3] Obviously, Long had not analyzed the plan very thoroughly. He could not guarantee that a one-year moratorium would eliminate the current surplus. He further indicated that he had not considered how farmers would live and what impact such action would have on cotton-related businesses.[4]

The problems notwithstanding, Long moved immediately to implement his plan. Since there seemed to be little consideration of seeking federal legislation, Long moved to get agreement from cotton-producing states. Texas was the key state in any such scheme since it produced over one-fourth of the nation's cotton. Thus, if Texas did not go along the plan might as well be abandoned.

Long called a conference of state governors to meet in New Orleans to discuss ways to implement the plan. The governors responded very cautiously to Long's invitation. Only

[3] T. Harry Williams, *Huey Long* (New York: Alfred A. Knopf, 1970), 531.

[4] McKay, *Texas Politics*, 222; Saloutos, *Farmer Movements*, 279-280; McKay and Faulk, *Texas After Spindletop*, 127-128.

two governors--from Arkansas and South Carolina--attended
while the others either declined or sent spokesmen. Therefore the meeting, held on August 21, was much less impres-
sive than Long had hoped it would be. Nonetheless, it was
an official conference and those in attendance agreed to re-
commend the Long plan to their respective legislatures. One
proviso was attached to the recommendation: states producing
at least three-fourths of the nation's cotton had to pass
such legislation before the plan would become operative.
This action was aimed directly at Texas because of its major
share of total production.[5]

The focus of attention was now on Texas, and especially
its governor, Ross Sterling. If such legislation were to be
enacted in time to affect the 1932 crop, Sterling would have
to call the Texas legislature into special session. When
asked his reaction to the action of the governors' conference, Sterling replied that Texas would not be the first to
pass restrictive legislation. He responded, "It's Governor
Long's baby; let him wash it first."[6]

Taking up the challenge, Long moved promptly. In a special session, the Long-dominated Louisiana legislature passed
the measure by August 27. Long immediately sent his assistant, O. K. Allen, to Texas by airplane to present a copy of
the Louisiana bill to Sterling in person. After missing
Sterling in Austin, Allen caught up with him at the Houston
airport where he is reported to have told the Texas governor,
"Here is Governor Long's baby, all washed, powdered, and
wrapped in a cotton dress."[7] Now the burden was on Sterling's
shoulders.

From the time Long announced his plan, Texas cotton farmers and other interested citizens debated its merits. Despite the difficulty of assessing public opinion, it seems safe

[5] Williams, *Huey Long*, 531.

[6] As quoted in *ibid.*, 532.

[7] *Ibid.*, 532-533.

to say that the Long plan was the most debated subject in Texas during the late summer and early fall of 1931.

The public responded overwhelmingly on the issue. A sampling of Sterling's correspondence shows that his staff was virtually overwhelmed with letters and telegrams on the issue. Objections included the charges that it was of no value, that it was unconstitutional, and that it was an unwarranted restriction on the rights of the farmer. In contrast, supporters of the special session and production controls believed that the Long plan or a variation of it was the only thing that could save farmers.[8]

The Long plan received most attention among Texans, and many of them were strongly for it. There were others, however, who did not favor total cessation of cotton raising, but who applauded Long for bringing the matter to public attention. Most Texans with personal reservations preferred some sort of acreage reduction; the sentiment ranged from thirty to seventy percent reduction. Some who took this milder position argued that the farmer must not be denied any income for 1932. Common decency, they reasoned, must not make the farmers bear the entire burden. Others stressed that a moratorium would have a disastrous impact on cotton-related businesses and industries such as gins, mills, and local merchants. They believed, therefore, that a milder action would obtain the desired results with as little suffering as possible.[9]

In addition to the correspondence directed toward Sterling, the issue was so controversial that the "Letters to the Editor" columns of the major dailies were filled with letters on the issue. Most of the farmers approved the Long plan or some other acreage reduction plan; most non-farmers were a bit more skeptical.[10] A farmer from Gilmer in his let-

[8] For examples of this sentiment see Sterling Papers, Box 176.

[9] Letters, August 4, 1931, August 28, 1931, September 1, 1931, September 2, 1931, Sterling Papers, Box 176.

[10] For examples see the following papers for August and September 1931:

ter to Sterling was probably correct in his assessment of the public attitude toward the Long plan. "Have discussed the so-called Long Plan of no cotton for 1932 with hundreds of people, and so far, not one has expressed himself as unfavorable to the proposition, tho--a few really prefer a reduction in acreage, rather than complete cessation, but all uniformly desire immediate action. . . ."[11]

Sterling was not the only governor to be bombarded about the Texas action. Long, widely admired in Texas, received much correspondence on the matter from Texans. Most of the letters and telegrams were similar to those received by Sterling. Many of Long's Texas correspondents were extremely complimentary to him and wholly endorsed his plan. Many justifications were given for such drastic action, including the elimination of cotton pests such as the boll weevil and the conservation of the soil.[12]

It must have been gratifying to Long to hear from prominent Texans adding their support. Included in this group were such men as the farmer from Highlands, Texas, who had 2400 acres in cotton but who wholeheartedly endorsed Long's plan,[13] and the farmer from Overton whose 800 acres of cotton would produce 800 bales at disaster prices.[14] W. L. Ellwood, a prominent Lubbock resident and owner of the Spade Ranch, told Long that he favored the plan because he knew farmers well, had sold them land, and knew that they favored it.[15] W. H. Moody, Jr. of Galveston, who called himself the largest cotton dealer in the state and probably the South, endorsed

Dallas *Morning News*, Galveston *Daily News*, El Paso *Times*.

[11]Letter, August 25, 1931, Sterling Papers, Box 176.

[12]Letters, August 15, 1931, August 17, 1931, Huey Long Papers, Department of Archives and Manuscripts, Louisiana State University, Baton Rouge, Louisiana.

[13]*Ibid.*, August 17, 1931.

[14]*Ibid.*, August 24, 1931.

[15]*Ibid.*, September 10, 1931.

the Long plan because it was the only solution. As he said, "I do not believe it right to dynamite houses and residences, but in case of serious conflagration this has often been resorted to and very properly so, and I think the same now applies to the cotton situation." He said he was willing to make the business sacrifice for the long-range public good.[16] Henning Newton, owner of several cotton gins, was so impressed by Moody's support that he also favored the Long plan despite personal losses he would sustain.[17]

Some of the critics of the Long plan and other reduction schemes maintained that such plans were useless since they were unenforceable. In answer to this charge, several people, including the county judge of Stonewall County, responded that partial acreage reduction was indeed unenforceable but that the Long plan had the special merit of being easily enforced.[18]

Long also received letters very much in opposition to his proposal. There were those like Congressman Thomas Blanton who said it was unworkable and would increase foreign competition.[19] Others said that it would cause too much hardship[20] and that it would shut down too many other industries.[21] Perhaps, the most cutting attack was the one from a resident of Beaumont who accused Long of being a cheat whose only goal was to aid the cotton capitalists by a scheme that would allow them to sell the nine million bales of surplus cotton.[22] It must have been a unique experience for Long to be called a front-man for capitalists.

[16]*Ibid.*, August 25, 1931.

[17]*Ibid.*, August 31, 1931.

[18]*Ibid.*, August 18, 1931, August 22, 1931.

[19]*Ibid.*, August 17, 1931.

[20]*Ibid.*, August 29, 1931.

[21]*Ibid.*, August 18, 1931.

[22]*Ibid.*, September 10, 1931.

From those not wholly in favor of the Long plan came
other suggestions of solutions. They ranged from those that
advocated partial acreage reduction[23] to such schemes as legislation requiring that all cement be sold in cotton bags[24]
and laws requiring everyone to wear cotton garments for five
years with stiff penalties of a $100 fine for the first of-
fense and $300 for the second and twelve months in jail.[25]
Several persons suggested acreage allotment plans that have
much similarity to the New Deal measures that came later.[26]
A banker from Midlothian suggested that such an allotment
should be set by a state board composed of twelve bank presidents and twenty-four farmers who would consult with other
state boards across the South. Banks would issue allotment
licenses. He was so convinced of the value of banks and bankers that he declared, "The farmers are ready for a Moses to
lead them out of the wilderness, and the bankers of the South
can do so."[27] One other person suggested that southern governors were the solution. He wanted a Southwide cooperative
established that would control cotton production and cotton
mills. In fact, he suggested a dictatorship of governors.[28]

Two very perceptive Texans told Long that there were hidden problems with acreage controls. J. F. Shaw of Atascosa
said that with the use of machinery and fertilizer the farmer
would be able to raise as much, if not more, than before on
smaller acreage.[29] Few, if any, Texans seemed to recognize
this possibility; it did prove to be a very real problem during the New Deal. Another wise Texan who signed himself "A.

[23]*Ibid.*, August 26, 1931.

[24]*Ibid.*, September 15, 1931.

[25]*Ibid.*, September 12, 1931.

[26]*Ibid.*, August 24, 1931, August 17, 1931.

[27]*Ibid.*, September 1, 1931.

[28]*Ibid.*, August 25, 1931.

[29]*Ibid.*, August 28, 1931.

Middleclass" told Long that his plan would make the cotton situation worse because a scarcity of cotton would simply encourage manufacturers to move more to rayon and other synthetics which would permanently reduce the potential cotton market.[30] That has indeed happened; one would have to question whether it was a result of controls or improved technology in the manufacture of synthetics.

Despite the intense debate in Texas about the Long plan, an accurate assessment of Texas attitudes is still most difficult. The Vernon Chamber of Commerce told Long in early September that Texas farmers were overwhelmingly in favor of his plan. The Chamber reported that in mass meetings in seventy-six Texas towns 11,954 farmers favored the Long plan, 2,684 opposed it, 7,330 favored some acreage reduction, and 166 opposed any reduction. In distribution by communities, twenty-eight towns favored the Long plan overwhelmingly, twenty-one favored acreage reduction, nineteen held miscellaneous views and nine took no action.[31] Whether these figures are representative of Texas opinion is impossible to know for sure. For example, other samples reveal that many Texans favored only partial reduction.[32]

Regardless of the exact division of public opinion, Governor Sterling came under intense pressure from both sides. In addition, Sterling's personal attitude was crucial. Apparently, he felt that the Long plan was either unnecessary or wrong. On one occasion, he said, "Yes I have been bombarded with thousands of telegrams and letters. I feel that the people are unduly excited. I will work it out someway."[33] Earlier he had replied to a telegram from the Governor of North Carolina by saying, "I am convinced that the majority

[30]*Ibid.*, August 24, 1931.

[31]*Ibid.*, September 4, 1931.

[32]October 24, 1931, Connally Papers, Box 15; August 21, 1931, Long Papers. See also Sterling Papers, Boxes 175-176.

[33]September 7, 1931, Sterling Papers, Box 176.

of farmers in Texas are opposed to Louisiana bill that pro-
hibits planting of cotton in nineteen thirty-two."[34]

If this was indeed the governor's view, it seemed un-
likely that he would call a special session of the legislature to deal with the question. Sterling was supported by
the stance taken by most newspapers in the state. Most editors of daily newspapers were opposed to any reduction proposal. They argued that it probably would be unconstitutional; it would stimulate foreign competition; it would add a
burden to the taxpayer and destroy the farmer; it would be
one step closer to State Socialism.[35] Most of the small town
weekly editors were completely opposed to the Long plan, but
some implied that they might be willing to agree to some limitation on production. The greatest opposition came from those
editors who were convinced that acreage reduction could not
be enforced.[36]

Despite the opposition of the press or his own personal
feelings, Sterling could not ignore the issue of a special
session. After receiving a copy of the Louisiana bill, Sterling refused to act immediately, waiting instead to hear
from members of the Texas legislature.[37] In the meantime,
a number of mass meetings were held by cotton farmers urging
the governor to call the session to provide some sort of agricultural relief.[38] Sterling, who had sent out a newspaper
questionnaire asking the opinion of farmers, was swamped
with replies. On September 1 the Galveston *Daily News* reported that 52,693 persons had declared in favor of a spe-

[34]*Ibid.*, September 2, 1931.

[35] Bonham *Daily Favorite*, August 24, 1931; Dallas *Morning News*, September 7, 1931; Galveston *Daily News*, August 12, 1931.

[36]*Ferguson Forum*, August 27, 1931; Fredericksburg *Standard*, August 7,
1931; *Texas Spur*, September 18, 1931; Weatherford *Democrat*, September 18,
1931.

[37]Galveston *Daily News*, September 1, 1931.

[38]*Ibid.*, August 30, 1931.

cial session, 6,799 had signed petitions, 44,256 had voted
for a session at mass meetings, and 1,638 had replied to
the governor personally. Only 514 persons had expressed
opposition to a special session. By September 5 the reports showed that between 70,000 and 80,000 people had expressed themselves on the issue.[39] Of the total replies
about one-half favored the Long plan and the others preferred a partial reduction in cotton acreage.[40] No longer
able to resist the pressure, Sterling issued the call for
a special session on September 5, 1931. He declared that
since the response had convinced him that the majority of
farmers favored an emergency acreage law, he was willing to
bow to public sentiment and allow the legislature to act.[41]

During the period when Sterling was considering the
special session, Long became impatient with the delay and
began to meddle in Texas politics. He attacked Sterling
as a tool of the rich; he said Sterling delayed in calling
the session because the wealthy interests in Texas did not
want it. Sterling publicly informed Long that he was not
running Texas and that it would be to the best interests
of all concerned if he would not meddle in Texas affairs.
"He [Long] may be able to demand that his legislature vote
whatever he wants, but we're a little more democratic in
Texas." Sterling, who was personally wealthy, left himself
open to further attacks for Long. "Yes you are more democratic. You have $35,000,000 while 2,000,000 farmers are
on the verge of starvation. Oh yes, you are democratic,
with money up to your eyes and every luxury, and deaf to
the cries of the children of the destitute farmers."[42]

In addition to his public attacks, Long apparently re-
quested information privately from Texas acquaintances about

[39]*Ibid.*, September 1, 1931, September 5, 1931.

[40]*Ibid.*, September 1, 1931.

[41]*Ibid.*, September 6, 1931.

[42]*Ibid.*, September 5, 1931.

Sterling's delay. J. E. McDonald, Texas Commissioner of Agriculture, told Long that the people of Texas and 110 members
of the legislature favored a special session. He was convinced that it would come soon.[43] Lt. Gov. Edgar E. Witt
told Long that he believed Sterling was delaying a special
session because of the turbulent condition in the East Texas
oilfields which had required the use of troops. Witt felt
that Sterling did not want the legislature in session while
troops were still on duty.[44] Two days later he told Long
that Sterling was delaying because "he is being influenced
by city folks who have not attended the farmers meetings and
do not know their wishes."[45]

When the Texas legislature assembled, Long was invited
to speak on behalf of his plan to the body and to a mass
meeting of citizens.[46] He received encouragement from Texans to come,[47] but such inducements were unnecessary. Long
was so excited by the possibilities that he temporarily put
aside his fear of flying in order to get to Austin as fast as
possible. However, a long-standing feud with his Lieutenant
Governor, Paul Cyr, prevented Long from leaving the state.
Long tried to get Cyr to promise that he would not act as
governor in his absence, but to no avail.[48] At least one Texan tried to prevail on Cyr to be reasonable for the good of
cotton farmers, but Cyr was not impressed by the request.[49]
Despite the disappointment of some Texans,[50] Long had to be

[43]September 4, 1931, Long Papers.

[44]*Ibid.*, September 3, 1931.

[45]*Ibid.*, September 5, 1931.

[46]*Ibid.*, September 6, 1931.

[47]*Ibid.*, September 7, 1931.

[48]Williams, *Huey Long*, 533.

[49]September 8, 1931, Long Papers.

[50]September 9, 1931, Long Papers.

content with addressing the mass meeting by radio.[51]

As the legislature delayed in taking action, Long's impatience prompted him to direct his attacks on that body. He stated that it was well-known "that the members of the Texas legislature have been bought like a sack of corn to vote against the cotton prohibition plan." He stated that the members had been paid by "the interests," but he never identified them. In fact, according to Long, the whole South, including Texas, was begging for the law, "but the corruption in Austin alone stands in the way."[52]

Since such an insult could not be ignored, the Texas Senate passed a resolution by a vote of twenty-one to seven declaring that Long's statement "is a lie made out of the whole cloth, and its author is a consummate liar."[53] The House of Representatives tempered the language by a vote of fifty-seven to forty-seven by striking out the section that called Long a liar. Instead the resolution stated that since the Texas Constitution prohibited membership to anyone who had participated in a duel, the members could not have the satisfaction in the gentlemanly fashion that any true Southerner should expect. Therefore, the only thing they could do was to resolve "that Governor Long has placed himself beneath the dignity of the further consideration of the Legislature." However, even after amending the resolution the House voted sixty-four to forty-seven to postpone its consideration indefinitely.[54] Despite this inaction the proposal did get statewide publicity which, after all, was the intent of the resolution.[55]

[51]Williams, *Huey Long*, 533.

[52]State of Texas, *Senate Journal*, 42d Leg., 2d Called Sess., 1931, 64.

[53]*Ibid.*, 64-65.

[54]State of Texas, *House Journal*, 42d Leg., 2d Called Sess., 1931, 132-134.

[55]Galveston *Daily News*, September 16, 1931, September 17, 1931.

In addition to official action, at least two members of the Texas legislature responded directly to Long. Dennis Ratliff of Haskell told Long that his statment was "an insult to every citizen of Texas,"[56] and H. H. Ray of Troy told him, "You run Louisiana if your people have no more sense than to permit you. We will try to run Texas."[57]

In addition to Long's attacks, the Texas legislature received pressure from other southerners who favored the Long plan. H. P. Fulmer, a member of Congress from South Carolina, urged the legislature to pass the measure as the only solution to the South's problems.[58] Harris County, Georgia, informed Sterling, "Georgia looking to Texas to adopt this plan."[59] A Louisianan told the legislature, "Governor Long sent a clean baby to Governor Sterling. Please send it back clean and don't dirty it up with a Texas baby."[60]

Rather than enact the Long proposal, the legislature passed a similar bill to limit cotton acreage in Texas. The law as finally passed provided that no one could plant cotton in 1932 to exceed 30 percent of the area he had in cultivation during the preceding year. After 1933 cotton could not be planted on the same land two years in a row.[61] The ostensible reasons for the law were conservation of the soil and the elimination of harmful pests. The bill was so controversial that numerous members of both houses felt obligated to explain their votes. Those opposing the bill believed that it was unconstitutional; that it prohibited a man from using his property as guaranteed to American citizens; or that it was unenforceable. Those favoring the mea-

[56] September 15, 1931, Long Papers.

[57] *Ibid.*, September 15, 1931.

[58] *Ibid.*, September 10, 1931.

[59] September 1, 1931, Sterling Papers, Box 176.

[60] Letter, n.d., Long Papers.

[61] *House Journal*, 187-188.

sure believed it to be the will of the people and the only thing that would save the farmer from destruction.[62]

Soon after the passage of the law, numerous people voiced the opinion that the legislature had acted wrongly. The editor of the Port Isabel *Pilot* believed that a precedent had been established that would allow government control of prices in any business. Likewise, individuals believed that the farmer had been hurt more than helped because he was now a criminal for trying to make a living by planting more cotton than he was allowed.[63] Only rarely did a newspaper editor believe the action was an honest attempt to find a solution to the farmers' problems.[64]

Much comment was forthcoming as to whether the law could be enforced. Plans were devised to avoid it legally, if possible, or illegally if no other choice was possible. The Galveston *Daily News*, one of those questioning the value and enforceability of the law, felt its position vindicated in October 1931 when the price of cotton dropped below five cents per pound. Some farmers, believing the law would not work, appealed to Senator Connally for a federal law that could be enforced.[65]

Many people, distressed because Texas did not adopt the Long plan, hoped the South would at least follow Texas in attempting to limit production. This hope was shattered, however, when Alabama, Georgia, Oklahoma, North Carolina, and Tennessee, states producing one-third of the nation's cotton, refused to enact such legislation. Thus, the attempt of

[62]*Ibid.*, 109-113, 177-179; *Senate Journal*, 138-139.

[63]Port Isabel *Pilot*, September 16, 1931; "Letters From Readers," Dallas *Morning News*, October 15, 1931, January 14, 1932.

[64]*Terry County Herald*, October 23, 1931.

[65]Karl E. Ashburn, "The Texas Cotton Acreage Control Law of 1931-1932," *The Southwestern Historical Quarterly*, LXI (July, 1957), 120-124; Galveston *Daily News*, January 20, 1932, March 8, 1932; Electra *News*, October 1, 1931; October 24, 1931, Connally Papers, Box 15.

those states that did pass legislation was undermined.[66]

Because of the actions of the other states, Texans began to challenge the constitutionality of the Texas law.
On February 1, 1932, Judge W. C. Davis in a district court
at Franklin, ruled the law to be in violation of both the
Texas and the United States Constitutions.[67] In a decision
by the Court of Civil Appeals meeting in Waco on March 5,
1932, the lower court ruling was upheld. The law was found
to be in violation of both federal and state constitutions
because it deprived the citizen of property without due process of law, because it impaired the right of contract, and
because it was a retroactive measure.[68] Thus, Texas was left
without any regulatory laws for cotton raising. The position of the farmer was the same as before the legislation
was considered.

Despite the failure of the southwide acreage reduction
plan, the legislation and the debate about it did have some
importance for the future. Farmers, and the public in general, had finally faced realistically the true problem of
agriculture and had devised a plan, albeit crude and ques-
tionable, to solve it. Moreover, the public debate had
sharpened the public's awareness and political consciousness
about the scope and intensity of the depression generally
and the agricultural problem specifically. When the agricultural measures of the New Deal were considered later, the
South was more agreeable to them than some sections of the
country.[69] Thus, the cotton holiday debate and the keen public interest in it may well have smoothed the way for the
innovations of Franklin D. Roosevelt.

[66] Johnson, "Farm Policy in Transition," 15-19.

[67] *Ibid.*, 18.

[68] *State v. Smith,* 47 *Southwestern Reporter,* 2d Series, 642-645.

[69] Saloutos, *Farmer Movements,* 284-286.

CHAPTER X

THE WAY OUT

When the existence of a depression could no longer be
denied, Americans were forced to face issues they had ignored earlier. As already discussed, efforts were made to
find the cause or causes of the depression. Americans, and
Texans as well, quickly searched for solutions or cures for
the economic distress.

Most Texans tried at first to find solutions within the
American tradition. Although some remedies suggested were
ludicrous, others were sincere attempts to deal with at least
a part of the real economic evil. Most of the proposals reflect a basic respect for the economic system and the pervasive influence of agrarian thinking in the state. There
were others, however, which took a more radical approach.
The plans, in fact, ranged "from orthodox marxism to native
cure-alls. . . ."[1] Persons in authority were flooded with
proposals, both of the crank and the serious variety.[2]
Texas did not escape this plethora of plans. So many
schemes, ranging from federal relief to "Buy Now" campaigns, were proposed that Senator Connally remarked that
his office force was overwhelmed by the deluge of mail proposing remedies that, in most cases, were of little value.
The Texas Weekly warned its readers to beware of plans that
came "from the half-baked doctrinaire, the business man of
limited experience, the shallow cracker-barrel economist. .
. ." Since professional economists did not know the solution, it stated, Texans would run a risk by relying on
amateurs.[3]

[1] Soule, *The Coming American Revolution*, 190; Rauch, *A History of the New Deal*, 10.

[2] Soule, *The Coming American Revolution*, 189; Joslin, *Hoover Off the Record*, 125-126.

[3] Steen, *Twentieth Century Texas*, 22; Beane, *Texas Thirties*, 64; *The Texas Weekly*, November 29, 1930.

Despite the uselessness of the unrealistic plans, they do serve as proof of the search for simple answers to a complex problem. A national lottery that would cause money to circulate and taxes to increase seemed to be the answer to some. Increased revenues from this source would make possible government aid to the destitute.[4] A Dallas businessman believed the answer to be the formation of "prosperity clubs" throughout the state. Only confident and optimistic people could be members; as the groups grew depression would vanish. A business magazine encouraged planning by the state and individuals alike for a grand celebration of the Texas centennial in 1936. The money spent by state and local governments for this event combined with the income from out-of-state visitors would restore Texas prosperity; it might even be the catalyst for national revival.[5] Some Texans believed that business recovery would come soon if retail products were packaged more attractively, or if everyone who owed money would pay his debts immediately. They did not seem to realize that people hit by depression did not have money with which to pay debts, and that, in those circumstances, packaging and better advertising techniques would not improve retail sales. The Huntsville *Item*, realizing that money was scarce, encouraged its readers to spend an extra ten cents per day to stimulate business. In just one year's time, purchases would increase by four and a half billion dollars; if that would not restore prosperity, nothing would.[6] A related proposal, that each family should drive its automobile an extra 300 miles in 1932, would increase the demand for gasoline, tires, repairs, and new cars. The editor of the Bonham newspaper, with tongue-in-

[4] FDRL, November 1, 1932, Box 732, December 13, 1932, Box 735.

[5] "Letters From Readers," Dallas *Morning News*, June 5, 1932; "Era of Development for Texas Foreseen," *Southern Florist and Nurseryman*, XXXIV (December 2, 1932), 12.

[6] FDRL, July 20, 1931, Box 721; Cameron *Enterprise*, October 1, 1931; Huntsville *Item*, December 4, 1930.

cheek, advocated that the nation should go farther by passing state laws that would require every automobile owner
to employ a chauffeur who was not a member of his own family. Since there were 32 million cars in the country, unemployment would vanish and Congress would be forced to lift
immigration restrictions. "How simple is the solution to a
great problem! Ah! don't go talking now about personal
rights and constitutions. Let's . . . settle a great problem."[7]

One solution attempted by the Hoover administration was
the passage of a national sales tax to balance the budget
and equalize the tax burden. Senator Connally, believing
it to be designed for the benefit of the wealthy at the
expense of lower income groups, fought the tax along with
liberal senators from other parts of the country. Texas
businessmen implied that they would support it if it meant
also a reduction in corporate income taxes, but those upon
whom the tax would fall most heavily vociferously opposed
it.[8] Although some supporters thought it was a way to end
the depression, most people did not seem to agree.

The "Buy Now" movement, begun as a national campaign,
received much support in Texas. Since the depression was
only psychological, confidence would return if people ignored hard times and bought goods as they had during prosperity. As soon as the citizens took "the padlock off their
purses" business would revive. Although the theory was
widely accepted, occasional editorials appeared, such as in
the Dallas *Morning News*, warning the people not to expect
too much from the "Buy Now" promotions.[9]

Related solutions included the "Give-a-Job" and clean-

[7] Electra *News*, May 26, 1932; Bonham *Daily Favorite*, July 29, 1931.

[8] Connally, *My Name is Tom Connally*, 135; Sec. Corres., Treasury Dept.,
October 27, 1931, Box 2; April 17, 1932, Rayburn Papers; Dallas *Craftsman*, March 25, 1932.

[9] Hannah, "Urban Reaction," 69-70; Haskell *Free Press*, October 16,
1930; Pecos *Enterprise and Gusher*, November 14, 1930; "Build Now," *County
Progress*, VII (November, 1930), 10; Dallas *Morning News*, October 7, 1930.

up campaigns. Everyone should do his part to hire the unemployed for any type of work for any length of time. If
each citizen were to clean-up, repair, or paint his property, many men would be employed, and if enough homeowners
were to do this, it would show the world that confidence in
the future had not been destroyed.[10] Likewise, any efforts
made on the local level to end the depression should give
preference to local citizens. So anxious was the state to
grasp at any straw of hope that Governor Sterling's unemployment committee officially endorsed the "Give-a-Job,"
the buy-at-home, and clean-up proposals.[11]

To some, all these plans were futile because the business depression was merely a reflection and extension of
the spiritual depression that the nation had suffered since
World War I. The only solution, therefore, was a religious
revival. Perhaps, a national day of fasting and prayer
would help. After all, when Abraham Lincoln and Woodrow
Wilson had proclaimed such days, military victories began
to occur.[12]

Occasionally solutions were proposed by cranks. A writer from Moulton informed President-elect Roosevelt that,
without revealing his plans, he would guarantee the end of
the depression if only Roosevelt would aid him.

> In all it will take me 120 days to put every single
> individual to work. I have an editor whom I prefer to
> be my secretary and you must give me this preference. I
> need 5 reporters and 5 secret service men for a body
> guard. I need an assistant secretary whom you may choose.
> I also need 2 stenographers and 2 messengers. Traveling
> expenses to be paid by the government. My salary will
> be $25,000 a year and expenses for a term of four years.[13]

[10]"Letters From Readers," Dallas *Morning News*, February 11, 1931; El
Paso *Times*, December 11, 1931; Austin *Statesman*, November 1, 1930; Weatherford *Democrat*, January 22, 1932; Rayburn Papers, June 1, 1930.

[11]Uvalde *Leader-News*, January 20, 1933; El Paso *Times*, June 27, 1930;
Bureau of Labor Statistics, *Committee for Unemployment Relief*, 7-10.

[12]Canadian *Record*, August 27, 1931; FDRL, October 17, 1932, Box 727.

[13]*Ibid.*, December 24, 1932, Box 736. Roosevelt's staff was so amazed

One of the most widely discussed proposals for ending the depression was the so-called "Back-to-the-Farm" movement. Although the idea was not new, it received new stimulus during the campaign of 1932 when Roosevelt suggested the moving of many of the city unemployed to unoccupied land in the country where they could engage in subsistence farming until the depression came to an end. His suggestion was so popular that he was deluged with letters of encouragement that provided detailed plans about how such a move might be accomplished. This was not an isolated reaction since people from all parts of the state responded.[14] A correspondent from Austin was so pleased that he wrote Roosevelt, "Mr. Hoover financed the big interests, the banks, the rail roads, the big corporations and the European Governments, you help your home farmers and laborers, and live in their hearts for ever."[15] Most of the proposed farm colonization plans involved some type of federal financing. There were those, however, that were based upon individual action, private companies, and Christian welfare agencies.[16] Although the idea of farm colonization was widely discussed by individuals, very rarely did the commercial press comment on it. The East Texas Chamber of Commerce journal and a Rio Grande Valley magazine, two publications that did speak out, both thought it was an excellent idea. Despite the few reservations of the East Texas Chamber it believed that, on the whole, a return to the soil was the only thing to be done at the present time.[17] The El Paso *Times* and the Austin *Statesman* both

by this letter that the following notation was made: "The 8th wonder of the world."

[14] See for example: FDRL, October 7, 1932, October 25, 1932, Box 727, July 3, 1932, Box 730.

[15] *Ibid.*, n.d., Box 725.

[16] "Letters From Readers," Dallas *Morning News*, May 14, 1932; "Public Opinion," Amarillo *Daily News*, March 30, 1932; "Letters From Readers," Dallas *Morning News*, March 16, 1932, February 2, 1931.

[17] Glen H. Davis, "Back to the Farm Movement Grows," *East Texas*, VII

believed it to be a good idea although the *Statesman* had a few reservations.[18]   The Dallas *Morning News* was a bit confused. When it first considered the idea in 1931, it was opposed because the nation already had too many farmers. About a year later, however, the editor considered it to be a good, although only a partial, remedy for the unemployment problem. A month later, he reversed his thinking again because such a plan was no solution to the depression.[19]   Those who were definitely opposed to the plan were convinced that the returning of people to the soil would only intensify an already serious farm problem. A farmer opposed to the idea suggested sending all people who supported the plan to the farm themselves. These city people who had become wealthy through the labor of farmers would then see how difficult farm life really was. They should take some of the money out of the cities and put it back into agriculture from whence it came. To this man, the settling of penniless people on farms would be useless since older, experienced farmers were failing daily.[20]

Despite the scattered opposition to such a plan some attempts were made to return the destitute to the soil. The city of Houston asked Sam Rayburn for his aid in leasing an abandoned military base where the city would locate 200 to 500 familes. Here they would be able to at least provide food for themselves until the depression ended.[21]   The base was not available, but some 1,000 acres was obtained under

---

(April-May, 1933), 14; "Musings of Monty," *Monty's Monthly*, XV (January, 1933), 12-13.

[18]El Paso *Times*, June 26, 1932; Austin *Statesman*, June 9, 1932, December 31, 1932.

[19]Dallas *Morning News*, April 15, 1931, April 17, 1932, May 16, 1932.

[20]"Ford Leads the Way to Chaos," *Hardware and Implement Journal*, XXXVII (February, 1932), 32; "Letters From Readers," Dallas *Morning News*, January 14, 1932.

[21]Walter Monteith to Rayburn, May 5, 1932, Rayburn Papers.

the leadership of Will Horwitz where a few families were set-tled.[22] Maury Maverick established a colony near San Antonio to provide for those who could get help in no other way. Organized on a collective basis, the colony made an attempt to become self-sufficient. The effort failed in the long-run, according to Maverick, because as soon as one of his colonists got a good job, he would "turn capitalist" and desert the enterprise. Although it certainly was no cure for the depression, it did provide shelter and food for many who might have starved otherwise.[23]

Technocracy was another widely discussed method of eliminating future depressions. Founded by Howard Scott, an amateur economist heavily influenced by Thorstein Veblen and Frederick Soddy, Technocracy was based upon the infallibility of science. The fullest use of machinery, engineers, and modern technology would make available the most luxurious life possible with the use of very little labor. The Technocrats believed that if the productive capacity were managed by competent engineers with an interest in maximum production rather than the profit motive it would be possible to produce enough goods with men working only four hours per day to provide every family with the equivalent of a $20,000 annual income. To the Technocrats the profit motive of laissez faire capitalism was outmoded; the new society would be one based on political and economic planning by engineers. In late 1932 and early 1933 the idea caught the imagination of the American public. Bankers and industrialists hailed Scott as the savior of America; Upton Sinclair and Stuart Chase thought it to be the most important movement of the twentieth century.[24]

[22] Montgomery, "Depression in Houston," 158-159.

[23] Maverick, *A Maverick American,* 167-176.

[24] Schlesinger, *The Crisis of the Old Order,* 461-464; Robinson, *Fantastic Interim,* 218-219; Dumond, *America in Our Time,* 456-457; Howard Scott, *Introduction to Technocracy* (New York: The John Day Company, 1933), 38.

> Radio comedians made jokes about it; a new dance was named
> after it at Roseland; in Chicago (according to *Time*) the
> sponsors of the anti-Rodeo League and the Mental Patients
> Defenders Association formed the Technocratic party of the
> United States.
>   Not everything, however, was acclaim. . . . Al Smith
> perhaps offered the definitive comment. "As for substitut-
> ing engineers for political leaders in running the country,"
> he said, "I cannot refrain from mentioning the fact that we
> have finished an era of government by engineers in Washington.[25]

After 1933 the public furor died, but the basic idea was not
destroyed. Although the solution proposed by the Technocrats may not have been practical, the very fact that they
had challenged the economic system and called for social and
economic planning undoubtedly helped mold public opinion toward a more receptive attitude for the New Deal.[26]

> But the Technocratic idea fitted precisely the American
> mood of the moment. It offered an answer to the pervasive
> riddle of the times. . . . It seemed to be scientific, and
> thus commended itself to a people who venerated science as
> the source of progress. . . . The very fact that it was ab-
> truse, that it broke clean away from the world of practical
> problems and intelligible statements, gave it a mystical
> irresistibility to a nation searching for a magic key to re-
> covery, for something which would both bring prosperity
> and serve as a religion.[27]

Quite a large segment of the Texas press commented on
Technocracy. Most of the publications noted the rise of
the theory, but withheld judgment, waiting instead to see
if anything concrete would result. The Electra *News* was
unwilling to criticize the idea until it was revealed if it
was "the greatest example of the power of man to visualize
and plan the future or the greatest hoax ever perpetrated
on the world." The Catholic weekly of San Antonio was dubious about the cure-all aspects of Technocracy and its Utop-
ian overtones, but it was "confident that technocracy will
expose some guiding principles of action that will aid man

[25] Schlesinger, *The Crisis of the Old Order*, 463.

[26] Mitchell, *Depression Decade*, 114.

[27] Frederick Lewis Allen, *Since Yesterday* (New York: Bantam Books
edition, 1961), 72.

in bringing about a readjustment of his relationship with the machine."[28] *Monty's Monthly*, noting Technocracy's attempt to solve the depression, remarked, "All we can say is that sump'n [*sic*] ought to be done about it." The Austin *Statesman* was dubious about its benefits because overproduction, both industrial and agricultural, was the basic cause of the depression. Therefore, how could increased production as proposed by the Technocrats be of any value? Other commentators believed it would not work since Americans were not willing to scrap an economic system that, despite its faults, had brought progress to the country. The Denison *Herald* thought it was merely another form of socialism; serious consideration of the idea was, therefore, disregarded.[29]

A proposal that received more support in Texas was the "soak-the-rich" plan. Although the idea was certainly not new, it received new impetus in 1932 when Huey Long, after becoming a United States Senator from Louisiana, launched his "Share Our Wealth" program. He agreed with Roosevelt that the problem was not a lack of money but the maldistribution of the nation's wealth. Long's plan was two-fold: to limit inheritances and to tax progressively large fortunes up to 99 percent for those over $8 million. Long stated that he bore no ill will toward the rich; in fact, he proposed to reduce their fortunes because he loved them so much. Since they were so blind and stupid, their reactionary and unfeeling attitude would result in the masses taking their fortunes violently; therefore, he was merely saving them from their own foolishness.[30]

[28] Electra *News*, January 5, 1933; *Southern Messenger*, January 5, 1933.

[29] "Musings of Monty," *Monty's Monthly*, XV (January, 1933), 13; Austin *Statesman*, December 27, 1932; Beeville *Bee-Picayune*, January 19, 1933; "Technocracy," *West Texas Today*, XIII (January, 1933), 8; Denison *Herald* as quoted in Bonham *Daily Favorite*, January 17, 1933.

[30] Dumond, *America in Our Time*, 458-459; Huey P. Long, *Share Our Wealth* (Washington, D.C.: n.d.), 5-6, 30.

The idea of limiting income and the amount of property a person could own was strong in Texas prior to Long's rise to national prominence. It did, however, gain in popularity after he became its champion. Most of those who supported it believed that the proposal would end the depression and perhaps save the American system.[31] The idea was so popular that a correspondent told Roosevelt, "If the democratic party does not do something to prevent concentration of Capital I believe we will be Russianized in ten years." State Senator Pink Parrish of Lubbock was so concerned about it that he made it a part of his campaign for congressman-at-large in 1932. He declared that since five percent of the American people owned eighty percent of the nation's wealth, they should pay eighty percent of the cost of government. Occasionally, a major daily paper such as the Austin *Statesman* indicated its supprt of the proposal. Only rarely did anyone defend the rich. A man who did told Roosevelt that excessive taxation of business and of the wealthy had caused the depression. The solution, therefore, was to reduce taxes on these groups and make up the deficit by a national sales tax that would force poor people who had never done so before to help support the government.[32]

The degree to which such a plan was supported indicates a growing feeling of desperation. Most Americans, Texans included, never before considered such a program because of the innate hope that they would someday be one of the wealthy. Perhaps the popular support for such a measure reveals the loss of hope among Texans. Because of the growing desperation they were willing to support measures that might, at another time, be considered radical.

Another such proposal that had widespread Texas support

[31] Connally Papers, October 27, 1931, Box 14, February 1, 1931, Box 24; Dallas *Craftsman*, October 30, 1930; "Letters From Readers," Dallas *Morning News*, September 12, 1931.

[32] FDRL, September 12, 1932, Box 730; Amarillo *Daily News*, June 16, 1932; Austin *Statesman*, October 3, 1931; FDRL, November 1, 1932, Box 734.

was the "Share the Work" program. This was not radical in itself, but the necessity of an administrative agency with coercive powers reveals that Texans were willing to accept methods to ease the depression that they would have abhorred at an earlier or a later date. This plan was quite simple. The number of hours or days worked per week should be reduced substantially. This would allow more people to have jobs, thus decreasing the problem of unemployment and increasing purchasing power. Despite the slight disagreement over whether the workers should receive the same pay for the shorter hours, the proposal was widely supported throughout the state by organized labor and private citizens.[33] The newspapers were not as enthusiastic. Since they did, however, recognize the inevitability of such a policy, they were willing to accept it.[34] The adoption of such a plan was undertaken in Lubbock and at least one state agency advocated it be used throughout the state.[35]

One of the major problems of the depression was the scarcity of money. As conditions worsened, credit was restricted, currency was hoarded, and many localities were forced to resort to barter or the printing of scrip that would be accepted by local merchants. When this did not ease the need for currency, the old Populist demand for inflation was revived. Hoover and others who believed the gold standard to be one of the major foundations of the American system were fearful that a panic situation might force the nation off the gold stan-

[33] Edward Ainsworth Williams, *Federal Aid for Relief* (New York: Columbia University Press, 1939), 32; *Weekly Dispatch*, January 9, 1932; Dallas *Craftsman*, November 18, 1932; "Letters to the Times," El Paso *Times*, January 29, 1931; FDRL, January 26, 1933, Box 733; Sterling Papers, October 13, 1931; Rayburn Papers, February 3, 1932.

[34] Austin *Statesman*, October 21, 1931; *Southern Messenger*, May 26, 1932; Galveston *Daily News*, May 31, 1931; Weatherford *Democrat*, December 16, 1932.

[35] "City Adopts Shift Crew Plan to Relieve Unemployment," *The Hub*, IV (December, 1930), 6; Bureau of Labor Statistics, *Committee for Unemployment Relief*, 7.

dard.[36] The problem of money was perhaps the greatest issue in Texas prior to the New Deal. Some people thought the problem was a lack of credit, but most believed the scarcity of a medium of exchange was the real villain.[37] Many were convinced that the monetary system was not working properly although they were not sure of the remedy except to have more money.[38] A Texan, very unhappy with Roosevelt's reluctance to advocate inflation, told the governor:

> Another thing why do you oppose the inflation of cur-
> rency when any man with the brains of a grasshopper can
> see that the people need that worse than anything else.
> Surely you know that the price of the dollar is too high.
> We contracted to pay debts, public and private, when the
> dollar was cheap and now we are forced to pay them dollar
> for dollar when prices are low and the value of the dollar
> is out of sight.[39]

That was the real crux of the problem. Money was so deflated that most people whose incomes and salaries had been reduced were unable to pay their fixed debts. To the Texan the solution lay in reinflating or expanding the currency. To a few Texans the answer was to control the money more carefully,[40] but to others the insistence on the gold standard restricted the circulating medium and hindered any improvement in the situation.[41]

The old issue of free silver was revived among Texans in the thirties. The free coinage of silver seemed to be the

---

[36]Hill, *The American Scene*, 410; Charles A. Beard and George H. E. Smith, *The Future Comes* (New York: The Macmillan Company, 1934), 11; Schlesinger, *The Crisis of the Old Order*, 233.

[37]Ross Sterling to John Garner, October 6, 1931, Sterling Papers, Box 180; FDRL, May 18, 1932, Box 718.

[38]*Texas Spur*, February 10, 1932; Rayburn Papers, March 29, 1932.

[39]FDRL, February 11, 1933, Box 731.

[40]Dallas *Morning News*, January 9, 1932; May 2, 1932, Dept of the Treasury, Box 3.

[41]FDRL, November 25, 1932, Box 731; "Letters From Readers," Dallas *Morning News*, January 8, 1933; "Public Opinion," Amarillo *Daily News*, May 18, 1932.

answer; perhaps there should be a fixed ratio, but certainly silver should be just as acceptable as gold in the payment of debts. Although most of the silver supporters were private citizens, Tom Connally and some of the commercial press were also favorable.[42]

A popular proposal was the simple expedient of issuing more money. A few farmers believed that agricultural products should be the basis of the new currency,[43] but most Texans did not concern themselves with its stability. They were convinced that the prestige of the government was strong enough to maintain the value of the new paper money. After all, they reasoned, why be concerned with the distant future? The need for money was immediate; problems of the long-run could be handled later.[44] A magazine editor stated the issue succinctly, "This government should . . . issue greenbacks equal to all its debts, retire the public debt and take this load from the backs of the people."[45]

The ideas and programs supported by many Texans indicate a change in their thinking. They had begun to abandon older ides of self-reliance, rugged individualism, laissez faire economics and small government. Their ideas and actions were also acquiring overtones of radicalism. These stemmed partially from older ideas of the late nineteenth and early twentieth centuries, but they were also new in some respects. The Texan became more critical of business

[42]"Letters From Readers," Dallas *Morning News*, June 10, 1931, June 22, 1931, August 16, 1931; "Pens of the People," Galveston *Daily News*, October 5, 1930; Connally Papers, August 5, 1931, Box 15; Cameron *Enterprise*, September 1, 1932; El Paso *Times*, May 29, 1932; Fredericksburg *Standard*, June 3, 1932.

[43]FDRL, December 15, 1932, Box 733; Connally Papers, August 17, 1931, Box 15.

[44]Claude *News* as quoted in *Ferguson Forum*, July 23, 1931; "Letters," *ibid.*, June 4, 1931; Connally Papers, February 14, 1931, Box 25; FDRL, September 21, 1932, Box 727; "Letters From Readers," Dallas *Morning News*, June 11, 1931.

[45]"Fooling the Farmers," *The Common Herd*, XV (March, 1930), 12.

leadership of government until many were openly criticizing the American political and economic systems. Some were, in fact, willing to abandon the system that would allow such a disaster to occur, hoping to replace it with something better.

CHAPTER XI

THE TEXAN AS A RADICAL

The depression brought as deep a questioning of American values as any other event in American history, for "the
time was ripe for a searching analysis of American society,
of the causes and cures for depressions, of capitalism's
basic inability to avoid periodical cyclical collapse."[1]
Americans were so stunned after the stock market debacle of
1929 that for some time they were unable to make a serious
assessment of the crisis. As the months passed with little
or no improvement, however, they began to question, to ana-
lyze, and to discuss the ramifications of the depression for
American society. The questioning of old values and the
search for solutions of the crisis has been summed up very
effectively by Dixon Wecter:

> Stereotypes of thought, traditional saws, the tribal wis-
> dom of the elders, all were challenged in books, maga-
> zines, and private talk. Perhaps, after all, the pro-
> mise of American life would turn out merely to be propa-
> ganda, the tyranny of words or the folklore of capitalism.
> But while youth was more prone to rebel, middle age and
> senescence often clung all the more stoutly to old loy-
> alties, particularly if they had a personal stake in the
> status quo--leaping to the defense of verities like hard
> work, thrift and individual enterprise, and opposing
> change in those concepts of law and government which they
> associated with happier days.[2]

One of the most striking social features of the depression was the lack of violence and revolt from the common
people. To be sure, there were a few outbursts, but most
were localized efforts with little chance of success. Certainly there was no uprising in the European or Latin American tradition. "Instead there was sullenness, anxiety,
fear and foreboding. The buoyant optimism familiar in American life was missing. Courage and faith in the future was

[1]Hannah, "Urban Reaction," 148.

[2]Wecter, *The Great Depression*, 34.

197

wanting. It seemed to many that a pall of gloom had settled over America."[3]

Texans, by and large, mirrored the national reaction to the crisis. People throughout the state were frustrated, unsure of what had happened, and afraid of the future. Some of them concluded that the only answer was to abandon the faltering capitalist system; for others, a minor repair job on the economic and social system would return the nation to "the good old days." Some Texans, on the other hand, concluded that nothing could be done. To them the depression was an inevitable phase of the business cycle, or it was punishment from a wrathful God for past sins, or it was merely the result of poor individual management. Although some Texans embraced socialist or communist ideology as alternatives, the great majority reacted in an agrarian fashion. They attempted to protect a way of life that had been challenged, and perhaps destroyed, by economic forces beyond their control. In such circumstances, many of them were willing to resort to whatever actions were necessary to protect this way of life, even if it meant embracing communism on the extreme left or fascism on the extreme right. In such a crisis, labels or ideology meant little; the important thing to Texans was the protection and restoration of rural society. As the depression worsened month after month, more people became convinced that it might even be necessary to resort to violent revolution to defend themselves and their society.

As the depression continued unabated, those demanding some sort of national planning became more vocal. They agreed that laissez faire individualism was out-of-date, but they could not agree if economic regulation should be public or private, voluntary or compulsory. Although some of them were convinced that it should be of a voluntary nature through private means,[4] most planners thought it should be done by

[3]Hannah, "Urban Reaction," 147-148.

[4]*Ibid.*, 267; E. P. Hayes, *Activities of the President's Emergency*

the government, coercively if necessary. The demand for reform, dormant since Progressive days, reasserted itself during the depression and culminated in the New Deal. During
the Hoover administration various agencies such as the Committee on Social Trends emphasized national planning to avoid
periodic slumps,[5] but the planners were generally ignored until the economic collapse restored their prestige.

Texans also believed more and more in collective action
to alleviate the depression and to avoid its recurrence in
the future. Most of the state believed that private, voluntary cooperation and planning was the best method. Economic
planning by any group was a violation of laissez faire economics, but the inconsistency of the thinking of Texans did
not appear to them since they usually justified collective
action and private planning as the only way to improve conditions.[6] Virtually all segments of the state believed that
unity and community organization would improve the economy;
some agreed that government encouragement of cooperative action would be of some value.[7] Before the government stepped
in with massive aid, many communities such as Kristenstad,
and private groups, such as the Houston bankers, had undertaken cooperative action and planning to prevent disaster.[8]

Committee for Employment (Privately printed, 1936), 89-90; Charles A.
Beard, *America Faces the Future* (Boston: Houghton Mifflin Company, 1932),
20.

[5]Beard and Beard, *America in Midpassage,* 115; Stuart Chase, *The Ne-
mesis of American Business* (New York: The Macmillan Company, 1931), 95-96;
Graves, *The Great Depression,* 189; Hofstadter, *The Age of Reform,* 302;
Soule, *The Coming American Revolution,* 198.

[6]El Paso *Times,* January 1, 1931; "Letters From Readers," Dallas *Morning News,* October 8, 1931, November 23, 1932; "Public Opinion," Amarillo
Daily News, January 7, 1931.

[7]"What the Campaign Reveals," *East Texas,* IV (July, 1930), 18; Bee-
ville *Bee-Picayune,* November 7, 1930; Huntsville *Item,* August 20, 1931;
"The New Deal is Cooperation," *Sheep and Goat Raisers' Magazine,* XIII
(May, 1933), 103; *Congressional Record,* 72d Cong., 1st Sess., 1931, LXXV,
Part 1, 735.

[8]"A Forward Going Program," *The Interpreter,* I (January, 1933), 3-12;
Jones, *Fifty Billion Dollars,* 23.

As conditions worsened more and more Texans became convinced
that state or national planning would be necessary if the
nation were to survive.[9] Senator Connally was informed that
political conservatism had been the cause of the trouble;
Texans were more likely to be lenient toward legislative
errors than they would be to no action at all. A correspondent to the Dallas *Morning News* was so convinced that national planning and action were necessary that he stated, "I
answer, hard times will not pass, and normal times will not
arrive, until Congress acts."[10] A Dallasite was so disgusted
with the talk about self-reliance and local initiative that
he wanted to awaken the farmer, and the public at large, to
the realities of the situation.

> As long as the farmer accepts the sop of the doctrine of
> individualism, he might as well be ginning his cotton by
> hand and plowing with a crooked fork. . . . The farmer
> ought to be investigating the potentialities of collective
> bargaining and quit plowing with the crooked stick of in-
> dividualism.[11]

Although he was most concerned about private group action
and planning, this type of thinking was easily moved to support government action.

The desire for governmental action of any type is often
charged with being of a radical nature. Most of the thought
and actions of Texans were not truly radical, even if they appear as such in retrospect. Instead, radicalism in Texas
was of a very practical nature. Unorthodox plans for ending
the depression were supported because they seemed to be the
only logical answers. Some of the schemes were unrealistic,
foolish, or the products of unimaginative minds; when no end
to the depression appeared in sight, more serious plans were

[9]
Dallas *Craftsman*, August 5, 1932; El Paso *Times*, August 24, 1931;
"After the Election, What?" *The Interpreter*, I (December, 1932), 4-5;
Waco Farm and Labor Journal, May 29, 1931.

[10]
Connally Papers, February 23, 1931, Box 16; "Letters From Readers,"
Dallas *Morning News*, September 3, 1931.

[11]*Ibid.*, January 1, 1930.

put forward as possible solutions. Some of them were perhaps radical for their time, but it was a practical radicalism. Although it is unfair to label them as radical, the plans did embody principles that were a break with the immediate past. Some people revived nineteenth century ideas, while others attempted to devise new methods for dealing with new problems. Most of the plans envisioned a broader role for the government, often without any consideration or recognition of the contradiction of the laissez faire philosophy of the twenties.

Of the many plans discussed by Texans, at least two have been discussed earlier and deserve mention again because they reflect upon the nature of radicalism as Texans perceived it. Technocracy, as promoted by Howard Scott, received much comment, but the number of Texans embracing the idea was quite small, probably because of the overtones of radicalism. Some commentators believed it would not work since Americans were not willing to scrap the capitalist system that, despite its faults, had brought progress to the country. Others thought it was merely another form of socialism; serious consideration of the idea was, therefore, disregarded.[12] A second proposal that received more support in Texas was the idea of limiting income and redistributing wealth, stimulated in part by Huey Long's "Share Our Wealth" program.[13]

The ideas and programs supported by many Texans indicate a change in their thinking. They had begun to abandon older ideas of self-reliance, rugged individualism, laissez faire economics, and small government. Their ideas and actions were also acquiring overtones of radicalism. These stemmed partly from older ideas of the late nineteenth and early twen-

[12]"Musings of Monty," *Monty's Monthly*, XV (January, 1933), 13; Austin *Statesman*, December 27, 1932; Beeville *Bee-Picayune*, January 19, 1933; "Technocracy," *West Texas Today*, XIII (January, 1933), 8; Denison *Herald* as quoted in Bonham *Daily Favorite*, January 17, 1933.

[13]Connally Papers, October 27, 1931, Box 14, February 1, 1931, Box 24; Dallas *Craftsman*, October 30, 1930; "Letters From Readers," Dallas *Morning News*, September 12, 1931.

tieth centuries, but they were also new in some respects.
The Texan became more critical of business leadership until
many were openly criticizing the American political and
economic systems. Some were willing, in fact, to abandon
the system that would allow such a disaster to occur, hoping
to replace it with something better.

On the national level there were many critics who demanded that the economic system be changed. Hoover stated
years later that he had been concerned during the depression
that the prophets of doom would gain a following. There were
the people who proclaimed the end of the American way of life,
the democratic political system, and the capitalistic economy.
President Roosevelt reminded Americans in 1938 about the
depth of despair just before he assumed the presidency. He
said that although the people were uncertain about the system that might be established, a growing number were concerned about the inadequacy of the old system.[14]

Opinion in Texas was much the same. Although Texans
were unsure of the remedy or were vague about a solution, a
growing portion of the citizenry was convinced that the American economic system had failed. Organized labor believed
that capitalism, as America had known it, was not worth
saving. Instead, some other system, based upon a democratic
foundation, should be devised. Any system that allowed the
workers to be exploited by starvation, low wages, and long
hours could not continue. As one of the most conservative
groups in Texas, organized labor did not advocate violence
or adoption of socialism, fascism, or communism; instead,
"whatever system a people elect to have is right, at the
time and for that people. The important thing, for all peoples, is the right to elect change--to move forward."[15]

---

[14] Stuart Chase, *A New Deal* (New York: The Macmillan Company, 1933),
153; Hoover, *The Great Depression*, 32; Rosenman, *Public Papers of FDR*,
II, 3.

[15] El Paso *Labor Advocate* as quoted in *Weekly Dispatch*, February 22,
1930; *ibid.*, November 28, 1931.

Many of the state's newspaper editors agreed that capitalism was under attack, but few of them were deeply concerned about its ability to weather such an attack. They agreed that evils did exist in such a system, but that they could be eliminated. Occasionally an editor, reflecting a latent fear, wondered aloud if the leaders of such a system could move fast enough to correct the evils before the demand for change became irrestible.[16]

Maury Maverick reported that most of the transients in the state with whom he had contact had little knowledge of politics or ideology. They were quite pragmatic in their ideas since they were willing to adopt any idoleogy that meant improvement in their own lives. The political immaturity was made clear when he revealed, "I found that their idea of 'capitalism' was a state of society in which you can be hungry for a while, but you will finally get a good job, and possibly have others that can either go hungry or work for you."[17] If this was a reflection of the attitude of the average citizen, it is little wonder that so many of the youthful transients considered capitalism a decaying institution.[18] Many average Texans not on the road were likewise convinced that capitalism was disintegrating and doomed to failure; only a radical change in the system would save the nation from complete destruction.[19]

In the face of the massive attacks made on capitalism numerous defenders came forward. The United States Chamber of Commerce, one of the greatest champions of the American economic system, was joined by Texas chambers in denouncing

[16]Austin *Statesman*, February 19, 1932; Galveston *Daily News*, June 16, 1931; Hebbronville *News*, June 17, 1931; *Ferguson Forum*, July 9, 1931.

[17]Maverick, *A Maverick American*, 170.

[18]Minehan, *Boy and Girl Tramps of America*, 163.

[19]"Public Opinion," Amarillo *Daily News*, February 17, 1932; "Letters From Readers," Dallas *Morning News*, September 16, 1931; FDRL, February 3, 1933, Box 734, n.d., Box 736.

anyone who advocated destruction of American capitalism. If change were required, it would have to be made without disrupting free enterprise. Since business had already been frightened by radical talk, the nation should simply work harder to end the depression.[20] Some of the other defenders were convinced that derogatory statements only helped to breed discontent. They questioned the motives, and almost the patriotism, of those who criticized the economic system.[21] Most of the vocal defenders of the system in Texas were the small town newspaper editors, who were convinced that the depression could be ended only through the free enterprise system.[22] Criticism, they believed, only frightened capital into hiding and thus prolonged the depression. The sooner people decided to stop complaining and go back to work, the sooner conditions would return to normal.[23]

Since a large portion of the nation was critical of capitalism, at least three alternatives were discussed. Those with small material possessions might turn to the Russian model of dictatorship while those with property and possessions to lose might very well go to the other extreme, advocating a conservative or reactionary dictatorship modeled after Mussolini's apparently successful system in Italy. By and large, most of those desiring a change took a middle position. They wished to maintain control over production and the economic system but without the complete destruction of private property.[24] So widespread was the discussion

---

[20] Chamber of Commerce of the U.S., *The American Economic System*, 8-36; "Politics," *West Texas Today*, XIII (July, 1932), 8.

[21] *Southern Messenger*, May 12, 1932; "Letters From Readers," Dallas *Morning News*, September 15, 1930.

[22] See for example: *San Patricio County News*, June 25, 1931; Fredericksburg *Standard*, July 31, 1931; Weatherford *Democrat*, January 16, 1931.

[23] Huntsville *Item*, January 28, 1932; Beeville *Bee-Picayune*, February 20, 1931.

[24] Seldes, *The Years of the Locust*, 223; Hannah, "Urban Reaction," 3.

that the eminent political scientist, Frederick A. Ogg, was prompted to write an article titled "Does America Need a Dictator?" In this paper he discussed the various proposals, reflecting all shades of opinion, that we needed a dictator. Although he doubted the possibility of the nation ever going so far as to give one man complete power, he concluded that since the business interests in the country were in control, any such action would probably result in a fascist dictatorship.[25] A number of contemporary observers were convinced that the ingredients for fascism, always present in America, were being molded into a cohesive force to suppress the growing discontent among the lower classes. A number of important business leaders were openly proclaiming that a Mussolini was all that America needed to solve its problems.[26]

A relatively small portion of Texans believed fascism was the answer. Individuals often voiced the need for a strong leader, a "Moses" to lead them out of the wilderness of depression.[27] Occasionally Texans spoke of the nation becoming fascist or the need for a man like Mussolini. When their statements are analyzed, however, the lack of understanding is apparent. They did not fully realize that fascism is

> *totalitarian in its objective:* to control all phases of human life, political or not, from the cradle to the grave. It begins the control even before the cradle, by pushing definite population policies, and has been known to reach into the grave, so to speak, to decide whether a dead person should have a burial at all, and if so, in what form.
> But fascism is also *totalitarian in its means.* It

[25]Frederick A. Ogg, "Does America Need a Dictator?" *Current History,* XXXVI (September, 1932), 641-648.

[26]Soule, *The Coming American Revolution,* 293-295; Lawrence Dennis, *The Coming American Fascism* (New York: Harper & Brothers, 1936), 209, 300; Schlesinger, *The Crisis of the Old Order,* 268.

[27]FDRL, September 7, 1932, Box 728; Connally Papers, January 18, 1931, Box 18; "Letters From Readers," Dallas *Morning News,* September 12, 1930.

will use any form of coercion, from verbal threats to mass murder, in obtaining its ends.[28]

Texans wanted a man of action who had the courage to take control and use the government apparatus for the benefit of the common man.[29] They were impressed, more than anything else, with Mussolini's decisiveness and ability to bring order out of chaos. Quite a number of editors could foresee the advent of a dictator, of the liberal or conservative variety, if something were not done quickly to end the depression.[30] Some of the group seemed quite pleased with the prospect if it were the remedy the nation needed.[31]

At the other extreme, communism was feared more than fascism. It is true that at the beginning of the depression, a widespread interest in the Russian experiment was apparent. There were communists in almost all groups, including students and teachers in the schools, among the tranients, and among the various groups of the unemployed.[32] Despite all the discussion the extent of communist membership was probably exaggerated during the early stages of the depression. Just as President Hoover and General MacArthur had misjudged communist strength within the Bonus Army, other studies showed that the percentage of communists among college students and the transients was rather small.[33]

Texans were indeed afraid of the "red menace," undoubt-

[28] William Ebenstein, *Today's Isms* (4th ed.: Englewood Cliffs, New Jersey: Prentice-Hall, Inc., 1964), 114-115.

[29] FDRL, September 27, 1932, Box 724; "Public Opinion," Amarillo *Sunday Globe-News,* March 29, 1931.

[30] Austin *Statesman,* November 12, 1932; *Weekly Dispatch,* January 16, 1932.

[31] Galveston *Daily News,* August 31, 1931; Haskell *Free Press,* August 20, 1931; Hebbronville *News,* June 18, 1930.

[32] President's Committee, *Recent Social Trends,* 430; Allen, *Since Yesterday,* 87; Davis, *The Lost Generation,* 39; Minehan, *Boy and Girl Tramps of America,* 163-164; Hallgren, *Seeds of Revolt,* 47.

[33] Warren, *Hoover and the Depression,* 235-236; Davis, *The Lost Generation,* 39; Minehan, *Boy and Girl Tramps of America,* 163-164.

edly due to the danger of private property being abolished. To some, however, such as the fundamentalist minister J. Frank Norris, communism was the "anti-Christ" that heralded the end of the world. Texans were also opposed to the Russian brand of communism because it was not in keeping with traditional democratic American values.[34] The extent of communism in Texas was small. Although there were occasional communist demonstrations in Austin, Houston, or Dallas, they were usually small and did not give any indication of a broad, well-organized movement.[35] Not many Texans were convinced that a soviet America was inevitable; however, if anything could stop it, it would have to be done soon.[36]

Socialism was the most popular alternative among those who were critical of capitalism. It offered the hope of government regulation without the destruction of private property or the strict regimentation of society offered by the other alternatives.[37] The Galveston *Daily News* believed that the socialist philosophy of Norman Thomas was one of hope instead of despair, and the Austin *Statesman* admitted that socialistic ideas did not seem nearly as radical as they once did. People were much more willing to admit to being socialists than they were of being communists or fascists. Roosevelt was informed that most of the dock workers in Galveston were socialists; many times when an individual offered a plan to a public official for ending the depression he might comment that it sounded socialistic. This was

[34]"Government Then and Now," *West Texas Today*, XIII (June, 1932), 8; Tatum, "Conquest or Failure," 245; M. C. Gonzales, "Beware of Communism," *LuLac News*, II (March, 1933), 1.

[35]Uvalde *Leader-News*, February 13, 1931; *The Texas Weekly*, February 14, 1931; "The Dallas Mob," *The Common Herd*, XVI (June, 1931), 2-6.

[36]FDRL, May 25, 1932, Box 721, September 13, 1932, Box 724; Connally Papers, December 8, 1929, Box 7; "Public Opinion," Amarillo *Daily News*, October 21, 1931; Haskell *Free Press*, October 23, 1930.

[37]Letter, June 12, 1933, Rayburn Papers; FDRL, February 3, 1933, Box 734, October 8, 1932, Box 730.

usually done without apology, however, although the admission was somewhat self-conscious.[38] A Snyder resident, believing that the Farm Board was an example of "the devil's own socialism," told Connally, "Now I wouldn't object to experimenting with Socialism, but when we do I want it to be the real article, and not the Devil's own."[39] Perhaps another of Roosevelt's correspondents best summed up the Texan's philosophy or his lack of one:

> I think sometimes I am unwittingly a bit of a socialist, and if a little socialism might help us at times, then I am for it. I am sure many people feel about it as I do, though they do not like to admit it openly. But when their ox is gored even the pronounced laissez faire type turn to the government for help and regulation. I am not radical and I do not want radical legislation; progress must be made slowly. But if the old ideas have failed, I am, like you, willing to experiment.[40]

The popularity of socialism in Texas was clearly demonstrated by the widespread demand for government ownership of essential industries. The business most in need of government control, according to many Texans, was banking. Banks had been responsible for the stock market crash, the restriction of credit, and the lack of circulating currency. Since the bankers were irresponsible men who had little concern for the average citizen, the federal government should take over the banks and operate them as one integrated system that would give fair and impartial service to everyone.[41] Some Texans were also concerned about the high rates charged by power and utility companies. Roosevelt was informed that the federal government had the responsibility to prohibit these outrages by confiscating and operating the utility com-

---

[38] Galveston *Daily News*, December 6, 1929; Austin *Statesman*, March 28, 1931; FDRL, October 31, 1932, Box 725, September 14, 1932, Box 729.

[39] Connally Papers, March 30, 1931, Box 15.

[40] FDRL, December 3, 1932, Box 733.

[41] *Ibid.*, June 22, 1932, Box 721, February 3, 1933, Box 735, November 27, 1932, Box 735; Hebbronville *News*, July 22, 1931; J. T. Canales, "Usury, *Lulac News*, I (July, 1932), 5.

panies.[42]   A man and wife from Palacious suggested that the railroads be nationalized under the leadership of William Gibbs McAdoo as they had been during World War I, since the public had received better service and the workers better pay and working conditions than under private ownership.[43]

Some Texans, still harboring a fear of the national government, believed the state of Texas should own and operate the basic industries. These included flour, cotton, and woolen mills, packing houses and canning factories. The editor of *The Common Herd* thought the state should own the banks, the bus lines, a coffin factory, and a cement plant.[44] The obvious goal of the various government ownership plans was to eliminate the exploitation of essential interests possible under private ownership.

For those advocating a change or a major modification of the economic system the means to be used to achieve their goals was of prime importance. Would they be willing to bring change through the traditional electoral process or would they resort to violence? This became a major question in the nation, as well as in Texas, in the early years of the depression. The debate among historians continues today.[45]

The possibility of a revolution in the United States during the depression has been widely discussed. Those who did not think the United States verged on a revolution had some very convincing arguments. The country was drifting rather than rebellious; the depression although bad, had not reached the point where the average citizen was willing

[42]FDRL, August 17, 1931, Box 721; Connally Papers, October 31, 1931, Box 15.

[43]FDRL, September 30, 1932, Box 729.

[44]"Public Opinion," Amarillo *Daily News*, July 7, 1931; "Letters From Readers," Dallas *Morning News*, April 1, 1931; "What We Propose," *The Common Herd*, XV (March, 1930), 13.

[45]For an excellent discussion, see the introduction to Bernard Sternsher, *Hitting Home: The Great Depression in Town and Country* (Chicago: Quadrangle Books, 1970), 3-44.

to rise against the government. The working class was not organized, had no fixed set of principles, and above all, had no national leader about whom it could rally.[46] Authorities have agreed that hunger alone will not drive men to revolt; they must have the conviction of an idea or a system which is better. Despite the growing radicalism, these men argued, America was still tied to the traditional folkways. Capitalism was still the rhetoric of the nation.[47]

On the other hand contemporaries and later historians were a bit more cautious about judging public temperament. People throughout the country were certainly discussing the possibility of "revolution." The use of this word was somewhat significant since it had rarely been used earlier in American history. Revolution was discussed by farmers, the unemployed, transients, and intellectuals.[48] The sincerity of the discussion is difficult to evaluate. It may have been discussed by intellectuals as a novel idea; those suffering from the depression may have been merely "blowing off steam" without any real thought of action. Wherever the truth may lie, it is evident that political leaders were worried about the possibilities of violence. Governors and mayors were very concerned; they were concerned so much, in fact, that the mayor of New York tried to reassure the city. "You're going to have a Mayor with a chin and fight in him. I'll preserve the Metropolis from the Red Army."[49] At the national level, Hoover was greatly concerned that there might

[46] Leuchtenburg, *FDR and the New Deal*, 26; Lens, *Left, Right & Center*, 265; Chase, *A New Deal*, 162.

[47] Hannah, "Urban Reaction," 262-263; Hallgren, *Seeds of Revolt*, 164-165; Stuart Chase, *Out of the Depression--and After* (New York: The John Day Company, 1931), 5; President's Committee, *Recent Social Trends*, 1533; Soule, *The Coming American Revolution*, 6, 69.

[48] Hallgren, *Seeds of Revolt*, 137-138; Seldes, *The Years of the Locust*, 289-290; Minehan, *Boy and Girl Tramps of America*, 170-171; Soule, *The Coming American Revolution*, 6; Cash, *The Mind of the South*, 372.

[49] Rollins, *Roosevelt and Howe*, 365; as quoted in Schlesinger, *The Crisis of the Old Order*, 4.

be violence. In 1931 he opposed the reduction of the armed forces because it would hinder the maintenance of domestic peace and order; when Congress in 1932 voted a ten percent pay decrease for all federal employees, Hoover begged exemptions for military personnel. He was concerned that the resentment caused by the reduction in pay might make the troops unreliable if they were needed to quell rioting and rebellion within the country. Hoover could see the Bonus Army as only the forerunner of violence and possible attempts on the government.[50] Roosevelt was also concerned. In his first inaugural address that gave so much hope to so many people, he stated that anyone who refused to recognize the realities of the moment was a foolish optimist. Afterward, he discussed the possibility of revolt in 1932 by explaining that the temper of the people caused him to act more decisively than he planned. He was told by a friend that if his administration were successful he would be remembered as the nation's greatest president; if he failed he would be the worst. To this he was reported to have replied, "If I fail, I shall be the last one."[51]

Revolution was also a very popular topic of conversation in Texas during the first years of the depression. Public officials were informed that unless something were done quickly, the nation would face a communist revolt.[52] Roosevelt was deluged with letters telling him that unless drastic action was taken and changes made quickly, "within four years, we shall have an armed revolution," or "the United States Government will be overthrown in the next fifteen years."[53]

[50]*Ibid.*, 256; Hoover, *The Great Depression*, 225-226.

[51]Rosenman, *Public Papers of FDR*, II, 11, V, 385; as quoted in Peel and Donnelly, *The 1932 Campaign*, 213.

[52]FDRL, July 5, 1932, Box 729; letter, September 1, 1931, Sterling Papers, Box 176; Connally Papers, September 30, 1931, Box 13; Rayburn Papers, January 5, 1932, June 14, 1932. Letters of this type were so common that the few examples are merely small samples of the opinion.

[53]FDRL, November 26, 1932, Box 734, February 7, 1933, Box 735.

Most of these people were unhappy about such a prospect, but there were some who welcomed it.[54] Some of the latter may have been trying to frighten Roosevelt into action by their descriptions of what might happen. One man informed him that unless something were done he would "live to see a condition here compared to which the French Revolution will have been as a Sunday School picnic."[55] A few newspapers agreed with these sentiments,[56] but the most prominent figure fearing revolution was former Governor Jim Ferguson who was convinced that only a spark was needed to start trouble. It might come at any moment, he believed, but the people still had a chance to avert it by using the ballot in 1932 to elect a Democrat who was more concerned with the plight of the people than with the wealthy.[57] Congressman O. H. Cross of Waco was also quite outspoken about his fear of violent revolution.[58]

In the early days of the depression, much of the state's press was convinced that the nation did not face revolution. They thought our system, traditions, and sense of fair play for all were too strong to be overcome by a small group of malcontents.[59] As the crisis worsened, however, many newspapers printed canned editorials praising the responsible manner in which Americans had acted during the depression, revealing perhaps an unspoken fear that violence might not be far from the minds of the poor and unemployed.[60] Organi-

[54]*Ibid.*, April 21, 1932, Box 719, January 15, 1933, Box 736.

[55]*Ibid.*, January 17, 1933, Box 731.

[56]Bonham *Daily Favorite*, January 13, 1933; Hebbronville *News*, June 3, 1931.

[57]*Ferguson Forum*, May 21, 1931.

[58]*Waco Farm and Labor Journal*, July 15, 1932.

[59]Amarillo *Daily News*, May 11, 1932; El Paso *Times*, December 2, 1931; Galveston *Daily News*, July 22, 1930, December 9, 1931; Huntsville *Item*, February 5, 1931.

[60]Amarillo *Daily News*, February 22, 1932; Austin *Statesman*, February 23, 1932; Canadian *Record*, July 14, 1932; Haskell *Free Press*, January 26, 1933.

zed labor in Texas comprised another group that continued to
deny the imminence of revolt, but it did warn business not to
expect this docile attitude to continue unless industry did
something to improve conditions.[61]

Just how widespread the feeling of rebellion was is difficult to assess. Occasionally demonstrations of the unemployed occurred, as in Houston in 1930 which displayed pic-
tures of Lenin and were influenced by communist organizers.
Other examples of violence can be found. For example, in
January 1930 a food riot occurred in Temple and on New Year's
Eve night of 1931 a series of cotton gin fires occurred in
Temple and several neighboring communities. These were really
only random acts of violence and had no overtones of radicalism although there was some fear that they might.[62] Although the people were hard-pressed to meet their obligations,
a sampling of the correspondence of one mercantile firm shows
that the overwhelming majority agreed with the man who said,
"I am broke like lots of others but if you and the others I
owe will give me time to make it I will pay ever [sic] penny
I owe."[63] Yet a resentment did develop among the poor because
of the way they believed they were being exploited by the
rich. The class consciousness is subtle, but it is there.
Some believed that the "country is being run in the interests
of big Banks, Insurance Companies, and Railroads," and others
stated that "the greedy, grafting and selfish rich are slow-
ly and surely bringing these United States to a very serious
and dangerous state of affairs." [64] The editor of the Hebbronville *News* expressed it rather succinctly. "The man of

[61]Dallas *Craftsman*, September 9, 1932; *Weekly Dispatch*, June 11, 1932.

[62]Austin *Statesman*, March 6, 1930; Galveston *Daily News*, March 7,
1930; Montgomery, "Depression in Houston," 28-30; Ozment, "Temple and Depression," 14, 75.

[63]Baker Mercantile Company, April 11, 1932, Customer's Letters,
1931-33.

[64]FDRL, September 12, 1932, Box 730, September 3, 1931, Box 721.

wealth, the big combines and monster corporations, the far-flung finance companies have fattened, grown opulent, and will be vulnerable targets for the extremist when the dam of conservatism breaks."[65]   One of the best examples of the class consciousness and growing hatred for the rich was a letter written to Governor Sterling by a poorly schooled war veteran:

> I do not intend to take my family and tramp up and down the roads and go cold and hungry this winter like I did last winter. We have picked cotton and slept on the cotton pile or anyplace we could until the cotton is gone and all we made is a few clothes about fifteen dollars worth and a little something to eat while we was working and now we are broke. I have been crippled up twice working for the incorporation and as I have stated if you and the House of Representatives would pay us boys for our service in 1918 we could live through this winter, but I do not intend to go cold and hungry this winter. If I have to take a gun and start out I can be killed but I can get about as many of them as they get of me. The Capitalists and the big businessmen hollowing be *patriotic* to your country during the world war and we was, but the government heads and the capitalists is not *patriotic* to us now. The government will not pay us for what we done and the capitalists will not give us work that we may supply ourselves and our families with the necessities of life.
> You may send your *Rangers* down if you like but I can burn as much powder as any one man, because life is nothing to me as it is no way. I want to see if you can get any action on payment of us boys salary of 1918 and it may save me from being killed or some other man for I do not intend to go hungry and cold as I did last winter.[66]

Texans may not have been on the verge of revolution by the beginning of 1933, but the discontent, resentment, and restlessness were growing. Had a strong leader of national reputation arisen with little concern for the democratic processes, many Texans would have been willing to join him in a violent revolution if it offered hope for betterment of their condition.

The Texan of the thirties was, to a degree, both a radical and a conservative. He was not doctrinaire like the de-

[65] Hebbronville *News*, June 17, 1931.

[66] Sterling Papers, October 17, 1931, Box 180.

vout communist; instead his radicalism was extremely pragmatic. The Texan was willing to abandon the current conservatism if there were an alternative that offered hope.
He was more of an agrarian radical than anything else. He
was so determined to maintain his way of life that he was
susceptible to many kinds of dogmas. He might just as easily have followed a communist, a fascist, or a socialist.
He wanted only to find a solution to his economic troubles.
Because he was an agrarian, and because he was trying to protect what he had and to return to a better life, the Texan
was conservative, or in some cases, reactionary. Therefore,
about the only conclusion possible is that the Texan was an
agrarian radical.

CHAPTER XII

THE BARD IN THE DEPRESSION: TEXAS STYLE

Texans reacted to the depression in many ways and through various media. One of the unknown--or at least overlooked--means by which people expressed their opinions was through verse. Although the United States has never been a haven for poets, there were a surprising number of persons in earlier days who read poetry and who tried their own hands at composing rhymes. No one should be surprised, therefore, to find that many Texans expressed their opinions to newspapers and public officials in this fashion.

Texas poets were a mixed group. Most of them were not professionals; they were concerned people trying to express their frustrations through traditional verse form. Thus, the amateur poetry often had a quality about it that can truly be called "folk expression." Many of the poems were not intended for publication; they were designed to influence the actions of public officials. Even among the published poems there is a quality of innocence and naivete that re-flects the simplistic view that Americans often take toward serious problems. In some newspapers and magazines the poems were published to influence public opinion. Very few of these poems are of any literary value, but they do have a message for anyone who will accept it: the discontent of the "common folk" could not be ignored indefinitely. By focusing on the verse of Texas, one can see some of what people were thinking and the type of solutions they were proposing. A perusal of such literature is often humorous or pathetic, but it also quite revealing of society.

Texans reacted to the stock market in many ways. (See Chapter II). Perhaps "Cyclone" Davis, an old Populist and a perennial Texas politician, expressed one point of view through poetry. Throughout his life Davis was a spokesman for the "plain people," but he was never one of them himself. Yet, his poetry probably said what many people wanted to say. As he reached old age his unhappiness with society was apparent when he said, "I am just one victim of malevolent minions and myrmidons of Mammon who have ruined millions of plain people."[1] Using his flowery language more effectively in verse form, Davis probably expressed the feelings of many people:

> Rank injustice and cruel outrage
> Meet our life at every stage.
> Government hears our complaint of wrong,
> As a stale demand, a hackneyed song.
> Discontent and dire despair
> Are seen and heard from everywhere.
> Millions of people drudge life thru
> To give more millions to a special few.
> When truth lies down forever crushed,
> And freedom's voice in fear is hushed,
> And the toiling man is made a slave,
> To add to the wealth ot a corporate knave.
> When riot rages throughout our land
> And crime is rampant on every hand;
> When moral codes and moral creed
> Shall have given way to lust and greed,
> I see our land in sad dismay
> While "wealth augments and men decay."[2]

When the stock market crash signaled the beginning of the depression Davis reflected the agrarian distrust of the "interests." His attack on Wall Street was one of the most vituperative and plainspoken of the period. While others hedged in their criticism he called a spade a spade:

> The Wall Street bandits
> In their lust
> Have trampled the people
> Into the dust.
>
> They have robbed millions
> Of all their feed
> In order to gorge
> Their sordid greed.
>
> They have robbed the populace
> Of their home
> And put them out
> On the earth to roam.

[1] Davis, *Memoir*, 44.

[2] *Ibid.*, 45.

217

They have gathered wealth
In great big stacks
And piled up debts
On the peoples backs.

In this grand style
They live at ease
They fear no law
And do as they please.

And the man who robs a country bank
He only robs by retail
These bandits who in millions rank
Rob by slaughter wholesale.

If hailed into court
By the powers that be
Most of our courts
Just set them free.[3]

Davis's view may have been cynical, but he was not the
only one who questioned how a depression could occur during
the "prosperous" twenties. Perhaps some of the "interests"
were controlling events for their own benefit, as Davis suggested. Taking a somewhat different approach, a magazine
from the lower Rio Grande Valley asked how such a depression
could exist. In publishing such a poem the editor was re-
iterating what he had heard from other people and what was
being stated in newspapers across the state. Numerous people
believed that money was not really scarce but that it was
being withheld from the people who really needed it. According to the following poem money was being spent foolishly:

Abnormal times; my nerves are shot
I'm chuck full of confusion,
The public tells me that it's broke;
There must be some collusion.

I know there's lots o'money here,
I've seen large rolls of "dough,"
But try and get it if you can,
You'll find the pickings slow.

Abnormal times, depressive thoughts,
The banks won't lend you money,
And yet large gobs of it are spent,
At any show that's funny.

At football, baseball, prize fights,
And that silly game of golf,
The spendthrifts find the money,
And quickly slough it off.

[3]*Ibid.*, 98.

And yet we have abnormal times.
Some call it a depression;
Let's keep on hanging crepe Old Top,
Let's make it an obsession.[4]

As the depression deepened and a mood of pessimism settled over the country, Hoover attempted to rally public confidence. To bolster public morale and to instill confidence, he constantly repeated his belief that the nation's economy was basically sound. Such optimism and hope were expressed in the theme song of the National Association of Credit Men meeting at its convention in Dallas shortly after the stock market crash. Obviously this poem did not originate with the "plain folks" nor was it an example of "folk expression." It was, in truth, an attempt by a middle class group to convince the general public (and itself, no doubt) that there was no serious depression and that a return of confidence would restore prosperity:

Let's sing-a song of hap-pi-ness
Shout till the raf-ters ring
Sing-a song of pros-per-ity
Let every loyal mem-ber sing

Smile--believe that times are good
And we'll make bad days--good days
Happiness is all that mat-ters
So keep it in your hearts al-ways

Here's a toast--to the world
Getting better and better in every way
Here's a Thanks--to our God
For giving us happiness every day
For our homes--our work
And all the good things that we have in store
May we prosper as ever before

We're the men of in-dus-try
Thir-ty thousand strong
We can build our pros-per-ity
By cheering up when things go wrong
Pas-sing clouds conceal the sun
But storms bring ran-bow hues
Show'rs are blessings good for everyone
So "Quit a-singing 'bout the blues."[5]

[4] "About Depressions and Obsessions," *Monty's Monthly*, XIV (November, 1932), 14.

[5] "Quit Singing the Blues," *Dallas*, IX (June, 1930) 12.

Opposing such Pollyanna statements were other publications, including the political newspaper of former Governor Ferguson that asked if the public was being deluded by the talk of prosperity and continued encouragement of confidence. Perhaps the situation was more serious than the Credit Men would admit. According to Ferguson, "This is not the time for handing out fine sounding phrases to the hungry."[6] By printing the following contributed poem, Ferguson was also warning the "interests" that the poor would not always be content with "fine sounding phrases:"

> The toad beneath the harrow knows
> Exactly where each sharp point goes;
> The butterfly beside the road
> Preached contentment to the toad.[7]

Ferguson's newspaper may have been politically motivated since Mrs. "Ma" Ferguson was again a candidate for governor. Even so, there were other anguished cries of discontent, perhaps best expressed by a young girl in her poem to Roosevelt on the eve of the 1932 election. Her description of Texas is very poignant and revealing of conditions there.

> The times are so hard
> You can't even buy lard,
> There's not enough money
> And we can't buy honey.
> It was 1931 and 1932
> And I do hope it will soon be through,
> We are all very sad
> Why not cheer up and be glad.
>
> The old men sit and gripe
> When they should be cheery and bright,
> The tramps walk the steet
> Asking for something to eat,
> And seeking places to sleep.
> We often hear
> That better times are near,
> So let's do our part
> And give Roosevelt a start
> And I do hope you are president.[8]

[6] *Ferguson Forum*, June 4, 1931.

[7] *Ibid.*

[8] FDRL, Box 732.

As conditions continued to worsen efforts were made to place the blame for the depression--to find a suitable scape-goat or a conspirator. Texans, and the average person every-where, most often blamed Hoover and the Republican Party for their problems. A popular form of protest was to rewrite the Twenty-Third Psalm to reflect changing conditions and atti-tudes.

> Depression is my shepherd; I am in want.
> He maketh me to lie down on park benches; He leadeth
>   me beside the still factories.
> He restoreth the bread lines; He leadeth me in the
>   paths of destruction for his Party's sake.
> Yea, though I walk through the Valley of Unemployment,
>   I fear every evil; for thous are with me; the Poli-
>   ticians and Profiteers they frighten me.
> Thou preparest a reduction in mine salary before me in
>   the presence of mine creditors; Thou anointest mine
>   income with taxes; my expenses runneth over mine
>   income.
> Surely unemployment and poverty will follow me all the
>   days of the Republican administration; and I shall
>   dwell in a mortgaged house forever.[9]

Many variations of "The 1932 Psalms" circulated throughout the country blaming both Hoover and the Republican Party.[10] Probably the rewriting of scripture to reflect current con-ditions had more of an impact with fundamentally religious Texans than would have been true in other parts of the coun-try.

Among the most bitter poems were those that attacked Hoover personally. This is not unusual since it is always easier to personalize evil than to blame some vague entity such as the Republican Party. Texans also remembered that a majority of them had deserted the traditional Democratic Party in 1928 partially to vote for Hoover, but particularly to vote against the wet-Catholic Alfred E. Smith. Now many of them felt they had been betrayed by the supposedly well-meaning Hoover. One such attack on Hoover was directed at

[9] Weatherford *Democrat*, June 10, 1932.

[10] In some cases the word "Hoover" or "Republican Party" was substitu-ted for the word "Depression" as in the previous citation. See for ex-ample: Haskell *Free Press*, September 1, 1932.

his unwillingness to give direct federal relief to the unfortunate, a particularly disconcerting action for those who remembered Hoover's outstanding service in providing relief for the destitute in war-torn Europe just ten years earlier. At that time the term "Hooverizing" was complimentary; one of the depression poets made it a term of opprobrium. In the days of the first World War to "Hooverize" had been patriotic; in the depression people were forced to "Hooverize" in the poet's definition of the word.

> Our country first was civilized,
>   And next to that was organized
> And then our nation Christianized
>   But now, oh boy, she Hooverized.
>
> George Washington was idolized
>   Abe Lincoln greatly eulogized
> And Woodrow Wilson highly prized
>   And now, just think, we're Hooverized.
>
> In Abraham's day they circumcised,
>   In Moses' day they sacrificed,
> In John's career they were all baptised,
>   But in Modern times were are Hooverized.
>
> Our chief sails high, rides most to the skies
>   And clothes his folks like butterflies
> But fails to hear the moans and sighs
>   Of us poor souls who Hooverize.
>
> Some men preach rank atheism
>   And others universalism
> And some poor souls preach socialism
>   While a few blame fools preach Hooverism.
>
> Now I'm quite sure you'll criticise
>   And with my rhyme not sympathize
> And maybe me you'll stigmatize,
>   But unless I'm fooled, you'll Hooverize.[11]

Some of the other amateur poets believed Hoover was completely indifferent; his motives may have been even worse. To the following poet he probably put political ambitions higher than public service.

> You cannot fool, said Honest Abe
> All of them all the time
> And while musing that great man's sayings
> I have written this humble rhyme.

[11] *Texas Spur*, August 14, 1931.

> For as one of the fooled and forgotten
> Who has finally seen the light
> I am convinced that Hoover had rather
> Be President than right.[12]

As the blame for Hoover became almost universal the answer to many people was to remove him from office through the electoral process. One poet, with tongue-in-cheek, wondered how Hoover had been elected in the first place since few of his supporters could be found as the 1932 election approached. His poem certainly reflected poor conditions within Texas and revealed the deep-seated religious beliefs of the people. He seems to be saying that God is concerned about average people and that He will help them if they will only help themselves.

> Hooverites are hard to be found!
> Since they brought this depression 'round!
> If to vote again I would vote for Democratic Day;
> I would vote for any one to keep this Hoover death away!
>
> Laborers, farmers and every kind of men are about to fall,
> Trying to eat and bed out of a Hooverite stall!
> If to do this over again, believe me, we'd do better with
>   whiskey or gin,
> Than to live a starving depression life and bring about so
>   much sin!
>
> Persons on highways, streets, and everywhere,
> Trying in every way to get one more fare.
> This is awful to think about--so many chidren with a scant
>   meal;
> For this depression has caused many good men to steal.
>
> If to live a godly life, you must live it true,
> Just to live for one another, and we all for you.
> If religion is what I think it is, it is hard to be found,
> But I am watching and praying that some day it'll come around.
>
> God never intended for us to oppress or swindle.
> Nor did He intend for us to wear a yoke like old Brindle.
> Now when you have another vote, place it on the right side,
> Just to see if we Democrats can not change the tide![13]

In line with this sentiment was a growing consensus that Hoover must be removed from office. Since he had probably been responsible for the depression in the first place, his

---

[12]FDRL, Box 727.

[13]*Texas Spur*, February 13, 1931.

223

actions to relieve conditions had been a total failure. Thus, a savior had to be found.

> There's a long, long rest awaiting for Herbert Hoover,
>   we know,
> He had made an awful mess of things as manager of the show.
> For the past three years he's straddled all of the fences
>   in the land--and now we crave the frankness of Roosevelt--
>   he's the man.[14]

Not everyone was willing to castigate Hoover completely. One poet believed the people had made a mistake in voting for a Republican, but thought that they had now learned their lesson. He said a person should not be blamed for voting for Hoover the first time because he may have been misled. It was the individual's responsibility, however, to vote "right" the next time. He implied that if the voter made the same mistake again he might not get another chance.

> Don't blame the Hooverite, he did not know what to do;
> His friend was voting for Hoover so he says I will vote too.
> With all his wealth and friends he is stranded in the sand;
> I doubt if he gets another vote if he takes a Hoover stand.
>
> I met a friend that used to dress up neat,
> But he was poorly clad, and you could see the 'Hoover seat'.
> I saw a little turtle crawling over land;
> He seemed to be trying to dodge the Hoover band;
>
> Birds and animals are getting awfully shy,
> There is no need for me to tell the reason why;
> Hooverite and Democrat are all just alike,
> On highways everywhere hitting the hike.
>
> Don't blame Hoover, he may get it straight
> But his work may be so slow, it may be too late
> Don't travel over land and wander all around;
> For when the wind blows it will turn the mill on your
>   own home ground.
>
> You may have to fight and fight mighty hard,
> If you ever get a hand to have the winning card.
> Now I am going to leave you, and leave you all alone,
> For I think the next time you have a vote you will cast
>   in in the interest of your home.[15]

As the years passed it became more apparent that Roosevelt would be the Democratic choice in 1932. After his nomination by the Democratic Convention comparisons were often

[14] FDRL, Box 718.

[15] *Texas Spur*, February 13, 1931.

made between Hoover and Roosevelt. Some of them indicated
that the people really had little choice, since Roosevelt
obviously had the answer to the problem. The following poet
indicated that there was really no comparison between the
two men. Hoover represented all the troubles of the previous
four years while Roosevelt symbolized progress and reform
for the future.

NO MORE

H oover and
  unger

with

C urtis and
  confusion

WE WANT

R oosevelt and
  efreshment

with

G arner and
  roceries [16]

Some of the others were even more vicious against Hoover
and laudatory of Roosevelt. Hoover was made the absolute
villain who was responsible for every bad thing of the past
four years. Roosevelt, on the other hand, was the knight on
the white horse come to rescue the people from their own
foolishness in electing a Republican to national office.

R oosevelt
  epeal
  eligious freedom
  eal Americanism

H oover
  ard times
  unger
  itch hiking
  uman bug
  11 [17]

Some, while making comparisons of the two men, also
suggested certain reforms that would help end the depres-

[16] FDRL, Box 728.

[17] *Ibid.*, Box 736.

sion. One poet tried to convince Roosevelt of the necessity
of prohibition repeal during the course of the campaign. Although he viewed the problem too simply and thought that repeal would solve all economic problems, he does represent a
large segment of public opinion. Since Texas was fundamental in religion and maintained many areas of local prohibition after the repeal of the Eighteenth Amendment, the poet
may not be representative of Texas thought on this issue.

> All minds are set on something,
> Wondering will 'twill come;
> And while we watch, we ponder
> Whence comes all the bootleg rum;
> But while our taxes, taxes
> Mount to a fearful sum,
> We wait in vain for that which would bring
> John Barleycorn back home.
>
> If Johnny came marching home again,
> Hurrah, hurrah!
> We'd give him a hearty welcome then,
> Hurrah, hurrah!
> The men would cheer, the boys would shout,
> The ladies they would all turn out,
> And we'd all feel gay
> If Johnny came marching home.
>
> We watch with keenest interest
> Each unofficial poll,
> As Al Capone's taxes
> Right into our treasury roll;
> While ever grow our army
> Of unemployed on dole,
> And more taxed things that somehow don't bring
> Our budget from the hole.
>
> The liberty bell would peal with joy,
> Hurrah, hurrah!
> To welcome home our long lost boy,
> Hurrah! hurrah!
> And all the lads and lassies say,
> With confetti they would strew the way,
> And we'd all feel gay
> If Johnny came marching home.
>
> We wait upon dear Congress,
> On them all eyes are set;
> But taxes and more taxes
> Are all that we seem to get;
> But we still have the ballot,
> And take it as a bet
> That yet, somehow--it won't be long now--
> Dear Congress will be "wet".

Oh, yet we'll have a Jubilee,
Hurrah! hurrah!
We'll give old Johnny three times three.
Hurrah! hurrah!
The ivy wreath is ready now
To place upon his martyred brow;
And we'll all feel gay
When Johnny comes marching home.[18]

After the election another Texan was convinced that Roosevelt had won because of the public dissatisfaction with prohibition. Despite his tortured style, the poet gets his message across.

Roosevelt in the big, white, the donkey at the barn.
Hoover on the elephant, ariding away in scorn.

Roosevelt in New York, a Real American born
Who but Hoover sir, says he's from down where da maka da corn.

One was dry the other was wet, with a full house you can bet
that Roosevelt will collect the debt.

A little booze, made a old beck a fighting foal, she broke the
elephant's neck in '32 by having a little white mule.

Roosevelt and the dripping mule with booze on every shoe, made
the Republicans mightly blue, the Fall of 32, that booze
the repub. used in '28 was out of date and it make Hoover
lose his great swine state.

It will be fine for the grape vines
When Roosevelt gives us beer and wine and not dine
with a shine, like Hoover did in '29.[19]

As the discontent continued to mount prior to the election, Roosevelt came to represent salvation for many of the unhappy and "forgotten" people. Perhaps to convince him of their support, he was deluged with letters of praise. One poet tried to use black dialect to show Roosevelt that his election was assured.

When de war quit, in nineteen eighteen,
    Our country was prosperous, serene,
Da Republican grabbed it,
    And since they Crabbed it,
She's as shakey as a Hula Queen.

Republicans have had their chance,
    And failed at the art of finance,
They've failed to hit,

[18]*Ibid.*, Box 724.

[19]*Ibid.*, Box 738.

    And will have to admit,
  That wid us, they've tore their pants.

  If we had what we haven't got,
      We certainly would have a lot,
  The Republican stroke,
      Has got us broke,
  So let us try to change the plot.

  Our present prosperity prevenshion
      Is causin lots of discontenshion,
  If the Democratic plan,
      Will help de po' man,
  It sho will be a great invenshion.

  Guvana Roosevelt is our best bet,
      We can't consida de Murray set;[20]
  We can't leave his pards,
      His national guards,
  And Alfred Smith is all wet.

  Guvana Roosevelt, de New Yorker,
      If he's appointed to be de stork-er,
  He'll deliver de child,
      In Democratic style,
  Because de Guvana'a a Corker.[21]

Other letters and poems were pleas for salvation from conditions that the public could not control.

  O Roosevelt! O Roosevelt!
  Canst thou deliver me
  From all the things on this old earth
  By Hoover caused to be.[22]

Perhaps Roosevelt did represent an American Moses to many people as he did to one lady from Laredo. The scriptural reference once again reflects the religiously-oriented thought of many Texans. This lady undoubtedly believed that an American Moses was needed to end such terrible conditions.

  Oh Roosevelt, ar thou a Moses,
  To lead this poor nation
  Whose sad purse deflation
  Has caused much vexation,
  And hot altercation,

---

[20] This refers to Governor "Alfalfa" Bill Murray of Oklahoma who had been mentioned as a possible presidential candidate in 1932. His use of National Guard troops in Oklahoma had weakened his support among many Texans.

[21] FDRL, Box 720.

[22] *Ibid.*, Box 724.

Not to mention starvation?
Oh Roosevelt, art thou this Moses?

I say, art thou the Moses
On whose reputation
We're promised salvation,
And tax regulation?
Is job consideration
Thine own specialization?
Thou art indeed this Moses!

Hail, Democrat Moses!
Accept our ovation;
Excuse it's duration,
And our agitation,
And attempted versification.
Your administration
I hail, Democrat Moses![23]

Just how accurately the letter-writer of the depression reflects the sentiments of the general public is impossible to determine. Nevertheless, more and more people were resorting to the pen to express their unhappiness. These actions also show how serious the depression was and how people were reacting to it. Although there are few studies with which to compare it, it is probably accurate to conclude that Texas poets expressed views similar to those across the nation.

[23] *Ibid.*, Box 735.

CHAPTER XIII

CONCLUSIONS

The Great Depression was one of the major events of the twentieth century; it had such a traumatic effect that the nation was permanently changed. The privations of the period affected the health of a whole generation, but the patterns of American thought were shaped, modified, and, in some respects, permanently transformed. This change is very apparent in Texas.

Texans, basically agrarian in background, had accepted laissez faire capitalism that resulted in the prosperity of the 1920s. During the boom years business and industrial giants had become the leaders of almost every phase of American life. The great respect and veneration for the captains of industry was shaken and in some cases shattered by the greatest stock market crash of all times in October 1929. From this time forward the nation continued to fall into a major depression despite the optimistic statements issued by business and political leaders in an attempt to maintain confidence. At first, Texans were unable to believe that the stock market could be such an important factor in the economy, but as it continued to crumble and business activity refused to revive, they were forced to recognize its pervasive influence on the American economy.

Texas reaction to the depression falls into a fairly discernible pattern. Since the Texan simply could not believe that a depression could occur, he continued for several months to deny the realities of the situation. He agreed with and joined in President Hoover's confidence-building crusade. Generally speaking the press of the state refused to acknowledge the existence of a depression until about a year after the market crash. There were newspapers, particularly those devoted to the interests of farmers and organized labor, that complained about hard times and warned of a general business depression; they were joined by a relatively small group of individuals. Generally, however, the people of the state seemed to think that if they ignored the bad conditions and did not heed the economic warning signs, boom days would continue. By the beginning of 1931 conditions were so bad that only the most blind optimist refused to recognize the serious economic crisis.

After the people of the state finally acknowledged depression, the press tried to convince the public that this was only a temporary crisis; they used statements of national figures, statistics, and favorable local events to prove their contentions. They tried to foresee the end of the depression by grasping at almost any indication of better business conditions. Much of the press and public alike decided to take a rather philosophical approach; since individuals could do little to end the depression, they should bear up under it with as little complaint as possible. In fact, they were able to find many beneficial effects resulting from the crisis.

Since the Texan was steeped in the agrarian myth there had to be an outside cause for the trouble; thus, a search for a villain (or conspirator in the populist tradition) began. President Hoover and the Republican Party were the most severely criticized, but businessmen of all types, especially bankers, were also blamed. Other causes discovered by Texans included the protective tariff, overproduction and underconsumption, the unequal distirbution of wealth, high taxes, war debts, and hoarding. To the religous fundamentalist the depression was only the punishment by God for past sins. Most Texans were never really able to look at the depression dispassionately; since they believed that agrarian society had been virtually perfect, the depression that destroyed it was the result of a sinister outside force.

During the depression Texans were forced to reevaluate and readjust some of their older concepts. The most important of these was the role of government. A depression of such proportions soon caused the collapse of private relief agencies and the bankruptcy of the local units of government. For a period of months, during which the unemployed and the destitute suffered greatly, a debate raged concerning the degree to which the federal government should intervene in the economic life of the nation. Although many Texans continued to cling to the shibboleth of states' rights, the Texans who believed in federal action prevailed. After the conclusion of this debate federal aid was more readily accepted; it was not until the advent of the New Deal, however, that massive federal intervention began.

Since much of Texas was rural, agriculture was one of the most seriously affected segments of the economy. The farmer, much more quickly than the other groups, overcame whatever aversion he may have had to government action. Although the farmer was anxious to get federal help, the most important governmental action in the early years of the depression was on the state level. Bowing to public pressure in 1931 the state legislature, in special session, passed a cotton acreage reduction law only to have it ruled unconstitutional by state courts.

Some Texans during this period became disillusioned with the American economic system. Many of them were concerned that America might become a communist, socialist, or fascist nation, while others would have been happy to see such a change. Prior to 1933, the possibility of a revolution in the United States and in Texas did exist although it was slight. As the depression worsened with little improvement in sight, disillusionment was widespread in Texas. Most Texans were simply bewildered by events which they could neither understand nor control. Had there arisen a popular national leader without respect for the democratic process, it is certainly possible that a minority of Americans might have been willing to attempt a violent overthrow of the government. Had this happened, a number of Texans probably would have constituted a contingent of the revolutionary force. Fortunately for the United States and the American political and economic systems, the election of 1932 brought a man to national leadership who had a healthy respect for the American system. Roosevelt had the saving grace, however, of being willing to experiment with the system to eliminate its weaknesses and to spread its benefits among all the citizens.

The major characteristic of the Texan that appeared during this period of crisis was his agrarian mentality. The Texas mind had been molded by the frontier experience, the agrarian myth, the conspiracy theory of history, and the fundamentalist mind. All of these conditioning forces can be seen at work during the depression. The attitudes of self-reliance and rugged individualism were challenged by the depression; the perfect society as envisioned in the agrarian myth was shattered. To the Texan who viewed the world in very simple terms, it was the work of a conspirator. In coping with the situation he overcame his aversion to governmental action, reverting to neo-populist ideas about the value of the government role. Some Texans became radicals, but only in the agrarian sense; they were not doctrinaire, only pragmatic.

The outstanding characteristic of the Texan mind during the depression was his pragmatic mind that made him willing to use whatever means necessary to alleviate the crisis. If this mean abandoning the business leadership of the twenties and returning more to the nineteenth century agrarian philosophy, he was willing to do so. If it required the reversal of older concepts about welfare and relief or about the value of the capitalist system, he was willing to change his position. Fortunately for the American system, Texans, and the nation as whole, did not succumb to ideologies and pressures that might have destroyed the good features of a system developed by trial and error for over a century.

BIBLIOGRAPHY

Manuscript Sources

Department of Agriculture, Secretary's Correspondence, Record Group 16, National Archives, Washington, D.C.

Baker Mercantile Company Papers, Southwest Collection, Texas Tech University, Lubbock, Texas.

Clay Stone Briggs Papers, University of Texas Archives, Austin, Texas.

Department of Commerce, Secretary's Correspondence, Record Group 40, National Archives, Washington, D.C.

Tom Connally Papers, Library of Congress, Manuscript Division, Washington, D.C.

Democratic National Committee Correspondence, 1928-1933, Franklin D. Roosevelt Library, Hyde Park, New York.

Herbert Hoover Presidential Library, Presidential Papers, West Branch, Iowa.

Huey Long Papers, Department of Archives and Manuscripts, Louisiana State University, Baton Rouge, Louisiana.

J. Frank Norris Papers in possession of Rev. E. Ray Tatum, University Baptist Church, Lubbock, Texas.

Oral history interviews by students at Panola College under the supervision of Professor Bill O'Neal, originals in Whisenhunt files.

Sam Rayburn Papers, Correspondence, 1932, Sam Rayburn Library, Bonham, Texas.

Morris Sheppard Papers, University of Texas Archives, Austin, Texas.

Department of State, Decimal File, 1910-1929; Records Relating to Internal Affairs of Mexico, 1910-1929; Record Group 59, National Archives, Washington, D.C.

Ross S. Sterling Files as Governor of Texas, Correspondence, Texas State Archives, Austin, Texas.

Texas Labor Archives, minute books of selected labor unions from Texas, The University of Texas at Arlington, Arlington, Texas.

Department of the Treasury, Secretary's Correspondence, Individual Case File, 1929-1933, Record Group 56, National Archives, Washington, D.C.

Government Publications

Hayes, E. P. *Activities of the President's Emergency Committee for Employment*. Privately printed for private circulation, 1936.

President's Research Committee on Social Trends. *Recent Social Trends in the United States*. New York: McGraw-Hill Book Company, Inc., 1933.

State of Texas. Bureau of Labor Statistics. *Report of Committee on Resolutions of the Joint Conference of the Legislative and Governor's Committees for Unemployment Relief*. Austin: Von Boeckmann-Jones Co., 1931.

State of Texas. *House Journal*. 42d Leg., 2d Called Sess., 1931.

State of Texas. *Senate Journal*. 42d Leg., 2d Called Sess., 1931.

State v. *Smith*. 47 *Southwestern Reporter*, 2d Series, 642-645.

U. S. Bureau of the Census. *Fifteenth Census of the United States: 1930. Population*, Vols. I-III.

U. S. Bureau of the Census. *Fifteenth Census of the United States: 1930. United States Summary, Unemploymnet*.

U. S. Congress, Subcommittee of the Committee on Manufactures. *Hearings on Establishment of National Economic Council*. 72d Cong., 1st Sess., 1931.

U. S. *Congressional Record*. Vols. LXXIV, LXXV, LXXVI.

U. S. Department of Labor. *Nineteenth Annual Report of the Chief of the Children's Bureau*, 1931.

U. S. Federal Emergency Relief Administration. *Unemployment Relief Census, October 1933*, 1934.

Memoirs and Documents

Beane, Wilhelmina. *Texas Thirties*. San Antonio: The Naylor Company, 1963.

Connally, Senator Tom as told to Alfred Steinberg. *My Name is Tom Connally*. New York: Thomas Y. Crowell Company, 1954.

Davis, Cyclone. *Memoir*. Sherman, Texas: The Courier Press, 1935.

Hoover, Herbert. *The Great Depression, 1929-1941*. Vol. III: *The Memoirs of Herbert Hoover*. New York: The Macmillan Company, 1952.

Hopkins, Harry L. *Spending to Save*. New York: W. W. Norton & Company, Inc., 1936.

Jones, Jesse H. with Edward Angly. *Fifty Billion Dollars*. New York: The Macmillan Company, 1951.

Joslin, Theodore G. *Hoover Off the Record*. New York: Doubleday, Doran & Company, Inc., 1934.

Kilpatrick, Carroll (ed.). *Roosevelt and Daniels*. Chapel Hill: The University of North Carolina Press, 1952.

Long, Huey. *Share Our Wealth*. Washington, D.C.: n.d.

MacArthur, Douglas. *Reminiscences*. New York: McGraw-Hill Company, 1964.

Maverick, Maury. *A Maverick American*. New York: Covici, Friede, 1937.

Myers, William Starr (ed.). *The State Papers and Other Public Writings of Herbert Hoover*. 2 vols. Garden City, New York: Doubleday, Doran & Company, Inc., 1934.

Perkins, Frances. *The Roosevelt I Knew*. New York: Harper & Row edition, 1964.

Rauch, Basil. *The History of the New Deal, 1933-1938*. New York: Capricorn Books, 1963.

Robinson, Edgar Eugene, and Edwards, Paul Carroll (eds.). *The Memoirs of Ray Lyman Wilbur*. Stanford, California: Stanford University Press, 1960.

Rosenman, Samuel I. (ed.). *The Public Papers and Addresses of Franklin D. Roosevelt*. 5 vols. New York: Random House, 1938.

Wallace, Ernest, and Vigness, David M. (eds.). *Documents of Texas History*. Austin: The Steck Company, 1963.

Waters, W. W. as told to William C. White. *B.E.F.: The Whole Story of the Bonus Army*. New York: The John Day Company, 1933.

Wilbur, Ray Lyman (ed.). *The New Day: Campaign Speeches of Herbert Hoover, 1928*. Stanford, California: Stanford University Press, 1928.

Newspapers

Amarillo *Daily News*. 1929-1933.

Austin Labor Journal. 1930-1932.

Austin *Statesman*. 1929-1933.

Beeville *Bee-Picayune*. 1929-1933.

Bonham *Daily Favorite*. 1929-1933.

Brady *Standard*. 1930-1933.

Cameron *Enterprise*. 1931-1933.

Canadian *Record*. 1929-1933.

Dallas *Craftsman*. 1929-1930, 1932-1933.

Dallas *Morning News*. 1929-1933.

Devil's River News (Sonora). 1929-1933.

Electra *News*. 1930-1933.

El Paso *Times*. 1929-1933.

Ferguson Forum (Austin). 1931-1933.

Fredericksburg *Standard*. 1929-1933.

Galveston *Daily News*. 1929-1933.

George West *Enterprise*. 1929-1931.

Hansford County News (Gruver). 1929-1930.

Haskell *Free Press*. 1929-1933.

Hebbronville *News*. 1929-1932.

Houston Labor Journal. 1929-1930.

Huntsville *Item*. 1929-1933.

Live Oak County Herald (George West). 1932-1933.

McAllen *Monitor*. 1929-1932.

New York *Times*. 1929-1933.

Pecos *Enterprise and Gusher*. 1929-1933.

Port Isabel *Pilot*. 1929-1932.

Roby *Star-Record*. 1930-1933.

San Patricio County News (Sinton). 1931-1933.

Santa Fe (New Mexico) *New Mexican*. 1933.

Seguin *Enterprise*. 1929-1933.

Southern Messenger (San Antonio). 1929-1933.

Sterling City *News-Record*. 1929-1933.

Terry County Herald (Brownfield). 1929-1933.

Texas Jewish Herald Voice (Houston). 1929-1933.

Texas Spur (Spur). 1929-1933.

Uvalde *Leader-News*. 1930-1933.

Waco Farm and Labor Journal. 1930-1932.

Weatherford *Democrat*. 1929, 1930-1932.

Weekly Dispatch (San Antonio). 1929-1933.

Periodicals

Acco Press. 1929-1933.

Alcalde. 1929-1933.

Baptist Standard. 1929-1930.

Bulletin of the Texas Library Association. 1929-1933.

The Cattleman. 1929-1933.

The Common Herd. 1930-1931.

Cotton and Cotton Oil News. 1929-1933.

County Progress. 1929-1933.

Dallas. 1929-1933.

East Texas. 1930-1933.

Editorials of the Month for Texas. 1930-1932.

Hardware and Implement Journal. 1929-1933.

Holland's. 1929-1933.

Houston. 1929-1933.

Houston Port and City. 1930-1933.

The Hub. 1929-1933.

The Interpreter. 1932-1933.

Lone Star Constructor. 1930-1932.

Lulac News. 1932-1933.

Monty's Monthly News of the Lower Rio Grande Valley of Texas. 1930-1933.

Sheep and Goat Raisers' Magazine. 1929-1933.

Southern Florist and Nurseryman. 1929-1933.

Southern Pharmaceutical Journal. 1929-1933.

Southwest Water Works Journal. 1929-1933.

Southwestern Life News. 1929-1933.

Texas Bluebonnet. 1932.

The Texas Outlook. 1929-1933.

Texas Opinion. 1932-1933.

Texas Municipalities. 1929-1933.

The Texas Monthly. 1929-1930.

Texas Law Review. 1929-1933.

The Texas Weekly. 1930-1932.

The Valley Farmer and South Texas Grower. 1929-1932.

West Texas Today. 1929-1933.

Contemporary Books

Adamic, Louis. *My America, 1928-1938.* New York: Harper & Brothers, 1938.

Adams, James Truslow. *The Tempo of Modern Life.* New York: Albert & Charles Boni, Inc., 1931.

Algren, Nelson. *Somebody in Boots.* New York: Farrar, Straus & Giroux, Inc., 1935, reprinted in Berkley Medallion paperback, 1965.

Allen, Ruth Alice. *Wage Earners Meet the Depression.* Austin: The University of Texas Bulletin No. 3545, 1935.

Ansley, Henry. *I Like the Depression*. Indianapolis, Indiana: Bobbs-Merrill Company, 1932.

Arnold, Thurman W. *The Folklore of Capitalism*. New Haven: Yale University Press, 1937.

Ayres, Leonard P. *The Economics of Recovery*. New York: The Macmillan Company, 1932.

Beard, Charles A. *America Faces the Future*. Boston: Houghton Mifflin Company, 1932.

_____, and Smith, George H. E. *The Future Comes*. New York: The Macmillan Company, 1934.

The Brookings Institution. *The Recovery Problem in the United States*. Washington, D.C.: The Brookings Institution, 1936.

Chamber of Commerce of the United States. *The American Economic System compared with Collectivism and Dictatorship*. Washington, D.C.: Chamber of Commerce of the United States, 1936.

Chase, Stuart. *The Nemesis of American Business*. New York: The Macmillan Company, 1931.

_____. *A New Deal*. New York: The Macmillan Company, 1933.

_____. *Out of the Depression--and After*. New York: The John Day Company, 1931.

_____. *Prosperity Fact or Myth*. New York: Charles Boni Paper Books, 1929.

Cole, G. D. H. *A Guide Through World Chaos*. New York: Alfred A. Knopf, 1934.

Davis, Maxine. *The Lost Generation*. New York: The Macmillan Company, 1936.

Dennis, Lawrence. *The Coming American Fascism*. New York: Harper & Brothers, 1936.

Dulles, Eleanor Lansing. *Depression and Reconstruction*. Philadelphia: University of Pennsylvania Press, 1936.

Dumond, Dwight Lowell. *America in Our Time*. New York: Henry Holt and Company, 1937.

_____. *Roosevelt to Roosevelt*. New York: Henry Holt and Company, 1937.

Fisher, Irving. *The Stock Market Crash--And After*. New York: The Macmillan Company, 1930.

Goslin, Ryllis Alexander and Goslin, Omar Pancoast. *Rich Man, Poor Man*. New York: Harper & Brothers, 1935.

Graves, Lloyd M. *The Great Depression and Beyond*. New York: The Brookmore Economic Service, Inc., 1932.

Hallgren, Mauritz A. *Seeds of Revolt*. New York: Alfred A. Knopf, 1933.

Hill, Edwin C. *The American Scene*. New York: Witmark Educational Publications, 1933.

Lynd, Robert S., and Lynd, Helen Merrell. *Middletown in Transition*. New York: Harcourt, Brace and Company, 1937.

Martin, Roscoe C. *Urban Local Government in Texas*. Austin: The University of Texas Bulletin No. 3637, 1936.

Miller, Ben F. *A Presidential Survey From Washington to Hoover Inclusive*. Slaton, Texas: Privately printed, 1932.

Minehan, Thomas. *Boy and Girl Tramps of America*. New York: Farrar and Rinehart, Inc., 1934.

Norris, J. Frank. *The Gospel of Dynamite*. no publisher, n.d.

Peel, Roy V., and Donnelly, Thomas C. *The 1932 Campaign: An Analysis*. New York: Farrar & Rinehart, Inc., 1935.

Scott, Howard. *Introduction to Technocracy*. New York: The John Day Company, 1933.

Seldes, Gilbert. *The Years of the Locust*. Boston: Little Brown, and Company, 1933.

Soule, George. *The Coming American Revolution*. New York: The Macmillan Company, 1934.

Tugwell, Rexford G. *The Battle for Democracy*. New York: Columbia University Press, 1935.

Wood, Clement. *Herbert Clark Hoover: An American Tragedy*. New York: Michael Swain, 1932.

Secondary Books

Allen, Frederick Lewis. *The Big Change*. New York: Harper & Brothers, 1952.

_____. *Since Yesterday*. New York: Bantam Books, 1961.

Beard, Charles A. and Mary R. *America in Midpassage*. Vol. III: *The Rise of American Civilization*. 3 vols. New York: The Macmillan Company, 1946.

Bernstein, Barton J. (ed.). *Towards a New Past: Dissenting Essays in American History*. New York: Random House Vintage Books edition, 1969.

Blum, John M., *et al*. *The National Experience*. New York: Harcourt, Brace & World, Inc., 1963.

Cash, W. J. *The Mind of the South*. New York: Random House Vintage Books, 1941.

Clark, James A., and Hart, Weldon. *The Tactful Texan: A Biography of Governor Will Hobby*. New York: Random House, 1958.

Cohn, David L. *The Life and Times of King Cotton*. New York: Oxford University Press, 1956.

Cotner, Robert C., *et al*. *Texas Cities and the Great Depression*. Austin: Texas Memorial Museum, 1973.

Current, Richard N., Williams, T. Harry, and Freidel, Frank. *American History: A Survey*. New York: Alfred A. Knopf, 1967.

Donohue, H. E. F. *Conversations With Nelson Algren*. New York: Hill and Wang, 1964.

Ebenstein, William. *Today's Isms*. 4th ed. Englewood Cliffs, New Jersey: Prentice-Hall, Inc., 1964.

Filley, H. Clyde. *The Wealth of the Nation*. Lincoln: University of Nebraska Press, 1945.

Fite, Gilbert C. *George N. Peek and the Fight for Farm Parity*. Norman: University of Oklahoma Press, 1954.

Flynn, John T. *Country Squire in the White House*. New York: Doubleday, Doran and Company, Inc., 1940.

Fusfeld, Daniel R. *The Economic Thought of Franklin D. Roosevelt and the Origins of the New Deal*. New York: Columbia University Press, 1956.

Galbraith, John Kenneth. *The Affluent Society*. New York: The New American Libary, 1958.

_____. *The Great Crash 1929*. New York: Time Incorporated edition, 1962.

Goldman, Eric F. *Rendezvous with Destiny*. New York: Random House Vintage Books, 1952.

Graves, Lawrence L. (ed.). *A History of Lubbock*. Lubbock: West Texas Museum Association, 1962.

Hicks, John D. *Republican Ascendancy, 1921-1933*. New York: Harper & Row Torchbooks, 1963.

Hofstadter, Richard. *The Age of Reform*. New York: Random House Vintage Books, 1955.

_____. *The American Political Tradition and the Men Who Made It*. New York: Random House Vintage Books, 1948.

_____. *Anti-intellectualism in American Life*. New York: Alfred A. Knopf, 1963.

_____. *The Paranoid Style in American Politics and Other Essays*. New York: Alfred A. Knopf, 1965.

Jones, Billy M. *The Search for Maturity*. Vol. V: *The Saga of Texas*. Edited by Seymour V. Connor. 6 vols. Austin: Steck-Vaughn Company, 1965.

Lens, Sidney. *Left, Right & Center: Conflicting Forces in American Labor*. Hinsdale, Illinois: Henry Regnery Company, 1949.

Leuchtenburg, William E. *Franklin D. Roosevelt and the New Deal, 1932-1940*. New York: Harper & Row Torchbooks, 1963.

Link, Arthur S. *American Epoch*. 2d ed. New York: Alfred A. Knopf, 1963.

Lydgate, William A. *What Our People Think*. New York: Thomas Y. Crowell Company, 1944.

Lyons, Eugene. *Our Unknown Ex-President*. Garden City, New York: Doubleday & Company, 1948.

McKay, Seth Shepard. *Texas Politics, 1906-1944*. Lubbock: Texas Tech Press, 1952.

_____, and Faulk, Odie B. *Texas After Spindletop*. Vol. VI: *The Saga of Texas*. Edited by Seymour V. Connor. 6 vols. Austin: Steck-Vaughn Company, 1965.

Michie, Allan A., and Ryhlick, Frank. *Dixie Demagogues*. New York: The Vanguard Press, 1939.

Mitchell, Broadus. *Depression Decade*. New York: Holt, Rinehart and Winston, 1947.

Nalle, Ouida. *The Fergusons of Texas*. San Antonio: The Naylor Company, 1946.

Nye, Russel B. *Midwestern Progressive Politics*. East Lansing: Michigan State University Press, 1959.

Pollack, Norman. *The Populist Response to Industrial America*. New York: W. W. Norton & Company, Inc., paperback edition, 1966.

Ratner, Sidney. *American Taxation*. New York: W. W. Norton & Company, 1942.

Richardson, Rupert Norval. *Texas the Lone Star State*. 2d ed. revised. Englewood Cliffs, New Jersey: Prentice-Hall, Inc., 1958.

Robinson, Henry Morton. *Fantastic Interim*. New York: Harcourt, Brace & Company, 1943.

Rollins, Alfred B., Jr. *Roosevelt and Howe*. New York: Alfred A. Knopf, 1962.

Roy, Ralph Lord. *Apostles of Discord*. Boston: The Beacon Press, 1953.

Saloutos, Theodore. *Farmer Movements in the South, 1865-1933*. Berkeley: University of California Press, 1960.

_____, and Hicks, John D. *Agricultural Discontent in the Middle West, 1900-1939*. Madison: University of Wisconsin Press, 1951.

Schlesinger, Arthur M., Jr. *The Crisis of the Old Order*. Vol. I: *The Age of Roosevelt*. 3 vols. Boston: Hougton Mifflin Company, 1957.

Schriftgiesser, Karl. *This Was Normalcy*. Boston: Little, Brown and Company, 1948.

Shannon, David A. *Between the Wars: America, 1919-1941*. Boston: Houghton Mifflin Company, 1965.

Sherrill, R. E. *Haskell County History*. Haskell, Texas: Haskell County Historical Society, 1965.

Shover, John L. *Cornbelt Rebellion*. Urbana: The University of Illinois Press, 1965.

Soule, George. *Prosperity Decade*. New York: Rinehart & Company, Inc., 1947.

Steen, Ralph W. *Twentieth Century Texas*. Austin: The Steck Company, 1942.

Sternsher, Bernard. *Hitting Home: The Great Depression in Town and Country*. Chicago: Quadrangle Books, 1970.

_____. *Rexford Tugwell and the New Deal*. New Brunswick, New Jersey: Rutgers University Press, 1964.

Timmons, Bascom M. *Garner of Texas*. New York: Harper & Brothers, 1948.

Tugwell, Rexford G. *The Democratic Roosevelt*. Garden City, New York: Doubleday & Company Inc., 1957.

Turner, Frederick Jackson. *The Frontier in American History*. New York: Holt, Rinehart and Winston, 1920.

Warren, Harris Gaylord. *Herbert Hoover and the Great Depression*. New York: Oxford University Press, 1959.

Wecter, Dixon. *The Age of the Great Depression, 1929-1941*. New York: The Macmillan Company, 1948.

Whisenhunt, Donald W. (ed.). *The Depression in the Southwest*. Port Washington, New York: Kennikat Press, 1980.

Williams, Edward Ainsworth. *Federal Aid for Relief*. New York: Columbia University Press, 1939.

Williams, T. Harry. *Huey Long*. New York: Alfred A. Knopf, 1970.

Theses and Dissertations

DeMoss, Dorothy Dell. "Dallas, Texas, During the Early Depression: The Hoover Years, 1929-1933." M.A. thesis, The University of Texas at Austin, 1966.

Dolman, Wilson Elbert. "Odessa, Texas During the Depression, 1932-1936." M.A. thesis, The University of Texas at Austin, 1968.

Hannah, James Joseph. "Urban Reaction to the Great Depression in the United States, 1929-1933." Ph.D. dissertation, University of California, Berkeley, 1956.

Jaffe, Madeline. "Rural Women in Unskilled Labor: A Study of Women from Country Districts in Unskilled Wage-earning Groups, Austin, Texas." M.A. thesis, The University of Texas at Austin, 1931.

Jenkins, Judith Geraldine. "Austin, Texas, during the Great Depression, 1929-1936." M.A. thesis, The University of Texas at Austin, 1965.

Johnson, William R. "Farm Policy in Transition: 1932, Year of Crisis." Ph.D. dissertation, University of Oklahoma, Norman, 1963.

McMillan, Mary Maverick. "San Antonio During the Depression: 1929-1933." M.A. thesis, The University of Texas at Austin, 1966.

Montgomery, William Edward. "The Depression in Houston During the Hoover Era, 1929-1932." M.A. thesis, The University of Texas at Austin, 1966.

Nickels, Leonara. "Public Services of Dan Moody." M.A. thesis, Texas Technological College, 1948.

Nordeman, Marion Martin. "Midland, Texas, During the Depression: 1929-1933." M.A. thesis, The University of Texas at Austin, 1967.

Ozment, Dianne Treadaway. "Galveston During the Hoover Era, 1929-1933." M.A. thesis, The University of Texas at Austin, 1968.

Ozment, Robert Allan. "Temple, Texas and the Great Depression, 1929-1933." M.A. thesis, The University of Texas at Austin, 1966.

Patenaude, Lionel V. "The New Deal and Texas." Ph.D. dissertation, The University of Texas at Austin, 1953.

Shapiro, Harold Arthur. "The Workers of San Antonio, Texas, 1900-1940." Ph.D. dissertation, The University of Texas at Austin, 1952.

Other Sources

Ashburn, Karl E. "The Texas Cotton Acreage Control Law of 1931-1932." *The Southwestern Historical Quarterly*, LXI (July, 1957), 120-124.

Ogg, Frederick A. "Does American Need a Dictator?" *Current History*, XXXVI (September, 1932), 641-648.

Tatum, E. Ray. "Conquest or Failure: a biographical study in the life of J. Frank Norris." Unpublished manuscript in the possession of the author at University Baptist Church, Lubbock, Texas.

The Texas Almanac and State Industrial Guide--1929. Dallas: A. H. Belo Corporation, 1929.

The Texas Almanac and State Industrial Guide--1931. Dallas: A. H. Belo Corporation, 1931.

The Texas Almanac and State Industrial Guide--1933. Dallas: A. H. Belo Corporation, 1933.

Whisenhunt, Donald W. "Maury Maverick and the Diga Relief Colony, 1932-1933." *Texana*, IX (Summer, 1971), 249-259.

I N D E X

Immigration: as cause of depression, 96; restrictions, 107-108
Immorality: as cause of depression, 93
Industrialization and impact on Texas, 5-6
Installment buying: as cause of depression, 97
Insull, Samuel: 75
International causes of depression, 94-95

"Jackass of the Plains": 69, 70
Jews in Texas: 20
Jones, Marvin: attacks tariff, 90; blames business for depression, 82

Kellogg-Briand Peace Pact, 25
Keynes, John Maynard: 100
Klein, Julius: predicts return of prosperity, 63

Lamont, R. P.: on stock market crash, 29-30
Lanham, Fritz: attacks tarriff, 90; opposes war debts moratorium, 95
League of United Latin American Citizens: 16n; blames banks for depression, 80
Legislative Efficiency and Economy Committee, 106
Libraries: impact of depression on, 104
Long plan: 168-182
Long, Huey: 201; cotton plan and impact on Texas, 168-182; meddles in Texas politics, 178-179; proposes "Share Our Wealth" plan, 191
Lottery: as solution to depression, 134
Lutherans in Texas: 19
Lynching: at Sherman, 17

MacArthur, Douglas: and veterans' bonus camp, 115
Maldistribution of wealth: blamed for depression, 88-89
Maverick, Maury: describes transients, 119-133; establishes community for transients, 123-124, 189; on radicalism, 203; on treatment of transients, 131-133;

on veterans' bonus, 111-112
McAdoo, William Gibbs: 209
McDonald, J. E.: 178
McNary-Haugen bill: 168
Mellon, Andrew: announces tax cut, 35; appointed ambassador to Court of St. James, 85-86; attempted impeachment of, 85-86; on stock market crash, 29-30
Methodists in Texas: 19
Mexicans in Texas: 14-15; illiteracy of, 16
Mexicans: attempts to limit immigration, 107-108
Milk War: 166-167
Minehan, Thomas: describes transients, 119-133
Money supply: as cause of depression, 193-195
Moody, Dan: appeals for federal aid for farmers, 158; on public works, 39, 55; starts "Buy a Bale" campaign, 161; supports cotton acreage reduction, 163; writes article on prosperity, 57
Moody, W. H., Jr.: 172
Morals: as cause of depression, 93
Morgan, J. P.: 81
Murray, "Alfalfa" Bill: 228n
Mussolini: as a popular figure, 205-206

National planning: 198-200
Negroes in Texas: described, 15
Newton, Henning: 173
Norris, J. Frank: on communism, 207; on government intervention, 144; on stock market crash, 49; predicted depression as sign of end of the world, 93

Organized labor: impact of depression on, 108-109
Overproduction: as cause of depression, 86-87

Paranoid style in Texas: 4
Parrish, Pink L.: attacks tariff, 90; on concentration of wealth, 192
Patenaude, Lionel V.: v, vi
Patman, Wright: attacks Republican Party, 77; attempts to impeach

247